THE FUNCTIONS OF LAW

The Functions of Law

KENNETH M. EHRENBERG

OXFORD
UNIVERSITY PRESS

OXFORD
UNIVERSITY PRESS

Great Clarendon Street, Oxford, OX2 6DP,
United Kingdom

Oxford University Press is a department of the University of Oxford.
It furthers the University's objective of excellence in research, scholarship,
and education by publishing worldwide. Oxford is a registered trade mark of
Oxford University Press in the UK and in certain other countries

First Edition published in 2016

Impression: 1

Published in the United States of America by Oxford University Press
198 Madison Avenue, New York, NY 10016, United States of America

British Library Cataloguing in Publication Data
Data available

Library of Congress Control Number: 2016930708

ISBN 978–0–19–967747–4

Printed and bound by
CPI Group (UK) Ltd, Croydon, CR0 4YY

For Sara

Acknowledgments

I would like to thank the following individuals and organizations, without whose support and advice this book would not have been possible.

Veronica Rodriguez-Blanco, Michael Giudice, George Pavlakos, Karin Boxer, David Enoch, Scott Shapiro, Detlef von Daniels, Tomasz Gizbert-Studnicki, Gurpreet Rattan, John Gardner, Les Green, Julie Dickson, Ken Himma, Norvin Richards, Fred Schauer, Ekow Yankah, Mark Murphy, Guyora Binder, William Twining, Dennis Patterson, Corrado Roversi, Zsofia Zvolenszky, Luka Burazin, Haris Psarras, John Searle, Amie Thomasson, Lucas Miotto, Cindy Phillips, James Specyal, Triantafyllos Gkouvas, Michael Pardo, Neil Williams, Randy Dipert, Barry Smith, Ken Shockley, my colleagues in the Philosophy Department of the University of Alabama, University College and the Oxford Centre for Ethics and Philosophy of Law, the University of Alabama Research Grants Committee, Mr. Ernest Sanford Williams and the Williams Fund of the University of Alabama, the Oxford Reading Group on the philosophy of action, the participants in the 2015 Krakow Workshop in Legal Philosophy, the participants in the 2015 Spring Workshops of the Edinburgh Legal Theory Research Group, my brother, Ethan, and my wife, Hanako.

I continue to be thankful to my dissertation committee, with whom I worked on some of these ideas in embryonic form: Jeremy Waldron, Joseph Raz, Jules Coleman, Stephen Perry, and Stephanie Beardman.

The following sections in the book draw on previously published work:

Chapter 5, Section C: Accepted for publication as 'Law as Plan and Artifact' (2016, forthcoming) 7 *Jurisprudence*.

Chapter 7: An earlier and much abbreviated version of this chapter first appeared in George Pavlakos and Veronica Rodriguez-Blanco (eds), *Reasons and Intentions in Law and Practical Agency* (Cambridge University Press 2015).

Table of Contents

List of Abbreviations

ELP	Exclusive legal positivism
ILP	Inclusive positivism
ITP	Interpretivism
PNL	Procedural natural law
SNL	Strong natural law thesis
WNL	Weak natural law thesis

1
Introduction

This book was conceived as a response to a certain surprise I felt as I began to investigate the methods of legal philosophy. It seemed surprising that some very prominent philosophers, with whose theories I largely agreed, tended to downplay the role of law's functionality in their explanations of the nature of law. At the same time, many of the philosophers with whom I had more points of disagreement were the ones who made law's functionality a matter of central concern.[1]

Of course, this led me to some doubt about my own convictions and powers of discernment. On the one hand, it seemed pretty obvious to me that law was a creation of human beings, a tool they used to alter or maintain social arrangements, to incentivize behaviors deemed valuable to the community (or to an influential subset of the community), and to solve certain social problems. As such, it seemed a natural starting place to analyze the nature of law in terms of those functions that its creators understood it to perform. (This does not imply anything about the relevance of drafters' intentions to the interpretation and application of law once enacted.) When we talk about individual laws, clearly there are a wide variety of purposes that legislatures, judges, monarchs, dictators, and caretakers have for their various legal enactments and decisions. It isn't immediately clear that these purposes can be systematized or described generally to capture an overall function for legal systems generally, or law itself. But my sense was that, as a kind of tool with many different applications, there would still be some general way of characterizing what law was for.

On the other hand, it seemed as though it was more common to find arguments from law's function among those philosophers who argue for an

[1] See, for example, Leslie Green, 'Law as a Means' in Peter Cane (ed.), *The Hart-Fuller Debate in the Twenty-First Century* (Hart Publishing 2010) 169–88 at 182; Anthony J. Sebok, 'Comment on "Law as Means"' in Peter Cane (ed.), *The Hart-Fuller Debate in the Twenty-First Century* (Hart 2010) 189–98 at 192: "The positivists claim that law is 'better understood' by focusing on its means while Fuller and Dworkin think that the law is better understood by focusing on its ends." I tend to see the law as a legal positivist would, but still think that it is best understood in terms of its ends.

essential goodness or moral purpose to law that extends beyond what we actually see in it or make of it. Natural lawyers hold that law's function is to provide for the common good, and that therefore there is an essential rationality against which laws as articulated by human beings must be measured. Insufficiently rational laws are therefore legally deficient (and not just morally or rationally deficient). Interpretivists such as Ronald Dworkin hold that the law justifies state action or inaction, especially regarding the use of force, by embodying and articulating the moral and political principles that the community holds dear. But then consistency with those principles is what determines whether some piece of legislation or a court decision is legally invalid. As a result, the legal validity of an enactment can be unmoored from the beliefs of those who create, follow, and apply the law. Theorists of these views tend to see their particular take on law's functionality as leading them away from seeing law as merely a tool of human creation, since it is somehow meant to capture or reflect these higher principles and aspirations.

It seemed like there was a missing position that was still appealing. This would be one that recognized the centrality of law's functionality to any adequate explanation of the phenomenon, but which didn't require the theorist to endorse that functionality or law as the best means of performing it.[2] Understood correctly, explanatory theories like those of most legal positivists should really be embracing the centrality of law's function to a proper explanation of law as a tool of human creation. Yet, it seems that many legal positivists believe that a method which emphasizes law's function is tarred by the central place given to it by their opponents, by the obvious problems with functional explanations in the natural sciences,[3] or by the somewhat mystical and conspiratorial role it sometimes plays in the social sciences. This ignores the differing ways in which functions can provide explanations, and that one is particularly well suited to the positivist picture.

Why think about the law in terms of its functions? One of the issues that have been bothering many of those more concerned with an explanatory account of law is how to explain law's normativity.[4] If we start from the

[2] A similar approach is called "thin functionalism" by William Twining, 'A Post-Westphalian Conception of Law' (2003) 37 *Law & Society Review* 199–258, 238–41, but is otherwise not clearly embraced much in the literature.

[3] These include problems of backward causation (wherein a beneficial result is imagined to bring about the structure that causes it) and problems of articulating goals or beneficial end states in the absence of a designer.

[4] For example, Gerald J. Postema, 'Coordination and Convention at the Foundations of Law' (1982) 11 *Journal of Legal Studies* 165–203, 182; Jules L. Coleman, *The Practice of Principle: In Defence of a Pragmatist Approach to Legal Theory* (Oxford University Press 2001) 65ff; Mark Greenberg, 'How Facts Make Law' in Scott Hershovitz (ed.), *Exploring Law's Empire* (Oxford University Press 2008) 225–64. But see David Enoch, 'Reason-Giving and the Law' in Leslie

belief that the law has a fundamentally morally important purpose that renders it morally valuable (as do natural lawyers), then explaining how the law generates obligations might be less problematic. If the law's morally important purpose requires it to be capable of imposing obligations, then that is a power it must have in order for it to do its job.[5] The morally important purpose would then lend its weight to the legal obligations posited as a result of human action. The law generates obligations where it is in service of that morally important purpose, and those obligations are necessary for it to carry out that purpose.

But if we wish to remain neutral about, or even to ignore, its purpose in our explanation, then it will be difficult to account for how certain social facts about law generate robust obligations. Avoiding an analysis of law in terms of its value appears to undermine the ability to provide an account of how it generates robust normativity. An account of law's purpose (even if we remain morally neutral about that purpose) would allow us to explain its creation of norms for the sake of accomplishing that purpose. It will then be an additional task to see how those norms might be obligatory. So one reason to see the law in terms of its function is so that we can begin an explanation of its normativity.

We could understand legal normativity in a purely contextually bound way, as H. L. A. Hart did,[6] saying that legal obligation was a context-dependent simulacrum of obligation.[7] We would therefore not need to explain or justify any inference from legal obligation to a wider moral obligation or the provision of a robust practical reason. But it would also not sit well with the way we understand law as a possibly sometimes legitimate practical authority. As a putative practical authority, it claims the right to issue directives that recipients have a practical reason to obey.[8] If, when, and where that claim is legitimate, we would have the obligations that it claims to impose. So accepting a

Green and Brian Leiter (eds), *Oxford Studies in Philosophy of Law, Volume 1* (Oxford University Press 2011) 1–38, arguing this focus is misplaced.

[5] John Finnis, *Natural Law and Natural Rights* (Clarendon Press 1980) 315–20; 'The Authority of Law in the Predicament of Contemporary Social Theory' (1984) 1 *Notre Dame Journal of Ethics and Public Policy* 115, 117.

[6] H. L. A. Hart, *Essays on Bentham: Jurisprudence and Political Theory* (Clarendon Press 1982) 159–60. See also Joseph Raz, 'Hart on Moral Rights and Legal Duties' (1984) 4 *Oxford Journal of Legal Studies* 123, 130–31; Kenneth Einar Himma, 'The Ties That Bind: An Analysis of the Concept of Obligation' (2013) 26 *Ratio Juris* 16–46, 18–19.

[7] More recent scholarship has shown that there are two ways of understanding such a notion of legal obligation: "adjectivally" (in which "legal" specifies a type of obligation) and "perspectivally" (in which "legal" specifies a point of view from which the obligation is seen). Scott J. Shapiro, *Legality* (Harvard University Press 2011) 184–88. See also Christopher Essert, 'Legal Obligation and Reasons' (2013) 19 *Legal Theory* 63–88, 67–68.

[8] Joseph Raz, *The Authority of Law: Essays on Law and Morality* (Clarendon Press 1979) 78–79.

merely contextually bound account of legal normativity threatens to undermine our tools for accounting for this other important feature of law. That is, if we finish our account of legal normativity with an understanding of it merely as the norms that law has created intra-systemically, then we miss out on what might legitimate its claim that those norms are applicable regardless of whether we consider ourselves to be within its system.

As Hume noted,[9] no amount of information about what is the case can be used by itself to reach a conclusion about what ought to be done. Every normative argument must have a normative premise smuggled in somewhere. The issue we are confronting here is an application of this problem. If we understand legal normativity purely contextually, then it is merely a descriptive fact about the system and cannot be used to reach any wider normative conclusions. A statement like "Legally, one ought not drive over seventy miles per hour" may use normative language, but is in reality merely standing in for descriptive historical facts about what legal officials said or did in the past. If we wish to make the jump to conclude "We ought not to drive over seventy miles per hour," then we need to understand more about what entitles us to this normative conclusion given the merely descriptive premises.

It is partially the hope of fording this gap that makes legal philosophy a compelling area of study. Whatever else law might be or do, it is a system of norms that are somehow founded upon social facts about what officials and legal subjects have done. While other areas of philosophy tend to work firmly on one or the other side of the gap, legal philosophy must contend with how to get from facts to norms.

More generally, the closest we seem to be able to get to bridging the gap is where the factual premises also contain some contextual information about the values or goals of participants. That contextual information can then be supplemented with arguments about the propriety of those values, and how wide-ranging the group of participants. Functions are the most useful and obvious way of packaging such a goal within a description. To take the simple case of an artifact like a hammer, the artifact is created to serve a purpose that is held by its creator (or supposed by its creator to be held by others). The artifact or tool (the hammer) serves to fulfill the goal (driving a nail) supposed for its use by its creator.

At first, however, that doesn't give us much more than a contextualized way of telling good exemplars from bad. If we say that the function of the hammer is to drive nails, I can use that information to tell the difference between at least some good hammers and some bad hammers. But

[9] David Hume, *A Treatise of Human Nature* (printed for John Noon 1739), bk 3, pt 1, § 1, 27.

I cannot use that information to say that it is good to drive nails. I must already believe (or at least have a good reason to believe) that driving nails is important in order to value the hammer. And even then, I might think that hammers are deficient tools because there are better ways to drive nails, such as nail guns.[10]

So, on the surface, the use of functions to explain an institution like law only gets us so far. Once we have a colorable articulation of what those functions might be, we can draw some plausible conclusions about how to tell good laws from bad laws in terms of their ability to accomplish that general purpose.[11] But we cannot thereby automatically say that they are creating reasons for people subject to those laws. Doing so requires the additional assumption that those people have either adopted the goals of law as their own and (possibly) that they agree the law is the best available means of accomplishing those goals, or that there is a good reason for them to adopt those goals, which they would see if they were looking clearly. (Or, at the very least, we must assume that following the law serves some possibly distinct goal that those people have adopted or have good reason to adopt.) That is, the primary way in which law seems to operate is by altering the reasons that people subject to those laws have, but it is not yet clear what legitimizes its claim to alter those reasons.

I have a good reason to drive safely, for my own benefit and for others'. But, if I am an exceptionally good driver, my reasons to get where I am going as quickly as possible in conjunction with my reason to drive safely may still allow for driving at very high speeds. The law at least purports to alter that by setting a speed limit as a maximum for everyone not in some emergency. Whatever the reasons behind the specific limit imposed by the law, however, I am supposedly subject to that law regardless of whether I have adopted the reasons for that specific limit and regardless of my driving skill. Hence the law is asking me to make a sacrifice, albeit in this case a rather small one.

[10] Jules Coleman notes that a hammer's function is likely integral to our concept of it, notwithstanding the fact that it might have other uses: Coleman, *Practice of Principle* 194. For an attempt (to my mind unsuccessful) to explain the concept of a hammer without reference to its function see Sylvie Delacroix, 'Six Paths to Vertigo-Free Legal Theory' in Michael Freeman and Ross Harrison (eds), *Law and Philosophy*, vol. 10 (Current Legal Issues series, Oxford University Press 2007) 36–48, 43 n. 37.

[11] We will see that law in general is a genre to which individual laws belong. This relation is not quite as straightforward as it was with hammers since individual laws must generally be a part of a legal system. It is therefore more correct to think of the legal system as an institutional exemplar of law as a genre. Individual laws could be (or create) institutions on their own, but are usually more properly considered applications of the legal system of which they are a part. I will argue later, however, that the purposes of individual laws are directly relevant to understanding the functions of law as a genre. If that argument is successful, then that will validate the claim made here that an understanding of law's institutional function can help to distinguish good laws from bad laws.

It is asking me to compromise my interest in getting to where I am going as quickly as possible for whatever wider good is supposedly effected by the speed limit law. (Even if I don't comply with the speed limit posted, if I drive more slowly than the maximum safe speed of which I am capable given my skill and the abilities of others around me, then the law appears to make a difference to what I am doing—although the difference in this case might have more to do with the threats the law makes than the rule itself.) If I do have sufficient reason to make the sacrifice the law is demanding of me, and my reason for making that sacrifice comes from the law itself, then it is successfully creating a non-prudential reason for me.

Now it might be suspected that much of what the law does, it does not by creating or changing reasons we have, but by altering the conditions in which pre-existing reasons are activated.[12] I have very good reasons to avoid unpleasant court proceedings, police intervention, the imposition of monetary fines, and imprisonment, not to mention the hopefully increasingly rare possibilities of corporal punishment and execution. It might be supposed that the law is simply informing me how to avoid these unpleasant eventualities.

There are a number of difficulties with this view, but one of my favorites is represented by the rules contained in 4 USC §§ 1–10, the Flag Code, which is a list of rules for the proper display and treatment of the U.S. flag. It just so happens that the U.S. Code did not initially provide any provisions for the violations of these rules,[13] specifically leaving that up to the individual states (of which at least two never instituted any repercussions for violations of the flag law). When those state provisions were struck down by the United States Supreme Court in *Texas v. Johnson*,[14] the 101st Congress did nationalize the penalties for flag desecration previously applicable only to the District of Columbia. That attempt was itself then invalidated by the Court in *U.S. v. Eichman*.[15]

The point of this example is that the law is still in force, originally and now again providing for no punishment for violations. (And it is instructive to consider that the Supreme Court could have struck down the law entirely, but rather decided only to strike down any punishments associated with its violation.) Nevertheless, it purports to alter or create the reasons people in the U.S. have in their behaviors toward the U.S. flag.

[12] For an argument that this completely explains legal normativity see Enoch, 'Reason-Giving and the Law.' For an application of this idea to the notion of legal authority see Lawrence Alexander, 'Law and Exclusionary Reasons' (1990) 18 *Philosophical Topics* 5–22, 8.

[13] From 1968 through the *Texas v. Johnson* decision in 1989, 33 U.S.C. § 700 did provide a penalty of up to $1000 and/or up to a year in prison for "publicly mutilating, defacing, defiling, burning, or trampling" the flag. But the Flag Code itself dates to 1942.

[14] 491 U.S. 397 (1989).

[15] 496 U.S. 310 (1990).

It may be that, without enforcement provisions, only those already motivated by patriotism or respect for the flag's symbolism will comply. But the law is there to instruct them on what is deemed the correct way to show that respect. (After the attacks of September 11, 2001, drivers in New York City took on the practice of showing their patriotism by dragging the flag on the road attached to their vehicles' rear bumpers, most likely in ignorance that doing so violated this law.) Additionally, if there is anyone motivated by the desire to be law-abiding independently of what that person believes about the importance of the flag, then, assuming that the flag law is valid and legitimately authoritative, that person's reasons for behaviors regarding the flag are changed.

More generally, any time we can think of a behavior we would not otherwise have performed absent the law, even when there is no chance for detection or reprisal, that is good evidence we are accepting the law as providing or altering our reasons for action. It may be true that, absent the threat of punishment, we must have other background motivations for following those reasons—patriotism, the desire to be like others, the desire to be seen (or to see oneself) as law-abiding—but if we have to look to the law for guidance to determine how to pursue that motivation, then we are seeing the law as reason-giving. If the law is creating the standards for those behaviors rather than merely reporting pre-existing standards, then we are not just getting information from the law about how to behave, but looking to the law to establish those standards.

Perhaps this is all that is required of an explanatory theory as opposed to a normative theory, which would seek to justify, criticize, or reform. If the explanatory theory could actually motivate an adherence to law by itself, then it wouldn't be merely an explanatory theory. While one might be motivated to do something by an explanation based on one's pre-existing commitments, if the explanation itself offered the motivation, it would have to include a justification. It may be enough to understand the law in terms of what it is supposed to do and to give a wider theory of what justifies legal obligation separately, if and when it happens to be justified.

The nagging kernel of the problem is that it seems to be part of the nature of law that it at least purports to create new reasons for action where they didn't exist before, and these reasons come packaged in the language of obligation. That would still need to be explained, even if not endorsed, by the legal philosopher. But if it were found to be part of law's function to create those new reasons, then we could begin to understand how and why it is in law's nature to do so without requiring us to endorse those reasons as our own and without requiring us to take a position on its chances of success.

It might be thought that we can understand law's claim to be reason-giving as an aspect of its claim to authority. If it is necessarily in law's nature to claim that authority, then it is thereby claiming to be reason-giving. The appeal to functions isn't meant to undermine this possibility but to answer the question more completely. What about law necessitates its claim to authority? How can merely descriptive facts about the actions of officials justify such a claim? My argument is that a clearer understanding of law's functions can answer these questions.

One promising place to turn in search of an explanation of law's purported ability to create new reasons is its institutional aspect. The law is an institution and institutions are human creations, one of the central purposes of which is to alter the normative relations among those subject to the institution. They do this by conferring statuses on individuals or groups who serve in defined roles; those statuses carry new rights and responsibilities within the confines of the institution. Institutions therefore create new reasons for action. From a perspective internal to the institution, it can create those reasons for those who are members of or subject to it without those members necessarily endorsing the specific reasons imposed on them. Hence, if it is possible to become subject to an institution without one's consent, it is possible to have reasons imposed on one without consent. This is a key step in understanding the possibility of the law creating non-prudential reasons such as obligations. Once I am subject to the institution (possibly, but perhaps not necessarily, as a result of my own choice or action), it can alter my reasons for action without my necessarily endorsing those specific alterations.

Think of a hospital. Clearly it is an institution whose primary purpose is caring for and curing of the sick and injured. Merely walking into a hospital alters one's normative space. One has new reasons to comply with the directions of doctors and nurses in the hospital that didn't necessarily exist before walking in. Rules in the hospital such as visiting hours and off-limit areas become applicable. A hospital administrator, in the performance of her job, can require that all visitors leave the hospital at once, which likely imposes an obligation on the visitors to leave. Norms of deference to people doing their jobs in the hospital may be considerably different than toward those same people outside the hospital.

Even if you had *some* pre-existing reasons to comply with the directions of doctors and nurses outside the hospital, being inside the hospital adds new ones and may alter the ones you already had. Sometimes these are just the triggering of reasons you already had. But it seems equally clear that doctors, nurses, and administrators can create entirely new reasons for those in the hospital by issuing directives or changing the rules. It is likely that one has moral reasons to back up these newly created reasons and give them legitimacy. Moral reasons such as not interfering in the expert care of a sick person will lend authority to new directives and rule changes made by hospital staff. Yet those changes still give rise to new reasons, which are created by the staff.

While one might object that these are merely corporate delegations of pre-existing legal authority, it seems fairly clear that these hospital norms would exist even if the hospital were located outside any legal jurisdictions, or if the legal system that did have jurisdiction made no provisions for hospitals, corporations, or other sub-institutional arrangements. An extra-jurisdictional hospital is still trying to cure and care for the sick and injured. And that gives us reasons to defer to its staff and administration. So entering the hospital gives rise to the possibility that hospital officials can create new reasons for you.[16]

One word of warning here is that there is an important difference between the reasons you actually have and the reasons you accede to or believe yourself to have. It is possible for one to deny that being in the hospital has altered one's reasons or imposed new obligations. One can be subject to norms without realizing it. My point here is that the norms one is subject to have changed whether one realizes it or not. If you do realize that those norms have changed, then they can serve as motivating reasons for your action. But even if you don't see them, they are there in the same way that you might have a moral reason not to eat meat which you don't yet realize or, if something like utilitarianism is true, a moral obligation to donate just about all your money to charity even if you wrongly believe yourself entitled to keep a greater portion to yourself.

Another important fact about institutions is that they can explain the distinction between actual and counterfeit examples of institutional norms: ones that the institution itself endorses and ones that may be purported but don't fulfill the institution's standards for validity within the institutional context. That is, institutions only claim to alter members' reasons in specified ways, usually by following specified institutional procedures that lend extra significance or status to certain people, objects, events, or behaviors. Only those norms that result from the specified procedures are to be credited with the status of institutional validity. This is important for two reasons. Not only does it explain how the contours of our normative space (the nature and extent of the norms we are supposedly

[16] One implication of this discussion is that an explanation of law (or some other institution) cannot be complete without some theory about what brings people into the ambit of the institution, making them subject to its norms. In the hospital example, it will be some theory about why walking into the hospital makes you subject to its norms. With regard to law, it will be a theory of what legitimates its authority. I thank Norvin Richards for pointing out this implication.

subject to) can be changed by the institution when those context-dependent reasons happen to be legitimately applicable, but also it shows how institutions can set their own boundaries, determining which norms are in play and which are not.

This talk of institutions sheds light on the law in a number of ways. It helps to understand the notion of legal validity in a broader way that relates it to law's institutional purpose. That is, it explains why questions of legal validity are so important to a well-functioning legal system in that those questions delimit the normative space of those subject to the system. Moreover, it suggests a way to understand how, once we become subject to the institution (itself a question of what legitimizes authority and possibly what grounds political obligation), mere facts about that institution can alter the norms that apply to us.

Since institutions are created by people to serve certain purposes, we might think of them as kinds of tools. Human beings have been making tools almost since our beginnings. While we no longer think of this as unique to humans, having found plenty of animals that make tools as well, it still seems a very characteristic aspect of humanity, given the multiplicity and complexity of the tools we make. So it is not much of a stretch to say that one cannot fully understand humans without considering this important aspect of our lives. While not everyone agrees on these classifications, tools themselves can be understood to be a subset of the broader category of "instrument"[17] or "use-object,"[18] which would include any object used purposely in an attempt to effect an intentional goal, and would include natural objects used by humans in an unmodified state. On this view, "tools" would be instruments that are intentionally modified in some way to serve the purpose for which they are to be used.[19] Some of those tools operate through symbolism, by standing for other things to make them easier for us to manipulate. Language itself can be considered a very complex tool in the sense that it is a use of sound or figures to symbolize things so that we can manipulate them and affect our interaction with them and each other.

Artifacts are a further subset of tools: instruments that are intentionally modified in such a way so as to be recognizable by others as a certain kind of

[17] Randall R. Dipert, *Artifacts, Art Works, and Agency* (Temple University Press 1993) 23–25.

[18] Amie L. Thomasson, 'Public Artifacts, Intentions and Norms' in Maarten Franssen and others (eds), *Artefact Kinds: Ontology and the Human-Made World* (Springer 2013) 45–62, 46, citing Edmund Husserl, *Studies in the Phenomenology of Constitution* (R. Rojcewicz and A. Schuwer trs., Kluwer Academic 1989 (1952)) 197.

[19] Dipert, *Artifacts, Art Works, and Agency* 27–28. But see Beth Preston, *A Philosophy of Material Culture: Action, Function, and Mind* (Routledge 2013), for an argument that tools and artifacts do not depend on intentionality for their functions.

thing.[20] Some tools or artifacts that perform symbolization and representation functions may themselves be abstractions. Institutions are certainly of this kind. A university is an institution and is not identical to its buildings, faculty, trustees, administrators, or students. Institutions are therefore generally abstract artifacts.[21] They are artifacts in that they are tools we create to be recognizable. But they are abstract in that they are not identical to any specific set of physical concrete entities.[22] Law is one such institution, one

[20] For the purposes of this introduction, this explanation of artifacts is somewhat vague so as not to take an immediate position on the differences between the views of Thomasson, 'Public Artifacts, Intentions and Norms' 46–47, and Dipert, *Artifacts, Art Works, and Agency* 29–30. Thomasson argues against the centrality of functions to the identification of artifact kinds but does so primarily in order to make room for artworks and similar examples. We will see later that her arguments, when applied to law, help the case that functions are central to its understanding.

[21] While in my way of understanding them, all institutions are artifacts (though not vice versa), not all need to be abstract. Certain ceremonial objects that have special symbolic meaning but need to have that status conferred on them might be one example. As we will see, formal institutions confer their institutional status on objects by type. Hence it is not quite correct to say of a given coin or piece of paper currency that it is an institution, even though money is an institution. On the other hand, I am open to the idea that where the institutional norms pick out only one unique object, such as a scepter to be used in opening the legislature of a country (without which the legislature's actions have no legal validity), we might meaningfully say that the scepter itself is an institution. There is no doubt that it is an artifact, but since its symbolic status and importance is conferred on it in such a way that it both confers deontic powers and counts for something more than its mere physical properties and attributes, it may make sense to call it an institution. In John Searle's original analysis, which was confined to institutional facts, there needed to be a pre-existing entity that had institutional status imposed upon it: John R. Searle, *The Construction of Social Reality* (Free Press 1995) 26–57. This is not itself at odds with my claim that institutions are generally abstractions, since the institution of money is not identical to a piece of currency. Rather, it is an institutional fact about that piece of paper that it counts as currency. Many noted problems with the difficulties of adapting his original analysis to the creation of new institutional facts without pre-existing entities upon which status is imposed (the so-called "freestanding Y term" problem from Searle's formula for constitutive rules creating institutional facts: "X counts as Y in circumstances C"). One useful example of this for law is found in Amie L. Thomasson, 'Realism and Human Kinds' (2003) 67 *Philosophy and Phenomenological Research* 580–609, 587. Another is by Barry Smith in Barry Smith and John Searle, 'The Construction of Social Reality: An Exchange' (2003) 62 *American Journal of Economics & Sociology* 283–309, 287–92, to which Searle makes an initial reply at 304–05. Searle did subsequently broaden his account somewhat to account for free-standing Y terms: John R. Searle, 'Language and Social Ontology' (2008) 37 *Theory and Society* 443–59, 453, broadening the account to "status function declarations," *Making the Social World: The Structure of Human Civilization* (Oxford University Press 2010) 19–20.

[22] See Gideon Rosen, 'Abstract Objects' (2012) *The Stanford Encyclopedia of Philosophy*, Edward N. Zalta (ed.) <http://plato.stanford.edu/archives/spr2012/entries/abstract-objects/>. Following Corrado Roversi, Anna M. Borghi, and Luca Tummolini, 'A Marriage Is an Artefact and Not a Walk That We Take Together: An Experimental Study on the Categorization of Artefacts' (2013) 4 *Review of Philosophy and Psychology* 527–42, 530, I see the "abstract" modifier as indicating only that the artifact is ontologically immaterial, citing Amie L. Thomasson, *Fiction and Metaphysics* (Cambridge University Press 1999). See also Zsófia Zvolenszky, 'Abstract Artifact Theory About Fictional Characters Defended' (2013) 5 *Proceedings of the European Society for Aesthetics* 597–612, 600.

that is also used to generate further institutions such as corporations, marriages, universities, and hospitals, although many of those could also be created without operation of law. Yet, when law is present, it tends to claim some monopoly on determining the conditions for the recognition of those other institutions (although perhaps only in its own contexts). So I will say that law is a genre of institutionalized abstract artifacts,[23] recognizing a certain redundancy in that calling it an institution generally implies that it is an abstract artifact, but using this terminology in order to underscore the importance of its functionality in order to understand its nature.

So artifacts and institutions are generally explained in terms of the functions that they are either designed or used to perform. However, I want to emphasize here, and throughout this book, that there are at least two different kinds of functions that are commonly used in explanations.[24] One classic

[23] I have been gratified to discover recently that others have begun to consider the possibility that laws, as institutions, are abstract artifacts. See, for example, Corrado Roversi, 'Acceptance Is Not Enough, but Texts Alone Achieve Nothing' (2012) 43 *Rechtstheorie* 1–30, 23; Corrado Roversi, 'Legal Metaphoric Artifacts' in B. Brozek and J. Stelmach (eds), *The Emergence of Normative Orders* (Copernicus Center Press 2015) 215–80; Roversi, Borghi, and Tummolini, 'Marriage Is an Artefact and Not a Walk That We Take Together', investigating the perceived distinction between institutional artifacts and other social objects; Luka Burazin, 'Can There Be an Artifact Theory of Law?' (forthcoming 2016) 29 *Ratio Juris*; Zvolenszky, 'Abstract Artifact Theory About Fictional Characters Defended' 608, using the law in an analogical argument. Hart claimed "that legal obligations are very often (though not always) human artifacts": 'Legal and Moral Obligation' in Richard E. Flathman (ed.), *Concepts in Social and Political Philosophy* (Macmillan 1973) 187–200 at 188 (and immediately extending this to include "rights, powers, immunities and disabilities"), the caveat likely reserved for customary laws and understanding the term "artifact" to refer to deliberate creation. See also Kenneth Einar Himma, 'Do Philosophy and Sociology Mix? A Non-Essentialist Socio-Legal Positivist Analysis of the Concept of Law' (2004) 24 *Oxford Journal of Legal Studies* 717–38, 731; Brian Leiter, 'The Demarcation Problem in Jurisprudence: A New Case for Scepticism' (2011) 31 *Oxford Journal of Legal Studies* 663–77, 666. While I may not consistently be quite so careful, John Gardner follows Hart in noting that law, as a generality, is a genre of artifacts. Individual laws and legal systems are the actual artifacts: John Gardner, 'The Legality of Law' (2004) 17 *Ratio Juris* 168–81, 171, noting further that law is a special genre of artifacts in that it contains both artifactual norms and systems of those norms (at least one to which those individual norms must belong). To call it a genre of artifact is notionally the same as what is called a "kind" of artifact (or an "artifactual kind") in the literature on the metaphysics of artifacts: Amie L. Thomasson, 'Artifacts in Metaphysics' in Anthonie Meijers (ed.), *Philosophy of Technology and Engineering Sciences* (Elsevier 2009) 191–212 at 195–97.

[24] Peter Achinstein argues there are three types (or senses) of functions as they are used in explanations: "design functions, use functions, and service functions" (what an artifact is designed to accomplish, how it is used by those who interact with it, and the benefit it provides to those who use it): Peter Achinstein, 'Function Statements' (1977) 44 *Philosophy of Science* 341–67, 349; see also Peter McLaughlin, *What Functions Explain: Functional Explanation and Self-Reproducing Systems* (Cambridge University Press 2001) 54; Karen Neander, 'The Teleological Notion of "Function"' (1991) 69 *Australasian Journal of Philosophy* 454–68, 462. While important to keep in mind for artifactual functions, many times these will overlap and I focus here on the distinction in kinds of functions by the class of explanandum (biological vs. artifactual), rather than which subset of

distinction is between biological functions and artifactual functions, the former characterized by their selected (-for) effects, the latter by their intended effects.[25] Many of the difficulties with which functional explanations are saddled tend to be associated with the selected effects, mostly seen in functional explanations in biology. These difficulties are not (generally) present with the intended effects seen in artifacts. Rather, for artifacts, the difficulties tend to be about the possible difference between the uses intended by an artifact creator and the uses to which the artifact is eventually put by its users.

A legal example of this is the use of certain statutes designed for one purpose but used in response to behaviors not within the ambit of that original purpose. For example, in *Bond v. U.S.*[26] the defendant pled guilty to a violation of the Chemical Weapons Convention Implementation Act, by which the U.S. Congress ratified the Chemical Weapons Convention, an international treaty. The defendant was charged with violating the act for attempting to poison her husband's lover with toxic chemicals. The Supreme Court held that the intention of the members of Congress in ratifying the treaty was merely to avoid the use of chemicals in warfare, and that the use of the ratification to prosecute Ms. Bond extended beyond the function for the law originally envisioned by its drafters and ratifiers.[27] (We will see that this is an instance of the "use function" differing from the "proper function."[28]) However, since we will be more focused on if and how we can get a generalized notion of law's function from the myriad individual laws and what they do, this kind of problem is likely to be smoothed out in the generalization process.

Instead, the difficulty for law will be in articulating the relation between the intended effects of particular laws and any functions that are used to characterize law more generally as a genre. And it certainly seems possible to imagine individual laws that fulfill their particular purpose while running afoul of a characterization of the function of law as such, more generally. Nevertheless, I will argue that there are a number of reasons to prefer the

the objects' properties are being emphasized in the explanation. In philosophical parlance, the "explanandum" is the thing being explained and the "explanans" is the explanation itself.

[25] Dan Sperber, 'Seedless Grapes: Nature and Culture' in Eric Margolis and Stephen Laurence (eds), *Creations of the Mind* (Oxford University Press 2007) 124–37 at 126, citing Karen Neander, 'Functions as Selected Effects: The Conceptual Analyst's Defence' (1991) 58 *Philosophy of Science* 168–84 and arguing for characterizing selected effects as "teleofunctions" to allow for biological artifacts.

[26] 572 U.S. ___ (2014)(Docket No. 09–1227).

[27] The point of this example is to show the possibility of repurposing, or having the use function differ from the design function. Note that I do not base any claims about the nature or operation of law in general upon any given decision by any court as such decisions could easily have been otherwise (and often are in other jurisdictions).

[28] Ruth Garrett Millikan, *Language, Thought, and Other Biological Categories: New Foundations for Realism* (MIT Press 1984) 2.

artifactual notion of function to the biological one for purposes of explaining law, and will remind the reader of this and the reasons for it in several places.

From this introduction, I will turn first to developing several ideas and distinctions that will be useful to us going forward. Then I will turn to the three main theories of general jurisprudence—interpretivism, natural law, and legal positivism—showing the dependence of each on its understanding of law's function and where potential pitfalls arise. Then, in what is intended to be an argument in favor of a broadly positivist view, I will develop and defend the metaphysical picture I have drawn here. While a central claim of this book is methodological—that the best way to understand law is by attempting to discover its social functions—the reason I first start with a metaphysical picture is that methodology needs to follow metaphysics. That is, one must first get a handle on the basic nature of what one is investigating in order to understand the best methods for performing that investigation. Those methods will then be suggested, if not determined, by the nature of the subject matter being investigated. I will end by considering several candidates for an understanding of law's overall function(s) and what their strengths and weaknesses might be for explanatory purposes.

2

Concepts, Distinctions, and some Preliminary Remarks on Method

We cannot really begin our analysis of the relation of law's nature to its function without first understanding just a little bit about what we mean by certain notions that will keep coming up in this book. So in this chapter I will merely lay out the basic contours of some of the ideas that will get heavy use. Some of these ideas and distinctions will seem a bit obvious. Others might instead be fairly controversial, and I will be unable to avoid taking a position in those controversies given the way those ideas will be used. Where I am aware of the controversy and unable to avoid it, I will at least try to motivate taking the position I do. In some places, I may instead sidestep the issue where the position doesn't matter directly to our topic, or where our treatment doesn't force us to take one side or another in the ongoing debate. Unfortunately, doing so may also sometimes require being less precise than would otherwise be desirable, so I will try to alert the reader whenever I am remaining purposely vague to sidestep an issue of less relevance.

A. Law

When we use the word "law," we could be referring to a number of different entities at differing levels of generality.[1] This means both that the word itself is generally ambiguous and that the references we make with it could come at different levels of generality. Nevertheless, there is some internal relationship among those entities when we limit the reference class to what is generally

[1] Much of my thinking here follows that of John Gardner in 'The Legality of Law' (2004) 17 *Ratio Juris* 168–81, 169. See also Chaim Gans, 'The Normativity of Law and Its Co-Ordinative Function' (1981) 16 *Israel Law Review* 333–49, 340, making an identical tripartite distinction, and H. L. A. Hart, *The Concept of Law* (Penelope A. Bulloch and Joseph Raz (eds), 2nd edn., Clarendon Press 1994 (1961)) 247.

the product of governmental enactments or declarations, and some of their derivations.[2]

We could be referring to a specific decision or piece of legislation, such as the speed limit, or the law requiring residents and citizens to pay income tax. Sometimes this might actually itself be a cluster of laws, or a number of decisions establishing a specific legal norm. As shorthand, I will generally use an indefinite article to indicate this: for example, "There is *a* law prohibiting the sale of alcohol to minors," although in common parlance this can of course be accomplished with a definite article as well.

A slightly different possibility (which is not always so clearly distinguishable from the first) is when we refer to what is still a specific legal norm, but do so without making reference to a specific legal enactment[3] that established the norm. In such cases we may be claiming that the norm is a member of the class of legally valid norms in the relevant jurisdiction, but we are not making any direct reference to the establishing enactment. Compare the statement "It's against the law to rob banks" to the statement above about selling alcohol to minors. While we can easily assume the existence of a specific legal enactment (or set of enactments) that establishes the norm not to rob banks, my language is more vague in that I am merely referring to law generally in my assertion that the norm against robbing banks is a member of the class of valid legal norms. In the statement "There is a law prohibiting the sale of alcohol to minors," I am asserting the existence of a specific enactment that establishes the legal norm, although I might not personally have ever read that statute or come into contact with its wording. (Note as well that the use of the definite or indefinite article does not determine whether the reference is specific or general. I can ask "What does the law about selling alcohol to minors say?", making a specific reference while using a definite article.) In general parlance, however, there isn't really much practical difference between these types of locutions. So for our purposes, I will group them together at one level of generality, using the indefinite article to indicate that we are referring to these specificities.

Sometimes it is important to talk about the set of all valid legal norms within a jurisdiction, perhaps to differentiate them from other jurisdictions, to discuss which norms might be members of one jurisdiction but not

[2] This should not be misunderstood to beg the question against legal anti-positivists. We could limit the reference class to products of governmental action and still impose further moral or rational restrictions to determine a final reference class.

[3] I intend the term "enactment" in a broader sense than its technical legal sense, covering any legally requisite establishing declaration. Hence it covers dictatorial fiat, administrative rule creation, and judicial (re-)interpretation or application, and even private exercises of delegated legal authority such as the formation of contracts and wills, as well as typical legislation.

another, or to understand that for legal norms to be valid they must generally be valid within such a jurisdiction. In such cases we generally speak of "legal systems" (the terminology I will use for this level of generality), although we sometimes instead use the ambiguous word, speaking for example of "the law of the United States" when referring to the U.S. legal system.

The possibility of nested jurisdictions can make this usage difficult and the boundaries of what constitutes a legal system can get confusing. In the U.S., there are generally sufficient distinctions between the roles and powers of the states and of the federal government for us to say that the federal government constitutes one legal system and each state also constitutes a distinct legal system. What is less clear is the relation of the states to their counties and other municipal legal regimes. Hence talk of "legal systems" will be somewhat vague and contextually bound, dependent upon the use to which the notion is being put. Even the relation between the states and the federal government might not be usefully considered to be that of distinct legal systems, for example in the context of a discussion of international law.

One important thing to keep in mind is that legal systems are often self-consciously designed to be frameworks for the creation of individual laws. Even when they are not so self-consciously designed, the officials who make, interpret, and implement those individual enactments are mindful of their impact on the system as a whole. An analogy that might come in handy is the relation of a computer operating system to the software that is written for running in that environment. Both are the products of human intentional activity even as the particular pieces of software must be written according to the specifications given within the operating system. Additionally, the various components of the operating system are themselves merely particular pieces of software.

The notion of a legal system is also somewhat problematic when dealing with non-political or non-nation-state legal systems. Do the Shi'ite madhaheb represent a distinct legal system from the various Sunni madhaheb or are they merely different instantiations of the same system?[4] While these are interesting questions, we will generally sidestep them, seeing "legal system" as referring to the set of laws and other legal norms within a referenced jurisdiction, even if that jurisdiction is subservient to, or not wholly separate from, another.

Another wrinkle is that I am using "jurisdiction" here not in its strictest legal sense, in which a single legal system can have multiple jurisdictions. For example, the various circuit courts of appeals each have their own jurisdiction in the U.S. federal justice system. But this doesn't mean that each circuit

[4] These are the systems of Islamic jurisprudence.

is a distinct legal system. Rather, I am using the term here as a placeholder for however one's favorite legal theory explains what unifies a set of legal norms into one system. For most analytic legal philosophers, this would be the ultimate criteria of legal validity. That is, a single legal system is differentiated from other legal systems by its having a distinct set of criteria for picking out what is legally valid.[5]

One thing that is important about the relation between individual laws and legal systems is that it doesn't generally make sense to think of a law independently of a legal system in which it is instantiated. That is, laws only exist within normative systems that validate them.[6] This is a facet of law's institutionality, which we will return to shortly.

Finally, we can refer to law as a type of human activity, a kind of institution, or a form of governance of conduct. When general jurisprudents offer theories of law, they are trying to account for this general type of activity. They may define their ambitions more modestly, usually to account only for municipal and nation-state law. However, they are attempting to explain or analyze this kind of law wherever it may be found.

We might be tempted to think that "legality" would be a better term to capture this most general notion, and I will sometimes use the term in this sense. But I also worry that it is too easily confused for more normatively pregnant notions of the rule of law. That is, we sometimes encounter the term "legality" as standing in for ideas about what makes a legal system a good exemplar of the kind, or for what is valuable about having a legal system as a form of governance. Granted, some of those considerations are very important to many legal philosophers. But since many others seek to explain law rather than to endorse it, we don't want the terms used in our theoretical focus to preclude *ab initio* the methodologies adopted by explanatory theorists. For me, this is especially true as I am hoping to count this as a contribution to that explanatory project. So here I merely caution the reader that I will not use "legality" in the more value-laden sense unless I specifically call attention to my doing so.

It might strike some as immodest that the general jurisprudent tries to offer up theories that explain the nature of law wherever it might be found. She will sometimes talk about offering "universal" or "conceptually necessary" features of law. This seems to suggest the jurisprudent is offering a

[5] I realize that this explanation might suggest that the laws of various counties or other municipalities might each form their own legal system (and in some contexts it would not be incorrect to say so). Generally, however, such regimes are much more heavily dependent upon the validity criteria of superior institutions than is seen between the federal legal system and those of the various states.

[6] Gardner, 'The Legality of Law' 169–70.

theory to arbitrate whether a given newly discovered society has law based merely upon the theoretical features she articulates. Mightn't some newly discovered community have a legal system with features that the jurisprudent neglected to consider? Absolutely. But that possibility serves as one constraint on theory construction. These new features would then need to be accounted for with changes to the theory. It also leaves open a possible empirical test of the jurisprudent's theory. I will discuss the relation between such possible empirical tests and the kind of conceptual analysis associated with universalist claims later in discussing the relation between metaphysics and methodology.

This constraint is also why one desideratum of an adequate theory of law is that it explains the features of law which help to distinguish it from other human activity. It is not because we need to use the theory to tell what law is when we see it, but rather because the theory is attempting to capture what we are already using to tell that a given system is law when we see it. If we discover a new community with a system we wish to call legal but our current theory does not account for it, that would be very good evidence that the theory needs revision, since it has not adequately captured what it was that tempted us to call that system legal.

The ever-present danger of this is that jurisprudents who are partisans of their favorite theories might be tempted to have their judgments about what counts as a legal system colored by their theories. However, the community of legal and jurisprudential scholars helps to keep its members on the right path. Scholars not over-awed by their own conclusions, or those of their mentors, do well to see a good reason to revisit their existing theory when they find a coalescing of opinion that a given newly discovered or newly imagined system counts as law but is not yet explained by their theory.

One additional factor to consider when disambiguating among these different senses of law is how the token/type distinction maps onto these different notions. Individual laws and legal systems can be discussed at the type level ("all laws must be valid to be binding," "legal systems must have a unified set of criteria of legal validity") or at the token level ("drive on the left," "the legal system of France").[7] The most general notion is always a type, although, of course, even that is a sub-type of even more general types. Law is one sub-type of the human institution type. However, sometimes it will

[7] Since, as we will see, laws are abstractions, it may be more correct to say that these are instances or occurrences of the type, rather than tokens. See Linda Wetzel, 'Types and Tokens' (2014) *The Stanford Encyclopedia of Philosophy*, Edward N. Zalta (ed.) § 8 <http://plato.stanford.edu/archives/spr2014/entries/types-tokens/>, noting that tokens "are concrete particulars." However, since the distinction itself is generally drawn in the literature as between token and type, I will continue using the common terminology and hope that logicians don't take affront.

make sense to see the general notion as a type that encompasses both laws and legal systems as sub-types, each with their own tokens.

Legal norms are another sub-type of law, distinct from laws and legal systems, although tokens of those will always also include one or more legal norms. Yet legal norms are also distinct. An early common law judge deciding that a given litigant had to pay an adversary a given sum in a case of first impression would be creating and imposing a legal norm without necessarily having a law to back that imposition up. It might also be possible to imagine legal norms (although not laws) independently of any legal system. For example, if the people in a Lockean state of nature wished to appoint a common judge over them for settling any disputes that might arise, that initial judge (prior to the formation of a state) would likely be imposing legal norms without a legal system being in place. Some might prefer to think of this as a primitive legal system, but nothing turns upon this preference for our purposes.

While some of these distinctions will not always be so clear, as the need to deal in generalities will sometimes require eliding them to reduce the complexity of presentation, I will try to make it clear which level of legal generality is in play.

B. Function

When we start thinking about functions we can easily get caught up in many ambiguities that appear in our usage of the term. Furthermore, much philosophical hostility to the notion of function likely stems from difficulties in pinning down exactly what they are and how they attach to the things they are supposed to explain, especially when thinking about them in the context of biology.

While it might be initially easy to think of functions in terms of the beneficial effects that something has, which it is either designed[8] to accomplish or selected to accomplish (perhaps even by a natural process),[9] there are at

[8] Larry Wright, 'Functions' (1973) 82 *The Philosophical Review* 139–68, 142, preferring "conscious" rather than "designed" functions as distinct from "natural" functions since it appears possible for artifacts to obtain functions with less effort than suggested by "design," following Richard Sorabji, 'Function' (1964) 14 *Philosophical Quarterly* 289–302, 290.

[9] See Karen Neander, 'Teleological Notion of "Function"' (1991) 69 *Australasian Journal of Philosophy* 454–68, 462; Harold Kincaid, 'Assessing Functional Explanation in the Social Sciences' in Michael Martin and Lee C. McIntyre (eds), *Readings in the Philosophy of Social Science* (MIT Press 1994) 415–28 at 417, distinguishing "functionalism" from "functional explanations." See also Carl G. Hempel, 'The Logic of Functional Analysis' in Michael Martin and Lee C. McIntyre (eds), *Readings in the Philosophy of Social Science* (MIT Press 1994) 349–75 at 353; John R. Searle,

least two different ways to use this idea. One is what is called a "selected" function in the biological literature, sometimes a "design" function in the artifact literature, or more generally a "proper" function.[10] A thing's proper function is the characteristic ends[11] that it yields (or is supposed to yield) which explain its presence, development, or selection.[12] Ruth Millikan introduced the idea of proper function to distinguish it from the ends that certain tokens might actually be used to serve.[13] Hence, the proper function of any carpenter's hammer is to drive nails (and pull them), even if I am using a particular hammer as a doorstop.

Millikan notes that there are two ways in which a proper function is acquired. One is where the token is made because previous members of that kind successfully performed the function (a "direct proper function"). The other is where the thing is created by a mechanism whose proper function is achieved by creating things like this to perform that function (a "derived proper function").[14]

Construction of Social Reality (Free Press 1995) 20, distinguishing "imposed agentive" functions from "discovered non-agentive" functions; Searle, *Making the Social World: The Structure of Human Civilization* (Oxford University Press 2010) 43–44, 58–60.

[10] The term "proper function" has gained wide acceptance in the literature but (in a non-mathematical sense) was introduced by Ruth Millikan in *Language, Thought, and Other Biological Categories: New Foundations for Realism* (MIT Press 1984) 17.

[11] I will use "ends," "purposes," and "goals" fairly interchangeably, although the last will be used more when emphasizing human intentions.

[12] See Neander, 'Teleological Notion of "Function"' 454, noting proper functions are both normative and teleological. See also John R. Searle, 'Social Ontology and the Philosophy of Society' in Eric Margolis and Stephen Laurence (eds), *Creations of the Mind: Theories of Artifacts and Their Representation* (Oxford University Press 2007) 3–17 at 8, noting that the difference between a mere causal explanation and a functional explanation is that the notion of function introduces normativity. The fact that functions introduce normativity in the form of benefits or goals should not be understood to preclude their use in a normatively neutral explanation of the phenomenon. See generally my 'Defending the Possibility of a Neutral Functional Theory of Law' (2009) 29 *Oxford Journal of Legal Studies* 91–113.

[13] Millikan, *Language, Thought, and Other Biological Categories: New Foundations for Realism* 2. Paul Griffiths understands proper functions to be any teleological usage, distinguishing "having the function F from merely functioning as an F": 'Functional Analysis and Proper Functions' (1993) 44 *The British Journal for the Philosophy of Science* 409–22, 410–12. Millikan does warn that her notion of proper function is meant to be for technical usage and not an analysis of function in general: Millikan, *Language, Thought, and Other Biological Categories: New Foundations for Realism* 18. But others have used it to develop a conceptual analysis of one usage of functions and it has come to reflect the philosophical usage that we are most concerned with here. See Mark Perlman, 'The Modern Philosophical Resurrection of Teleology' (2004) 87 *Monist* 3–51, 17.

[14] Ruth Garrett Millikan, *White Queen Psychology and Other Essays for Alice* (MIT Press 1993) 13–14. See also Amie L. Thomasson, 'Artifacts and Human Concepts' in Eric Margolis and Stephen Laurence (eds), *Creations of the Mind: Theories of Artifacts and Their Representation* (Oxford University Press 2007) 52–73 at 56–57.

A slightly different but frequently overlapping notion of function is what Millikan calls a "Cummins function," after work by Robert Cummins.[15] These are the benefits that a given trait or aspect contribute to a wider system of which it is a part. Many theorists appear to be invoking Cummins functions in their explanations or in their arguments about why functions are not necessary or valuable to a complete understanding of law.

The issue with Cummins functions is that the wider system of which the element is a part is not generally fixed. Unless we can fix that wider context in which the functional ascription is made, and fix it independently of the functional ascription, the explanation is always open to being challenged by another competing context in which the advantage is different.[16] That is, if we understand a part's function to be its contribution to the whole, then we must also specify which whole we are considering. Otherwise, our explanation will be open to challenge merely by specifying a different whole for that part. In Millikan's example, a leaf might have one Cummins function for the tree on which it grows, another for a wider ecosystem that includes local insect and bird life, and still another for the biosphere as a whole to which it contributes oxygenation.[17]

Since the functional explanation itself cannot be an argument in favor of one context or another, an argument over Cummins functions must involve an independently settled context. Where that context is not settled, the arguments over functions are likely to be hopelessly confused. Furthermore, when it is understood as a theory of functions generally, Cummins' theory (as a result of the unfixed contexts) leads theorists to make attributions of functions that appear flatly wrong or to things not ripe for functional explanations.[18]

[15] Ruth Garrett Millikan, 'An Ambiguity in the Notion "Function"' (1989) 4 *Biology and Philosophy* 172–76; Ruth Garrett Millikan, 'Biofunctions: Two Paradigms' in Andre Ariew, Robert Cummins, and Mark Perlman (eds), *Functions: New Essays in the Philosophy of Psychology and Biology* (Oxford University Press 2002) 113–43, citing Robert Cummins, 'Functional Analysis' (1975) 72 *The Journal of Philosophy* 741–65. These are also sometimes called "causal-role" functions: Christopher Boorse, 'A Rebuttal on Functions' in André Ariew, Robert Cummins, and Mark Perlman (eds), *Functions: New Essays in the Philosophy of Psychology and Biology* (Oxford University Press 2002) 63–112 at 64. Griffiths agrees with the distinction between proper and Cummins functions, in that the one does not assume the other, but doesn't think that they come apart as frequently: Griffiths, 'Functional Analysis and Proper Functions' 410, citing Ruth Garrett Millikan, 'In Defense of Proper Functions' (1989) 56 *Philosophy of Science* 288–302.

[16] See Griffiths, 'Functional Analysis and Proper Functions' 411, noting that one Cummins function of the liver is to host liver flukes.

[17] Millikan, 'An Ambiguity in the Notion "Function"' 175.

[18] Perlman, 'The Modern Philosophical Resurrection of Teleology' 15, quoting Boorse, 'A Rebuttal on Functions' 65, collecting criticisms: "the function of mists is to make rainbows, the function of rocks in a river is to widen the river delta, the function of clouds [is] to make rain with which to fill the streams and rivers, and the function of a piece of dirt stuck in a pipe is to

Thinking about the function of law in terms of a Cummins-style function can be seen in the somewhat mysterious or controversial functionalisms of some legal theories of the early to mid-twentieth century. One can say that the function of law is to provide for economic efficiency, or to consolidate power in the elite, or to provide a *post facto* rationalization for judicial decisions precisely because each of these benefits is brought by law to a slightly different wider system of which it is a part. Law is an element of an economic system, a social class system, and a governmental system, and brings a slightly different benefit to each of these systems. Arguments among these theories over the function that best explains law appear fruitless because these theories do not usually explicitly fix the context in which the function is to be assessed. When they do, it is generally done by fiat or assumption. Such arguments are in reality over the context in which to adduce a function for law rather than over what functions law has.

Whether they fix the context or not, such explanations are always open to a competing explanation that relies on law's function in a competing context. This is why a deeper understanding of many of these theories leads one to think that they are arguing past each other. Without recognizing that there are other valuable notions of function available, many subtle thinkers see the misuse of Cummins functions in this way and despair of the utility of the notion of function to explain law.[19]

Of course, the Cummins function and the proper function will often coincide where the focus is on a specific wider context. In the tree example, if the context is limited to the tree itself as a member of a specific type of organism, then the Cummins function is likely to match the selected function that explains the presence of the leaf. So we should not be surprised to see functional explanations that involve both mentioning of a wider context to which the explanandum contributes in performing its function, and a proper function that is the selected-for or designed-for element of the explanation.

Therefore this is a word of warning: reference to a wider system in a functional explanation strongly suggests some notions of Cummins functions are slipping in. Where the context is clearly fixed, this is not necessarily pernicious, but there is no necessity for a functional explanation to involve a wider system. (It is, however, still relevant to ask where the benefit is, as functional

regulate the water flow," citing respectively John Bigelow and Robert Pargetter, 'Functions' (1987) 84 *Journal of Philosophy* 181–96, 184; Philip Kitcher, 'Function and Design' (1993) 18 *Midwest Studies in Philosophy* 379–97, 390; Millikan, 'In Defense of Proper Functions' 294, and Griffiths, 'Functional Analysis and Proper Functions' 411.

[19] See for example Leslie Green, 'The Functions of Law' (1998) 12 *Cogito* 117–24, 118.

explanations always involve some evaluative stance.) In general our focus will be on proper functions.[20]

When it comes not to biological entities but to artifacts, proper functions are generally understood to be design functions as opposed to use functions. Design functions are tasks that artifact inventors or designers envision for the artifact when fashioning it.[21] Use functions are the ways in which the artifact is used when people actually employ it. (Peter Achinstein separates this last category into use functions, understood as the intended or expected results of the person using the artifact, and service functions, understood as the benefits that actually result from the usage.[22] I will group these together and call them "use functions" generally except if and where this particular distinction is important to the analysis.)

It is possible, however, for a use function to become the proper function of an artifact when its usage differs from its intended purpose and comes to dominate people's conception of the artifact. Proper functions are most commonly seen among artifacts in understanding the artifact to be created by a person for a purpose.[23] However, this does not account for how an artifact's function might change or how it might differ when seen with the eyes of its creator from the eyes of its later users. To embellish upon an example from John Searle,[24] someone could build a stone wall that was originally designed to keep intruders out, which over time and with some deterioration comes to be used as a boundary between municipalities. We are here thinking about this repurposing[25] as changing how we identify the object by changing its proper function. We no longer conceive of the object as a wall, but rather as a boundary marker. Where we have maintained our understanding of the object's identity but merely use it in a new way, we do not yet change its proper function.[26] We will revisit some of these complexities below in our discussion of artifacts.

[20] See Thomasson, 'Artifacts and Human Concepts' 56, recommending the use of proper functions when discussing the functions of artifacts.

[21] Peter Achinstein, *The Nature of Explanation* (Oxford University Press 1983) 272. This is somewhat controversial as it assumes an intentionalist account of how an artifact comes to be associated with its proper function, but we will see this problem is not as large for law. See also Griffiths, 'Functional Analysis and Proper Functions' 418–19, arguing parts of artifacts developed by trial and error may have functional contributions unappreciated by designers.

[22] Achinstein, 'Function Statements' (1977) 44 *Philosophy of Science* 341–67, 349. See also Neander, 'Teleological Notion of "Function"' 462, distinguishing "design functions," "user functions," and "occasion functions."

[23] Perlman, 'The Modern Philosophical Resurrection of Teleology' 31–32.

[24] Searle, 'Social Ontology and the Philosophy of Society' 12; *Making the Social World* 94–96.

[25] See Beth Preston, 'Philosophical Theories of Artifact Function' in Anthonie Meijers (ed.), *Philosophy of Technology and Engineering Sciences* (Elsevier 2009) 213–34 at 215–16, calling it "recycling."

[26] But see Neander, 'Teleological Notion of "Function"' 432, arguing "the function of an artifact is always whatever it was selected for."

Apart from the less problematic way in which functions help to explain artifacts as opposed to their role in explaining natural biological entities,[27] another advantage of focusing on artifact functions as opposed to biological functions is that it allows for one-off idiosyncratic functions that attach only to specific unique artifacts. That is, while biological functions generally must be understood to explain a type rather than a token organ or part of an organism, we can make sense of functions for artifacts that only appear once in history.[28] It is important to remain open to this possibility for law precisely because special laws with unique functions will present a challenge for any view that seeks to generalize from individual laws to typify the functions that law performs as a genre.

Of the various ways of conceptualizing functions, the one that is generally most suited to discussions of artifacts is what John Bigelow and Robert Pargetter call a "representational theory," in which a mental representation of a future causal result is used to form a plan for how to achieve it, a kind of "goal theory."[29] One aspect of functions we've already seen is that they are value-laden, in that they refer to a benefit that the explanandum brings about through the performance of its function.[30] Artifact functions are therefore less problematic than biological ones since designers, creators, and users can all be understood to be interacting with the artifact for the reason that they believe it brings some benefit or value into the world (even if that value or benefit is only to one person or is otherwise localized, perhaps even while being of large disvalue to just about everyone else).

Mark Perlman provides a kind of taxonomy of philosophical theories of functions that covers their usage across explananda (including both biological and artifactual), and also a kind of scorecard for the debate among the myriad competing theories.[31] He groups the various theories into nine distinct types of position, plus an eliminativist position that sees all functions as chimerical.[32] Since many (though certainly not all) of the complexities have to do with examples and counterexamples from biology,

[27] Wright, 'Functions' 142; Perlman, 'The Modern Philosophical Resurrection of Teleology' 32, "even if there is a problem ascribing teleology to natural objects, there is no problem putting it into human artifacts" (noting as well that some writers disagree). See also p. 35 (admitting to "the philosophical bias that artifactual functions are far less problematic than natural functions").

[28] Neander, 'Teleological Notion of "Function"' 462. But see Perlman, 'The Modern Philosophical Resurrection of Teleology' 39–40.

[29] Bigelow and Pargetter, 'Functions' 184–85.

[30] Perlman, 'The Modern Philosophical Resurrection of Teleology' 8–9, noting this is not a universal view. Searle, 'Social Ontology and the Philosophy of Society' 8.

[31] Perlman, 'The Modern Philosophical Resurrection of Teleology' 6–23.

[32] Ibid 6, 12.

we can sidestep some of the debate just by limiting our focus to the use of functions in artifacts.[33] That is, we do not need to take a clear position on the metaphysics of functions, or a side in these debates, if our use of them to explain law or artifacts more generally is compatible with several positions.

To support this claim, let us look briefly at just a couple of the distinctions to see how the focus on artifacts avoids the issues being debated. Within the realm of naturalistic theories,[34] which hold that functions arise in the natural world or our place in it, Perlman distinguishes between theories that reduce the idea of function to more basic natural properties (such as goals and causes) and theories that do not. Searle's view is understood to be an example of the latter in that all functions are observer-relative, and are one way in which we map value onto the world.[35] But since Searle understands the social reality created by this process to be natural (in that our representations of the world are themselves natural processes), it isn't an attempt to eliminate functions at all.[36] While I am partial to this understanding of functions since it appears to me that their value-laden aspect requires some form of observer relativity,[37] our focus on artifacts means we don't really have to make a choice between Searle's conception and "reductionist" theories that explain functions in terms of more basic natural properties like etiology or goal contribution.[38] That is, our focus primarily on design functions with regard to artifacts means that we are not forced into a choice between seeing

[33] For the reasons stated immediately above, I do think that Cummins functions, which Perlman discusses as a causal role theory, are not a helpful way of understanding functions when it comes to artifacts such as law: ibid 12–15. So we cannot remain entirely neutral in these debates if Cummins' theory is seen as covering artifacts as well. While Cummins seemed to think so, he also noted that the scientific use of functions (which is what he was trying to capture) is not generally employed to explain artifacts. Cummins, 'Functional Analysis' 747 n. 3, 754. He did imply that his theory was more adept at explaining sub-systems within artifacts: ibid 746 n. 2.

[34] These are opposed to "non-naturalistic" theories such as Plato's forms and religious conceptions of functions as God's intentions, as well as some "quasi-naturalistic" theories: Perlman, 'The Modern Philosophical Resurrection of Teleology' 6, 7–10.

[35] Ibid 11, citing Searle, *Construction of Social Reality* 14. See also Searle, 'Social Ontology and the Philosophy of Society' 8.

[36] Perlman, 'The Modern Philosophical Resurrection of Teleology' 11–12.

[37] This doesn't mean that I'm a moral relativist or value pluralist. Rather, it simply seems to me that to have a value, there must be someone doing the valuing. There can still be right and wrong answers about those evaluations. It may also be that I am led to this partiality by the fact that seeing functions as Searle does allows for a kind of intentionality more generally, my partiality arising from my focus on artifacts. See ibid 33; Searle, 'Social Ontology and the Philosophy of Society' 8. See also Thomasson, 'Artifacts and Human Concepts' 52, noting that artifacts depend upon intentionality, and Risto Hilpinen, 'Artifact' (2011) *The Stanford Encyclopedia of Philosophy*, Edward N. Zalta (ed.) § 4 <http://plato.stanford.edu/archives/win2011/entries/artifact/>.

[38] Perlman, 'The Modern Philosophical Resurrection of Teleology' 6, 15–20.

such a function as a basic feature of our interaction with the world or as standing in for a more basic natural property.[39]

Similarly, if we do choose to see such functions as representing something more basic, the design focus means we don't have to choose between conceiving them as the expected causes and effects that the designer envisions in planning out the artifact, and the goals that the designer adopts in making those plans. Clearly, elements of both are necessarily present in the intentions of the designer, and we need not claim either to be more basic than the other in the explanation of function.

We will see that there are notions of artifacts in which intentionality is not central. However, there we will also see that those notions aren't applicable to law.

We will also need to avoid one common understanding of function when used in social sciences. This is the idea that a social institution has a function only if the beneficial effect is "unintended" by those who create or maintain the institution and the effect or causal relation between it and the institution is "unrecognized" by those who benefit from it.[40] While there is a certain kind of social theory that relies heavily on notions of functions that must remain mysterious to institutional participants in order to do their explanatory work, our exploration of law is not one that depends in any way upon its function being hidden from those who benefit from or create it. Quite to the contrary, by seeing law as a kind of artifact, we are imagining that those who create individual enactments do so with an intention in mind about what the enactment is to accomplish. We then hope to gather those functions together and characterize them in a general way as much as possible in order to understand law as an institution. It is this methodological difference that leads us away from focusing upon "latent" functions to do the explanatory work.

Social theories that are dependent upon mysterious functions envision the social institution they are attempting to explain as arising in a way akin to biological natural selection.[41] This is supposed to explain why participants

[39] For an interesting discussion of the different kinds of social kinds and how they can be both mind-dependent and still objective (even sometimes natural), see generally Muhammad Ali Khalidi, 'Three Kinds of Social Kinds' (2015) 90 *Philosophy and Phenomenological Research* 96–112, with thanks to Lucas Miotto for the reference.

[40] Jon Elster, *Ulysses and the Sirens: Studies in Rationality and Irrationality* (Cambridge University Press 1979) 28; G. A. Cohen, 'Functional Explanation, Consequence Explanation, and Marxism' (1982) 25 *Inquiry: An Interdisciplinary Journal of Philosophy* 27–56. See also Hempel, 'The Logic of Functional Analysis' 356, distinguishing "latent" from "manifest" functions, citing Robert King Merton, *Social Theory and Social Structure* (1968 enl. edn., Free Press 1968 (1949)) 51.

[41] Certainly, many artifacts do exhibit functions that arise in ways akin to natural selection, for example, trial and error. And there are also artifacts or artifact-parts that have functions of which users and designers are not aware. Neander, 'Teleological Notion of "Function"' 462 n. 11.

are unaware of the benefit directly or of the relation between the institution and the benefit.[42] Instead, where the institution is self-consciously developed, participants are likely to believe it aids in a distinctive benefit that is of a more local value inside their social context. Also, it is likely that many such social theorists are considering the functions that explain social institutions to be Cummins functions and then assuming that the wider contexts in which the benefits can be perceived are not themselves accessible by participants.

Because we are not thinking that law developed according to some social analogue of natural selection,[43] we can see more of a continuum and communication between participants in legal institutions and the theorists who explain them. Hence it makes more sense for the theorist to work toward a characterization of law's function by collecting and generalizing upon the particular functions adduced by those drafting and deciding upon individual enactments. While those participants may not be directly aware of these characterizations as explaining legal institutions generally, nothing depends upon that lack of awareness. Indeed, there is no reason to expect that self-aware participants would be unable to perceive generalizations about the functions they have for individual enactments.

One final, very anti-Aristotelian thing we might notice about functions is that for something to have a function, it has to be capable of failure. I say this is "anti-Aristotelian" because, due to other metaphysical commitments which need not concern us here, Aristotle believed that when he was explaining something using its function, he was defining it as a thing that performed that function. Hence things that failed to perform their functions were not members of the class being defined, since they therefore fell outside the definition. That is, success (or at least the structural capacity for success in entities not yet put into operation) in the performance of the function was a necessary condition for being a member of the class being explained. For us today, this is not only implausible (broken chairs are still chairs), but belies our current way of conceptualizing functions. For something to be ripe for a functional explanation, it must be conceptually possible for it to fail to

[42] Hempel, 'The Logic of Functional Analysis' 356, giving the examples of religion and magic, citing A. R. Radcliffe-Brown, *Structure and Function in Primitive Society* (Cohen & West 1952) and Bronislaw Malinowski, *Magic, Science and Religion, and Other Essays* (Doubleday 1954). See also Perlman, 'The Modern Philosophical Resurrection of Teleology' 33–34.

[43] I do not deny the possibility that authority relations may have developed in some kind of evolutionary process, nor that there are customary laws that arose in some kind of less self-conscious way. But the commonly found municipal legal enactment, and the system of which it is a part, was most likely designed and developed by a legislator at some point. Even if we cannot really be sure of the nature and genesis of a legal prototype, it is clear that the legal enactments of today are mostly the product of self-conscious design.

perform that function.[44] If failure is not a conceptual possibility, then the entity might have causal properties that are possibly or actually valuable to an agent, but we don't think that those properties would count as the entity's point or purpose. If it is conceptually impossible for that valued effect not to take place, we don't tend to think of the cause in terms of its utility to bring about that effect; we will tend instead to group cause and effect together as a single entity, event, or process, and not see one as useful for the sake of the other.[45] This will be particularly important to keep in mind when we consider the appeals by some theorists to functions in explaining law.

C. Artifact

Randall Dipert was one of the first analytic thinkers to tackle the notion of artifacts directly, giving us a useful way of conceiving of what differentiates artifacts from other "products of intentional behavior,"[46] seeing artifacts as a specific type within more general classes of such products. For Dipert, an "instrument" is generally anything that someone has considered useful as a means to some end and has been used in an attempt to achieve that end.[47] The next step in his taxonomy is a "tool," which is an instrument that has been "intentionally modified" in order either to allow it to serve as a means for a goal, or to enhance its ability to achieve that goal.[48] The key distinction here is modification. If I smash a nut against a rock on the ground in order to open the nut, I am using the rock as an instrument but not a tool (in Dipert's

[44] I originally encountered this point in John Gardner, 'Law's Aims in *Law's Empire*' in Scott Hershovitz (ed.), *Exploring Law's Empire* (Oxford University Press 2006) 207–24 at 216, although I intend to draw some wider conclusions from it than does Gardner. For further support of this claim see George Letsas, 'Monism, Interpretivism, and Law's Aim' in Michael Freeman and Ross Harrison (eds), *Law and Philosophy*, vol. 10 (Current Legal Issues series, Oxford University Press 2007) 49–59 at 50; Preston, 'Philosophical Theories of Artifact Function' 217, claiming that "malfunction" must be accounted for in any theory of the relation between artifacts and their functions; Perlman, 'The Modern Philosophical Resurrection of Teleology' 34, "teleology requires the possibility of malfunction"; and Lynne Rudder Baker, 'The Metaphysics of Malfunction' (2009) 13 *Techne* 82–92, 82, "There is no ... function without the possibility of malfunction."

[45] See Peter Geach, 'Teleological Explanation' in Stephan Körner (ed.), *Explanation* (Basil Blackwell 1975) 76–95 at 94: "If God is almighty, he can get anything he wants by the thoughts of his mind, so there cannot be ascribed to him any adaptation of means to ends" (which suggests that if failure is conceptually impossible we don't explain the process in terms of means and ends).

[46] Randall R. Dipert, 'Some Issues in the Theory of Artifacts: Defining "Artifact" and Related Notions' (1995) 78 *Monist* 119–35, 121.

[47] Ibid.

[48] Ibid 123, noting as well that natural language will not always match perfectly with these explanations.

terminology). If I smash the rock a few times to give it sharp edges the better with which to open my nut, then I am making it into a tool.

The step from tool to artifact comes for Dipert when the tool also serves to communicate its identity. That is, it has been modified in such a way that it "signals" its purposive usability.[49] Here, signaling just means that there is some (usually structural) aspect of the object that communicates its usefulness to an intended audience. In our nutcracker example, there tend to be specific forms of the sharpened edges, or the location of the pivot point, that suggest that an object is a nutcracker. Alternatively, there might be design elements that are not directly related to its function which do the communication. Perhaps more elaborate nutcrackers characteristically come in the form of a soldier from an earlier period. Of course, the communication need not be successful, and the intended audience might be quite circumscribed.

One aspect important to emphasize for the legal realm in which we are going to use this signaling idea is that part of the artifactual property itself is that it be useful in producing the belief that the object has a specific sort of usability.[50] Artifacts "have a form which indicates, but might not be identical to, their (tool) function."[51] This is not to say that other tools cannot accidentally communicate their use to potential future users. Rather, artifacts are special in that there is generally something about them that is designed to suggest their usability to a given audience.

This is one thing that many theorists cite as differentiating artifacts from other human creations: that an artifact is created in such a way so as to communicate its identity as the kind of thing it is to other members of a community of users.[52] This identity is generally, though not always, conceived in terms of the artifact's function.

Caution is in order with this facet, however, as some artifacts may be designed to deceive some who interact with it into believing it is a different artifact, or even a natural object.[53] Think of an artificial hollow rock that is used in one's garden to keep spare keys to the house. The whole purpose of

[49] Ibid 127–29. [50] Ibid 129. [51] Ibid 130.

[52] Perlman, 'The Modern Philosophical Resurrection of Teleology' 40, citing Randall R. Dipert, *Artifacts, Art Works, and Agency* (Temple University Press 1993). There is a wider sense of "artifact" that includes anything "modified by humans, either intentionally or unintentionally." Hilpinen, 'Artifact,' quoting Kathy Diane Schick and Nicholas Patrick Toth, *Making Silent Stones Speak: Human Evolution and the Dawn of Technology* (Simon & Schuster 1993) 49. But this wider usage is usually confined to the realm of archeology. The "strict or proper sense" of the term generally refers to products of intentional action: Hilpinen, 'Artifact.'

[53] Dipert, *Artifacts, Art Works, and Agency* 31; Hilpinen, 'Artifact' § 5, giving the example of a mechanical shark used in making a film; Thomasson, 'Public Artifacts, Intentions and Norms' in Maarten Franssen and others (eds), *Artefact Kinds: Ontology and the Human-Made World* (Springer 2013) 45–62, 50.

the artifact is to fool others who see it into thinking that it is a real rock, and hence to keep one's keys safe from potential intruders. So it would seem to be an artifact that is designed not to signal its usability. The answer to this problem is that the intended audience of users to whom the artifact creator is communicating via the artifact may be quite circumscribed.[54]

Amie Thomasson acknowledges the possibility that there are artifacts in some broader sense that are not intended to be recognized by anyone (including the creator), and so suggests that we limit our focus to "public artifacts" that are "intended to be recognizable as artifacts of that kind by a certain intended audience."[55] We will follow her lead; when I use the term "artifact" I generally mean a public artifact in her sense.

The type/token distinction is similarly important when it comes to artifacts. An artifact can be a specific object, a type that has many tokens, one of those tokens, or an abstraction.[56] So hammers are an artifact type of which there are many sub-types and tokens, with a variety of forms. We will see that this is similarly true of institutions like hospitals and universities, as well as even more abstract ones like marriages and legal systems. A small point of terminology here: we can refer to a type (kind or genre) using singular or plural terms, and sometimes mass nouns.

When it comes to artifacts, we should first remember that the role of functions in explaining artifacts is much less problematic, although certainly not completely unproblematic. Karen Neander notes that "the function of an artifact is the purpose or end for which it was designed, made, or (minimally) put in place or retained by an agent."[57] Thomasson argues that, while some *kinds* of artifacts are understood in terms of their functions, others are understood in terms of their structural characteristics.[58] This particular distinction is made primarily in order to provide space for artistic artifacts, which may not have a function.[59] When it comes to law, it will be clear that it is the kind of artifact that is understood in terms of its function.

While functions in general are important to the understanding of most (though not all) artifact types (or kinds), they are certainly not sufficient. Also, saying that the function of an artifact is important to its understanding does not imply that success or even having the characteristic function is

[54] Dipert, *Artifacts, Art Works, and Agency* 31; Hilpinen, 'Artifact' § 5; Thomasson, 'Public Artifacts, Intentions and Norms' 50.

[55] Thomasson, 'Public Artifacts, Intentions and Norms' 50.

[56] Hilpinen, 'Artifact' § 2.

[57] Neander, 'Teleological Notion of "Function"' 462. See also Herbert A. Simon, *The Sciences of the Artificial* (3rd edn., MIT Press 1996 (1969)) 5; Baker, 'The Metaphysics of Malfunction' 84 ("artefacts are defined by their intended functions"); and Hilpinen, 'Artifact.'

[58] Thomasson, 'Public Artifacts, Intentions and Norms' 47–48.

[59] Ibid 48.

necessary to be a member of that kind. It's certainly possible to create a member of a given artifact kind without ever intending that the object be used as others of the kind are used.[60] Instead, the kind is generally conceived in functional terms, but membership of a given token depends more upon the intentions of the designer that are communicated through formal elements of the token to mark it out as belonging to the kind.[61]

Beth Preston gives a list of characteristics frequently seen in the relation of artifacts to their functions. While we will return to this list in greater detail later when we look at its applicability to law, I mention it here to help us see the potential advantages and pitfalls in thinking about artifacts in terms of their functions. Artifact functions are generally "multiply realizable," in that there are many artifact types that perform the same function and there are many different sub-types within given artifact types that perform the function in slightly different ways.[62] Artifacts are frequently "multiply utilizable," in that a given type of artifact can often perform more than one function.[63] Artifacts can generally be "recycled," in that they can be used for a different purpose than originally intended.[64] They exhibit "reproduction with variation," in that members of an artifact type change over time with the innovation and adaptation of designers hoping to improve upon the artifacts' ability to perform their tasks.[65] They can "malfunction," in that they can fail to accomplish their purpose.[66] Finally, they can also have "phantom functions," in that they can be intended to accomplish the impossible because the task itself is conceptually or physically impossible to achieve.[67]

D. Institution

An institution is a special kind of artifact.[68] Institutions are generally social arrangements in which members have defined roles that carry specially

[60] Paul Bloom, 'Intention, History, and Artifact Concepts' (1996) 60 *Cognition* 1–29, 5.

[61] See for example ibid 10.

[62] Preston, 'Philosophical Theories of Artifact Function' 214–15.

[63] Ibid 215.

[64] Ibid 215–16. This is sometimes called "repurposing" elsewhere in the literature and this book.

[65] Ibid 216–17. See also Baker, 'The Metaphysics of Malfunction' 84, distinguishing between malfunctions and functions that are impossible to fulfill.

[66] Preston, 'Philosophical Theories of Artifact Function' 217. See also Baker, 'The Metaphysics of Malfunction' 84 and n. 44 of this chapter.

[67] Preston, 'Philosophical Theories of Artifact Function' 217.

[68] Corrado Roversi, 'Acceptance Is Not Enough, but Texts Alone Achieve Nothing' (2012) 43 *Rechtstheorie* 1–30, 19; Corrado Roversi, Anna M. Borghi, and Luca Tummolini, 'Marriage Is an Artefact and Not a Walk That We Take Together: An Experimental Study on the Categorization of Artefacts' (2013) 4 *Review of Philosophy and Psychology* 527–42; Luka Burazin, 'Can There Be an Artifact Theory of Law?' (forthcoming 2016) *Ratio Juris* 8.

created rights and responsibilities. They are therefore primarily for creating and marshalling deontic powers, giving those subject to them new reasons for action.[69]

Institutions sit between more basic social forms like conventions or rituals and more complex or complete ones like cultures or societies.[70] Unlike some of these other forms, and in keeping with seeing them as a kind of artifact, institutions are also self-consciously created in some way. Hence they are a social arrangement for pursuing certain ends by creating and altering the normative relationship among members.

Searle's theory is the most discussed theory of institutions and is usually a jumping-off point for other discussions and amendments,[71] so we will generally follow it here. His analysis is actually of institutional facts, rather than institutions themselves. But since it is an account of the creation of these facts, the theory of institutions is a big component of the account.

He begins with a distinction between brute facts and social facts. The former are not dependent upon observers, while the latter are dependent in some way upon collective intentions.[72] An institutional fact is then a social fact in which a "status function" is assigned by collective intention via the adoption of a constitutive rule to an object, person, practice, event, or another entity (possibly thereby bringing the entity into existence).[73] These status functions carry deontic powers to create or alter "desire-independent reasons for action."[74] Put slightly more simply, something is endowed with special value or power, or someone is given special rights or responsibilities, by someone declaring it to be so in a formal context. This makes a new kind of social activity possible, further emphasizing the artifactual nature of institutions.

For our purposes, there is something a bit unfortunate in Searle's use of the phrase "status function" to describe this. It is clear that here the notion of function is the more mathematical one of mapping values onto a domain. The status function is used to impose a status on something, but that does not mean that imposing statuses is the ultimate proper function of the institution. Rather, institutions generally create and manipulate statuses as a

[69] Seumas Miller, 'Social Institutions' (2007) *The Stanford Encyclopedia of Philosophy*, Edward N. Zalta (ed.) § 2 <http://plato.stanford.edu/archives/fall2012/entries/social-institutions/>, claiming it is "self-evident" that social institutions have deontic properties; Searle, *Making the Social World* 23, 85–86.

[70] Miller, 'Social Institutions.'

[71] Thomasson, 'Realism and Human Kinds' 584–85.

[72] Searle, *Construction of Social Reality* 26–27, 229 n. 1, citing G. E. M. Anscombe, 'On Brute Facts' (1958) 18 *Analysis* 69. See also Searle, *Making the Social World* 10, Smith and Searle, 'The Construction of Social Reality: An Exchange' 304.

[73] Searle, *Construction of Social Reality* 23–26, 40–45.

[74] Searle, *Making the Social World* 23, 99.

means of accomplishing a more basic end. Hence it will be important going forward to keep in mind that talk of "status functions" does not invoke the mechanisms of functional explanations that I argue for. (I will occasionally insert a reminder of this in a footnote where necessary.)

The status function is generally conceived in the form "X counts as Y in context C."[75] But it need not always be so,[76] and it is also possible to declare the creation of institutions or institutional facts without there being a pre-existing X.[77] The institutional fact is created when the rules constituting the new status are adopted.

The point is that we create this institutional status, enabling the recipient (if any) to serve a function that it could not otherwise have served.[78] In the example mentioned before, the decayed stone wall serves as a boundary because we continue to treat it as such.[79] It must be done by collective intention because there must be more than one person to recognize the status in order for it to be a social fact. The deontic powers conveyed by the new status must be interpersonal, otherwise they merely look like personal plans or promises to oneself at best, delusions at worst. If I declare myself president, I cannot thereby get any power to change the rights or responsibilities of others unless people start to go along with that declaration.

An instance of that status, something or someone bearing it or having it bestowed, is called in the literature an "instance" of the institution and is to be distinguished from the institution itself.[80] However, one complicating issue is that institutions can also be seen as types, with individual institutions as tokens of the type, and actions by the individual institution as instances. This is complicating because sometimes we will see individual institutions as instances of a type, and sometimes the instance will be an application of the institution's status rule to something.[81] So a given contract is an instance

[75] Searle, *Construction of Social Reality* 28.

[76] Searle, *Making the Social World* 19–20; Smith and Searle, 'The Construction of Social Reality: An Exchange' (2003) 62 *American Journal of Economics & Sociology* 283–309, 301.

[77] Amie L. Thomasson, 'Realism and Human Kinds' (2003) 67 *Philosophy and Phenomenological Research* 580–609, 587, using the example of law to show that new institutional entities can be brought into existence by mere declaration; Searle, *Making the Social World* 85–86.

[78] Searle, *Construction of Social Reality* 88–89, 'Social Ontology and the Philosophy of Society' 12.

[79] Searle, 'Social Ontology and the Philosophy of Society' 12.

[80] Neil MacCormick and Ota Weinberger, *An Institutional Theory of Law: New Approaches to Legal Positivism* (D. Reidel Pub. Co. 1986) 54. See also Dick W. P. Ruiter, 'Structuring Legal Institutions' (1998) 17 *Law and Philosophy* 215–32, 215–16. I will sometimes call these "members" of the institution when I wish to specify them in personal or set-theoretic ways (in the sense that the institution determines a set of its applications).

[81] See for example Ruiter, 'Structuring Legal Institutions' 217, grappling with this difficulty as it applies to the institutional differences between legal and non-legal institutions.

of the institution of a given legal system, but a particular hospital is itself an institution and an instance of the hospital institutional type. Some might see this as a good reason for disambiguating the notion of institution even further, but as all are characterized by the creation and marshalling of deontic powers by setting statuses, I prefer to see them as different applications of the same idea.

When I call law a kind of "institutionalized" abstract artifact, I do so in order to call attention to the fact that we are not always so precise about the level of granularity with which we refer to institutions. That is, since we can use the word "institution" to refer either to institutions on the one hand, or applications or instances of institutions on the other, understanding law to be a genre of institutionalized artifact allows for multiple levels of granularity, while calling attention to the fact that we might be dealing with either an institution or an instance of one.

In general, for something to become institutionalized, the status must be assigned by type rather than by token. What lends the status its institutional character is the possibility of iteration and repetition, so that the same status can be applied at different times and possibly in different places, to different people, objects, or events. By applying the particular status function to a type, rather than a token, the institution is able to perform its task across time and space via multiple tokens. To do this, the specifications of what is to receive the status are set by "codification."[82] For a social fact to be a candidate for institutionality, it must be capable of having its status function codified.[83] Where the status function is uncodified, the status must be assigned token by token and the institution is at best "informal."[84] Cocktail parties are informal institutions because there are no codified rules determining what counts as a cocktail party; we determine what counts as a cocktail party on a token-by-token basis.[85]

Informal institutions also may not have quite the same level of self-conscious design that are found in formal institutions. One might think that this threatens to undermine the claim that they are still artifacts. But artifacts can also be created and signal their usage without being quite so self-consciously designed to do so. Perhaps a creator only really intended to build a tool and needn't have included any elements that signaled its usability to

[82] Searle, *Construction of Social Reality* 53. Searlean codification is more general than the legal variety, which would be a paradigm instance of it.

[83] Ibid 87–88.

[84] Searle, *Making the Social World* 91. See also Neil MacCormick, 'Norms, Institutions, and Institutional Facts' (1998) 17 *Law and Philosophy* 301–45, 323; Neil MacCormick, *Institutions of Law: An Essay in Legal Theory* (Oxford University Press 2007) 22–24.

[85] Searle, *Construction of Social Reality* 87–88.

others, yet others came to see some elements of the tool as characteristic and useful for identifying it for the kind of thing it is.

When I say that informal institutions have less self-conscious design to them, I mean this in the fashioning of the institution as a new type. Individual instances are usually explicitly designed. Cocktail parties are quite self-consciously planned out. It's just that the first person to plan a cocktail party probably wasn't doing so as a new type of social gathering.

The notion of codification (and hence the distinction between formal and informal institutions) is very important for our purposes because it explains the notion of validity in its institutional context, legal validity being one example. That is, when there is explicit codification, "specif[ying] the features a token must have in order to be an instance of the type,"[86] any token that does not have all of those features is deemed to be institutionally counterfeit or invalid. Imagine an exact molecular copy of a U.S. ten-dollar bill, except that the copy bears a distinct and unique serial number. It is still a counterfeit piece of currency because it does not have all the properties specified by the law for legal tender—it wasn't printed by the Bureau of Engraving and Printing, nor was it issued by the Federal Reserve.[87] It doesn't have the correct historical properties. To be legally valid, legislation and other enactments must conform to the specifications that are codified in Searle's sense within a constitution or other foundational sets of rules.[88]

Since Searle's codification must be "official" for the institution to be formal (and hence for it to convey status by type),[89] law can be seen as a special institution for generating other institutions.[90] It is the formal social mechanism by which we convey deontic powers to create and alter the rights and responsibilities of members of society, altering their relationship to one another by changing their status with regard to each other. (Of course, this is not meant as a definition, and other social mechanisms might do similar things.) It is the way we formalize the imposition of those status functions toward whatever ends officials and private individuals have in mind when creating new institutions within its ambit.

[86] Ibid 53.

[87] Ibid 32–33. See also Frank A. Hindriks, 'The New Role of the Constitutive Rule' (2003) 62 *American Journal of Economics & Sociology* 185–208, 203–05.

[88] This does not imply that such codification must be in written form. It is enough that there be some "official" acceptance or adoption of the constitutive rules reduced to some set of symbols, which could be verbal.

[89] Searle, *Construction of Social Reality* 53, keeping the term "official" within quotation marks but not explaining the term or use of quotation marks any further.

[90] Miller refers to these as "meta-institutions," although they are still institutions themselves: 'Social Institutions' § 1.

While we will focus on Searle's theory of institutions throughout this book, two other theorists of institutions bear mention here. Bracketing reductionist accounts that seek to reduce institutions to simpler social forms like conventions and holistic theories that are only interested in the relation between institutions and wider social arrangements, Seumas Miller divides theories of social institutions into "collective acceptance" theories, such as Searle's, and his own "teleological" theory.[91] As we've seen with Searle, collective acceptance theories depend upon some form of collective intentionality to validate the institutional arrangement. *Pace* Miller, however, there is no reason these theories cannot be compatible with a notion of collective intentionality that reduces them to individual intentions—at least, intentions held in the brains of individuals and without positing "a supra-individual entity not reducible to the individual agents and the relations among them."[92]

Miller's own account is teleological in the sense that it focuses on the ends (understood as social goods) that institutional participants thereby jointly pursue, which they do from their functionally described institutional roles.[93] Given our focus on the notion of function to explain law, one might think therefore that Miller's theory would be the best one to adopt for our explanation of law's institutional nature. But Miller's conception of function leads him to think that he is offering a normative theory of institutions rather than a "descriptive" (or explanatory) one.[94] By this he seems to understand not that he is saying institutions ought to be understood functionally, but rather that institutions ought to be aiming at some human good that is morally valuable. As such, any institution that aims at morally reprehensible ends is "deficient qua institution."[95]

In many ways, this view is therefore parallel to the views of modern natural lawyers, and we could apply many of the same arguments I will make in the chapter on natural law to Miller's view of institutions. For our purposes here it is enough to say that it is not neutral with regard to the functions that institutions can meaningfully follow.

[91] Ibid.

[92] Ibid § 2. Miller touts as one advantage of his own theory that it is compatible with individual intentions, claiming that collective acceptance theorists generally rely on positing such supra-individual entities. But see John R. Searle, 'Collective Intentions and Actions' in Philip R. Cohen, Jerry L. Morgan, and Martha E. Pollack (eds), *Intentions in Communication* (MIT Press 1990) 401–16 at 406, noting that "society consists of nothing but individuals … there cannot be a group mind or group consciousness." "All consciousness is in … individual brains." According to Searle and several others, the *content* of the collective intentionality held in those individual minds may be irreducibly we-intentions.

[93] Seumas Miller, 'Institutions, Collective Goods and Moral Rights' (2003) 18–19 *ProtoSociology* 184–207, 184–85.

[94] Ibid 185. [95] Ibid 186.

What's more, however, it is not clear how Miller's normative view is necessarily at odds with the collective acceptance descriptive views he criticizes. While Miller thinks that his view is more accommodating of atomistic individual intention and action in his notion of joint action,[96] collective acceptance views like Searle's do not need to posit some kind of supra-individual collective mind to hold the collective intentions that maintain institutions.

One advantage to Searle's theory of formal institutions (correctly understood) is that it helps to explain away certain problems of malfunction that might tempt some to remove the malfunctioning member from the class being explained. Miller argues that the functions provided for by the assignment of status come apart from the relevant deontic powers, seeing this as a point against Searle's theory of institutions. He gives the example of an "incompetent surgeon" who cannot perform any successful operations (needing to rely on others to perform all his operations), although authorized and accredited by the relevant professional body (an institution) to do so.[97] Miller's point is that this person cannot perform the functions of a surgeon, and therefore the deontic powers conveyed by his status do not confer any ability to perform the contemplated function. Therefore, Miller believes, collective acceptance of the status function is not sufficient to enable the status holder to perform the function the status is supposed to accomplish.

There are a number of problems with this criticism. One is that it misses the distinction between *status* functions and proper functions more generally.[98] (Miller calls them "substantive functions."[99]) Miller misses this distinction even after he has artificially limited the discussion of functions. Noting that the "term 'function' is multiply ambiguous" (but forgetting this caveat when engaging in his criticism of Searle's theory), he settles upon a specific meaning for it: "a state of affairs that is aimed at by institutional actors, albeit not always consciously."[100] But if this is what the term "function" means to Miller, it is not clear why an incompetent surgeon is not still aiming at a successful surgery, especially by getting others more competent than he involved.

This is especially baffling given Miller's accommodation of global malfunctions and deficiencies in his own theory. Where institutions are aiming at morally reprehensible ends, he has no problem pronouncing them merely

[96] Ibid 189, 'Social Institutions' § 3.

[97] Miller, 'Institutions, Collective Goods and Moral Rights' 205.

[98] Keep in mind that the notion of function in "status functions" is the mathematical sense, not the sense we use to explain artifacts.

[99] Miller, 'Institutions, Collective Goods and Moral Rights' 205.

[100] Ibid 185 n. 2.

deficient institutions. But he is not willing to admit that Searle's theory can accommodate such local malfunctions as incompetent surgeons.

The clear reply is in seeing that Searle's notion of status functions is not so teleological and, as previously mentioned, is more akin to the mathematical understanding of functions. It focuses instead on the institutionally defined role that is to be played by the recipient of the status.[101] We may argue with the propriety of granting this person the status of a surgeon, but once the person has this institutional status there are certainly other deontic powers that are appropriately attendant. As a surgeon, his demand that we vacate the surgical theater gives us a reason to do so even if, as hospital employees, we had an otherwise good reason for being there. (Granted, the safety of the patient—itself an institutional, as well as moral, mandate—may well override the surgeon's directives. But his status gives us considerable prima facie reasons for compliance.)

Miller's criticism also misses the distinction between mere social facts and formal institutions. To put it in terms of the example, the surgeon's inability to perform surgery might tempt us into thinking that he is not a "real" surgeon in a social fact sense. But once there is an institution that sets forth who is to be officially accredited the title and status of surgeon, then for institutional purposes he's a surgeon no matter how incompetent. This is the mirror image of Searle's example of the Korean War: a war in the social fact sense, but merely a "police action" in the institutional sense so as to avoid the legal requirements attendant upon an official declaration.[102] The point is that the institutional status can come apart from the social fact sense of the same term on which the institutional status usually rides.[103]

The main thing to keep in mind for now is that statuses are understood in terms of the functions that the possessor of the status is to perform within the institutional context. The status is generally one of the *means* by which the institution performs its function. The key step in institutional creation is therefore the assignment of function. It underscores the importance of understanding institutions like law (the quintessential institution for creating institutions) in terms of those statuses it creates and the functions it thereby performs.

The other theorist of institutions we need to examine is Neil MacCormick. He was engaged in the very similar project of understanding law as a means

[101] Searle, *Construction of Social Reality* 20; *Making the Social World* 43–44, 58–60.

[102] Searle, *Construction of Social Reality* 89.

[103] In correspondence, Lucas Miotto notes that Miller's criticism also appears to miss the distinction between a person's physical ability and an institutional notion of power, which does not necessarily imply any physical ability.

of imposing a kind of institutional reality. He did not think of law itself as an institution or kind of institution, but rather of things like contracts as institutions of the law.[104] Part of his reason for this was a difficulty he had in accepting Searle's picture of the relationship between institutional facts and institutions themselves: "Lurking in some Platonic cave behind the institutional fact lies the institution itself."[105] (Even though he is dismissive of the opacity of Plato's cave for understanding the relation of the institution to the institutional fact, he had no problem invoking Platonic forms for explaining the relation of an institution to an instance of the institution.[106])

Once we understand better Searle's notion of the declaration as a kind of speech act for creating the institution and instances under it,[107] the relation of the institution to facts about it need not be so opaque. An institutional fact is a descriptive fact about the declaration, about its context, and about the collective acceptance of whatever changes that declaration purports to make.[108] The context, and the rules that govern that context, is the institution itself.

Searle makes a point of noting that "Status Function Declarations," which constitute social and institutional facts, need not be seen as mysterious in the way of which MacCormick complains. He gives the example of buying drinks for a couple of friends in a bar, bringing the drinks back to the table and announcing "This one is Sally's; this one is Marianne's; and this one is mine."[109] In so doing (and to the extent that the others accept that pronouncement), one alters the rights and responsibilities those at the table have toward each other regarding those specific drinks. Since it is about rights and responsibilities, and depends upon collective acceptance, the statement can "create a reality by representing it as existing."[110]

MacCormick also distinguished between social institutions like universities, hospitals, parliaments, courts, etc., and institutions of the law like contracts. So, for him there were two senses in which law is an institutional phenomenon. The former is an institution in the social sense (including the various arms of government). But the legal rules and norms by which those social institutions are put into effect are institutional facts, not institutions

[104] Neil MacCormick, 'Law as Institutional Fact' (1974) 90 *Law Quarterly Review* 102–29, 105.

[105] Ibid. [106] Ibid 109.

[107] "They ... change the world to match the content of the speech act": Searle, *Making the Social World* 11. "In a Declaration we make something the case by declaring it to be the case": ibid 69.

[108] Ibid 85. Searle makes a point of noting that the "Status Function Declarations" which constitute social and institutional facts need not be seen as mysterious in the way MacCormick would seem to complain.

[109] Ibid 88, noting as well that it is sufficient to simply push the drinks toward their intended owners without saying anything.

[110] Ibid 89.

themselves.[111] He also distinguished a "triad" of rule-types that govern institutions: institutive rules (specifying when an instance of the institution has come into existence); consequence rules (specifying what its effects are); and terminative rules (specifying when the instance passes out of existence).[112] He argued that this triad captured the norms that governed institutions in general better than Searle's notion of the constitutive rule.

It seems, however, that in MacCormick's criticism of Searle he failed to grasp that Searle's notion of constitutive rules is more basic than his triad. We might ask what makes the institutional fact that a given triad governs an institution true. What makes those rules authoritative for that institution? The answer to such questions requires another level of rule that is endemic to institutions: basic rules of validity. But in Searle's picture, basic rules of validity, as well as MacCormick's triad, are all sub-instances of the more basic notion of constitutive rules. Hence, while MacCormick's picture of rules that all institutions generally must have in order for them to perform their functions is quite valuable, it needn't have been understood in opposition to Searle's.

MacCormick does criticize Searle's picture of constitutive rules for blurring the distinction between constitutive and regulative rules. Constitutive rules specify the contours of an activity or institution, bringing it into existence and differentiating it from other areas of human endeavor. Regulative rules then determine how the activity or institution is to operate. But Searle's distinction is not meant to be a mutually exclusive one. Rather, constitutive rules "do not just regulate, but they also create the possibility of the very behavior that they regulate."[113] This is entirely to be expected, as we can appreciate if we consider the rules of a game like chess,[114] which set forth both what the game is and how it is to be played. We expect many rules to perform both functions, so blurring the distinction in this manner should be seen not as a demerit of Searle's theory, but rather as a strength, in that it is accurately capturing how we use these rules.

Another complaint MacCormick makes about Searle's notion of constitutive rule is that it is overbroad, noting that Searle's formula "X counts as

[111] MacCormick, 'Law as Institutional Fact' 110–11.

[112] Ibid 106–07; MacCormick, 'Norms, Institutions, and Institutional Facts' 335. His idea of the triad of rules associated with institutions was another reason he rejected seeing the law itself as a kind of institution, since the law as a whole is not defined and regulated by a given set of institutive, consequential, and terminative rules. MacCormick, 'Law as Institutional Fact' 111f.

[113] Searle, *Making the Social World* 10. See also John Rawls, 'Two Concepts of Rules' (1955) 64 *Philosophical Review* 3–32, 25 (using the term "practice rule").

[114] Chess is Searle's example: *Making the Social World* 10. Rawls uses baseball: 'Two Concepts of Rules' 25.

Y in circumstances C" could be used to describe a bottle used as a weapon in a pub brawl.[115] In doing so, MacCormick seems to miss the distinction between the content of the constitutive rule (which tends to have the characteristic form of Searle's formula) and the relation of that rule to the institution. Institutions are constituted by constitutive rules (and create further instances through them) when they are declared to be enforced or enacted (and that declaration is collectively accepted by the relevant audience). It is not the form that gives the rule its institutional character; it is the circumstances of its use. The fact by itself that other practices or behaviors can be described using the characteristic form of a constitutive rule does not make those practices or behaviors into institutions, nor does it make the use of the formula by institutions problematic.

The other aspect of the institutional use of the constitutive rule is that the status it conveys doesn't usually have any meaning outside the institutional context. The institution generally creates the status. So even if the drunken brawler first declares his bottle to be a weapon and everyone in the pub dutifully accepts the truth of that declaration, he has not created an institutional fact, because the declaration was superfluous and the bottle would have the (social fact) status of a weapon in many other contexts as well.

MacCormick claims that he's led to his views about the triad rules for institutions and the weaknesses in Searle's picture precisely by the fact that institutions are understood in terms of their functions (which he sometimes refers to as "final causes," following Aristotle).[116] The idea is that institutions are individuated by their functions, as expressed in their institutive, consequential, and terminative rules. But it is far from clear that the triad rules are so closely related to functions ("final causes" or sometimes also "underlying principles" for MacCormick). One danger here is that seeing institutions as individuated via their triadic rules threatens to re-create the problems we've seen with considering institutions to be functional kinds. I see no reason why two institutions cannot share the same function even as they differ in their triadic rules. Searle certainly would not have a problem saying that institutions with the same function could have differing constitutive rules.

One move that MacCormick makes which helps to diagnose both the reason he sees a link between the institution's function and its triadic rules and why that link is weak can be seen in the following statement: "Unless you know the underlying principle or final cause of a given institution, it profits you nothing to know how an instance of it can be established."[117] But this cannot be right. Following the rules (whether we call them constitutive or

[115] MacCormick, 'Norms, Institutions, and Institutional Facts' 334, n. 25.
[116] Ibid 335. [117] Ibid.

triadic) about how to establish and implement an institution can profit you greatly without knowing anything about the purpose of the institution. Just consider all of the possible social rewards for establishing certain institutions, and the penalties for failing to do so when required. Those are awarded or exacted without the establishing party necessarily knowing anything about the purpose of the institution.[118] We again need to be wary about too closely identifying the purpose, final cause, or function of the institution with its means of fulfilling it or the process by which it comes into being. One advantage of Searle's picture is precisely that these distinctions are maintained while still allowing us to understand institutions in terms of their functions, as MacCormick would have us do.

E. Law's Relation to its Function

Someone approaching the explanation of law in terms of its function might do so in at least four different ways. The most ambitious would be to say that the function the theorist adduces for law is both necessary and sufficient for the presence of law. In other words, the theorist claims that the explanation is offered as a kind of definition that differentiates law from all other possible human activities, that the explanation itself uniquely picks out legal activity without capturing anything else. To do this in functional terms is to say that the function one adduces for law is only and always performed by law. Difficulties with this approach will be apparent when considering seeing law's function as a necessary condition and as a sufficient condition independently. But it seems exceedingly hard to imagine a function that only law performs, and yet always does so perfectly.

A slightly less ambitious option is to say that anything that performs the function is a member of the class of law (which includes laws, legal systems, and wider legal norms), but that law might not always accomplish this task, or perhaps might not even always aim at it. Nevertheless, since the performance of that function is unique to law (since anything that performs it is law), one only needs to account for that function in one's theory, since it is that which sets law apart. This is to see law as a functional kind, which is to say that performance of (or, perhaps, aiming at) the function is sufficient for membership in the class being explained. It allows that not every instance of law successfully performs the function. But since its doing this sets it

[118] I could, for example, ask someone to establish a secret club without telling him what the purpose of the club was to be.

apart from everything else, performance of the function explains what it is by showing what distinguishes it from other areas of human activity.[119]

Leslie Green's example of a functional kind term is a "leader."[120] Perhaps not every leader successfully leads, but anyone who is successfully leading is a leader, even if she might not be a specific kind of leader like a president or a general. And anyone who has the task of leading is a leader.

The problem with this approach is that most of the functions we usually associate with law are also performed by other institutions, normative systems, or areas of human behavior such as morality, etiquette, organized religion, and contextual rules in formal or informal associations. So it is hard to imagine that there is any one function that is uniquely performed by law.[121] On the other hand, we should remain open to the possibility that, when we have aggregated all of the various functions performed by individual laws and systems of those laws, there will be some unique set of functions any one of which could be performed by law, seen as an aggregation of those more basic components. But that unique set might also be so complex and myriad that we don't get much explanatory utility from it.

Another option is to say that the functions one adduces for law are necessary for the presence of law, but not sufficient. This gives up on differentiating law from other forms of human behavior in the specification of function, although it still leaves open the possibility that law is differentiated by non-functional explanatory elements. It admits that the functions law performs are also performed by other institutions or areas of behavior or normativity, but still says that an adequate theory of law must account for what law is supposed to be doing.

The danger of this methodological route, taken without modification or caveat, is that it tends to trap the theorist into problems with deficient members of the class. If it is necessary for the law to do something specific in order to be law, then anything not doing that cannot be law.[122] So if it is failing to perform (or aim at) its task, perhaps because it is defective in some way, then we are left claiming that it cannot really be law. If a function we

[119] This would not explain malfunctioning members and what entitles them to membership in the class of law. But a theorist employing this explanatory method might have a different argument as to why explaining the inclusion of malfunctioning members is not necessary.

[120] Green, 'Functions of Law' 109.

[121] See for example Himma, 'Do Philosophy and Sociology Mix? A Non-Essentialist Socio-Legal Positivist Analysis of the Concept of Law' 728.

[122] One way to avoid this danger would be to introduce a distinction between an artifact having a function that it is intended to perform, and actually performing the function. Then the membership condition could be tied to the possession of the function without its fulfillment. However, this solution would just push the problem back to instances where the law did not even aim at its intended function.

consider necessary for law were something like the coordination of behavior, this methodological tack would require us to say that any legislation which did not coordinate behavior or which perhaps increased behavioral entropy could not be law. Another side of this same problem is that it doesn't allow for failure or malfunction, which we have seen is necessary for any useful functional explanation.[123]

One might reply to this problem by relying on the different senses of "law." Even if a theorist articulates a function as necessary for a legal system, this does not entail that every single legal enactment within the system must be performing or aiming at the function in order to be a member of the class of law (or even of that legal system). In other words, it's possible that there is one function necessary for legal systems (or one for each system), perhaps a distinct separate one for each law, and a third for law in general as a type of human activity.

I don't deny this possibility in its entirety, but there are a few things to note. For one, this move doesn't solve the basic problem of seeing function as a necessary condition for membership, even if we divide the class up according to the different kinds of referents for "law." It still would exclude failures from membership in whichever class is being explained. Second, however, we will see later that the relationship among the different referents for "law" is such that the most broad and general referent will likely be best explained by combining the functions adduced for individual laws and legal systems, finding what is common among them. Hence the broadest functions we can adduce for law would include all possible functions for laws and legal systems. Then any of those more particular instances of law that fail their more particular functions would, on this model, also fail to fulfill the functions of the broadest category.[124] As a result, this model would create an additional pressure to exclude even individual legal enactments and legal systems that fail to fulfill (or aim at) their functions from the class of law in general.

[123] See for example Himma, 'Do Philosophy and Sociology Mix? A Non-Essentialist Socio-Legal Positivist Analysis of the Concept of Law' 731, and generally Gardner, 'Law's Aims in *Law's Empire*' 216, Perlman, 'The Modern Philosophical Resurrection of Teleology' 34, Letsas, 'Monism, Interpretivism, and Law's Aim' 50, Preston, 'Philosophical Theories of Artifact Function' 217, and Baker, 'The Metaphysics of Malfunction' 82–84.

[124] One exception to this would be where in failing one function, those instances would be fulfilling another that still comes under the broadest description. That is, if the particular instance of law somehow succeeds in fulfilling a distinct function by failing to perform the function we have in mind for it, and if that distinct function in which it now succeeds comes within the description for the broad function we have assigned to law in general, then this failure would not run afoul of the broader function associated with law in general. This is likely to be rare and does not detract from the point made here: that seeing functions as necessary conditions for membership in a given class makes it difficult or impossible to accommodate failures.

A final option is the least ambitious. It is to say that any adequate explanation of law must do so in terms of the social functions it performs, without making any extra claims that performance of those functions are either necessary or sufficient for membership in the class of law. This is to say that one cannot understand law without reference to these functions, even though those functions are not always successfully accomplished and other entities might accomplish the same tasks.[125] It is to see the function as explanatorily necessary but not to see performance as necessary for membership. That is, an adequate understanding requires articulating what law is for. However, this does not imply that it must always accomplish, or even aim at accomplishing, its function. Furthermore, it is not to say that anything performing or aiming at the function is law.

One might initially think this method is too weak to generate a theory of law. After all, what good is this talk of functions if the law doesn't necessarily always accomplish (or even aim at) them and if other things can do the same thing? We often understand functions themselves as characteristic purposes in order to avoid being led to exclude defective members from the class being explained, since any good explanation in terms of function must accommodate the possibility of malfunction. Furthermore, when we envision giving theories of other human institutions, such as hospitals or universities, it is difficult to imagine doing so without giving a central place to their functions. We are not thereby tempted to claim that performing those functions is either necessary or sufficient. Hospitals that fail to heal are still hospitals (although admittedly very bad hospitals). Not every institution for higher education and research is a university. But healing in the first instance, and education and research in the second, are still the functions that explain what those institutions are. If we encounter someone unfamiliar with them, we are likely to start with those functions as central to our explanations.

Even if this makes it seem as though having, although not necessarily performing or aiming at, the explanatory function is now the necessary condition, we would still have to explain how something comes to have a function if it isn't necessarily even aiming at it. So this leaves open the question of what the theoretical role of function in the explanation might be.

However, when we consider the law to be a kind of abstract artifact, this becomes less problematic. In general, any artifact that is intentionally created will have a purpose that the creator had in making it. While that intention might only apply to a token artifact that the inventor makes, as the inventor

[125] See Kenneth Einar Himma, 'Do Philosophy and Sociology Mix? A Non-Essentialist Socio-Legal Positivist Analysis of the Concept of Law' (2004) 24 *Oxford Journal of Legal Studies* 717–38, 732.

and others make other tokens with the same or similar purposes, we can begin to speak of that artifact as a type. Some perhaps generalized or aggregated way of describing the purposes of the tokens can then be associated with the type as its function. The first shoe was likely made to protect a specific foot from a specific danger or discomfort. But as its utility came to be seen for other feet and other dangers, and other shoes were made, the shoe—as an artifact type—came to be associated with the function of protecting feet.

One might say that functional explanations of law are not complete because they do not explain how law arose in society. Was it an accretion of customary norms into something more institutional, or was there some first designer who envisioned a system of norms to be declared officially enforced? The details of the first law are likely as shrouded in the mists of prehistory as those of the first shoe. It is true that a functional explanation will be very unlikely to be historically complete on its own. However, that does not mean that it isn't still an explanation of what law is. To specify something's origin itself does not explain it more fully than to specify what it is for. And from a philosophical point of view, it would seem more valuable to explain law's social functions than its historical development.[126]

There are also, admittedly, further theoretical complexities, such as the fact that it is not generally possible to conceive of a law without a legal system of which it is a part. If that conceptual limitation is correct, then the first law could only have come about within the context of the first legal system. But this doesn't prevent us from seeing law as an artifact type, albeit an abstract one, in the same way we think of shoes, hammers, hospitals, universities, and corporations.

The token/type distinction is especially important in discussions of law's functionality. When speaking of specifics, it is generally quite easy to tell whether we are talking about one specific piece of legislation or court decision, or of all legislation and judicial decisions in a given jurisdiction. But when we are speaking abstractly about law's success or failure in the performance of its function, we may be speaking about specific enactments, of legislation as a type, of a specific legal system, or of legal systems or law in general. This last category could include, for example, a global skeptical claim that law as a type of institution is not suited to its task and is always doomed ultimately to fail to fulfill its function(s).

[126] See Kincaid, 'Assessing Functional Explanation in the Social Sciences' 426, making this argument in favor of functional explanations (and citing Darwin's inability to explain how new biological traits arise) as against Hallpike's criticism that functional explanations cannot explain the origins of social institutions, referring to C. R. Hallpike, *The Principles of Social Evolution* (Clarendon Press 1986).

Borrowing terminology from Jeremy Waldron, we might distinguish between law's "retail" function and its "wholesale" function.[127] A piece of legislation that increases the penalties for tax evasion might have the retail function of increasing compliance with the tax code or getting more people to meet their tax burdens more completely. It might have the wholesale function of increasing government revenue or inculcating more respect for law among the populace. Note that this distinction can be a bit slippery as, for example, the function of increasing government revenue could also have been a retail function if it was one of the express justifications for the passing of the specific piece of legislation. Since we are dealing with proper functions here, the distinction of retail and wholesale is not the distinction between what a drafter envisions and the actual utility of the law. Instead, it is between the function(s) the drafter uses to "sell" the legislation (e.g. to voters and/or other legislators) and the perhaps wider or distinct set of actual benefits she expects will result from the legislation.[128]

When it comes to legal systems, we might say that the retail function is whatever improvements its founders used to argue in favor of its adoption over a preexisting arrangement. Again, its wholesale function would be the actual benefits they expect to result from the change. Here we might be talking about the adoption of a new constitution, or merely a package of laws that fundamentally alters the criteria of legal validity.

Of course it is possible that laws will have effects that their drafters do not envision for them. It is also possible that a package of laws developed for one purpose has the effect of fundamentally altering the criteria of legal validity such that we would say a new legal system has come into being. However, to the extent that those effects are valuable and not seen as reasons to repeal the laws, they would be more on the order of use functions of some kind rather than proper functions. Hence they are not as explanatorily valuable for our purposes here.

When it comes to law as a whole, the distinction is a bit more complex and may tend to veer more explicitly into the values usually associated with "legality." One can imagine selling the idea of legality to a pre-legal people by enumerating the oft-cited benefits of an authoritative means for settling disputes and an official procedure for changing rules to adapt to changing

[127] Jeremy Waldron, 'Does Law Promise Justice?' (2001) 17 *Georgia State University Law Review* 759–88, 772; 'Is the Rule of Law an Essentially Contested Concept (in Florida)?' (2002) 21 *Law and Philosophy* 137–64, 145.

[128] This discussion of the relationship of drafters to the retail and wholesale functions of pieces of legislation does not favor any particular interpretive strategy for courts seeking to apply the legislation later on. There may be a host of good reasons for saying their intentions are irrelevant for courts performing interpretations.

circumstances.[129] These would then be serving as the retail functions, while wholesale functions might include increasing coordination of behavior, inducing a regulated market to facilitate trade, or even something more nefarious like making the population easier to subjugate.

The important point here is that the wholesale function is not merely a generalization of the retail, nor is it necessarily some form of latent function, which we've rejected above. Rather, the distinction is merely a reminder that not every function for law is worn on its sleeve, even if we are rejecting the mysterious feedback mechanisms sometimes cited by social theorists.

Hence we might be thinking of law's functions as setting success conditions for individual legal enactments and norms, or we might think of them as giving success conditions for law as a means of accomplishing the ends articulated within the functions. To say that law is understood by its functions is not to say that it necessarily is the best method for accomplishing those ends, just as we would say that a hammer is understood as a tool for driving nails, even though a nail gun arguably does a much better job.

There is also the likelihood that a sufficient amount of success or failure among specific laws has an overall impact on the system. If over-many laws are failing to accomplish their purposes or are disregarded by too many of those supposedly subject to them, then we are likely to see a breakdown in the legal system.

Furthermore, some specific laws may be uniquely placed to have a greater impact on the system as a whole. That is, for a variety of reasons, it is possible that certain otherwise unimportant laws serve as lynchpins in the stability of a legal system. So if a lynchpin law fails to perform its function, then that specific system itself will also fail, perhaps in that citizens or officials would stop seeing the law as normatively binding or guiding, or perhaps its failure would lead to too many conflicts among the other laws. For example, perhaps a certain society has a law that citizens must salute the flag every day upon waking up. The stated function of this law is to engender respect for the national institutions, especially the legal system. Yet perhaps in the context of this country's legal system, it is a relatively minor law, with minor penalties for violations, and one that people violate all the time (perhaps with few detections). Up until now it has been enough that many people follow the law and have respect in the country's institutions as a result. Some who don't follow the law still have the respect that having the law engenders. But perhaps if those following the law begin to lose that respect anyway, so that the law is no longer performing its intended function, enough people will start to

[129] See for example Hart, *Concept of Law* 91–94.

lose respect for the legal system. As a result, people all over the country start ignoring too much of the law for the government to effectively respond. The legal responses the government attempts are seen as oppressive and the entire system collapses, leading to a coup or constitutional crisis. I admit that this is an unlikely scenario in most countries. However, the point of the example is to show that it is possible for certain laws to serve as lynchpins in order for the wider legal system to work.

Inattention to the distinction between different notions of function when applied to law can sometimes lead theorists to error. One example is that of Michael Moore, whose article 'Law as a Functional Kind' exhibits a number of such problems.[130] One issue is that seeing law as a functional kind is to understand its function to be a sufficient condition for membership in the class of law.[131] Under such a view, anything that performs law's characteristic function is thereby understood to be law (or at least a part of law). This implies the need for law's function to be unique to it, which, when we think of law as an artifact, is neither helpful nor necessary.

We might think that explanatory uniqueness is important for any adequate theory of law. However, we need to remember that it is a desideratum of the theory as a whole, not necessarily of the function used to explain the law. We do not understand what a hospital is without understanding its function, even though that function is shared by other institutions and organizations.

The other error in Moore's article involves his confusion of proper functions with Cummins functions, leading him to a kind of systems theory for every biological function and thinking it therefore appropriate to claim that the function of the body is to be healthy.[132] One pernicious thing about these errors is that they lead other theorists who appreciate them as errors, notably Leslie Green,[133] to see them as reasons to reject a functional analysis for law altogether.

We cannot immediately assume it will be enough to explain the function of law in general by simply aggregating all of the retail functions of individual laws and legal decisions. The reason for this can be seen by imagining a religious artifact.[134] The creators and users of such artifacts would explain their purposes from inside their religious context, while sociologists and anthropologists might give them another explanation that harnesses some

[130] Michael S. Moore, 'Law as a Functional Kind' in Robert P. George (ed.), *Natural Law Theory: Contemporary Essays* (Clarendon Press 1992) 188–242. In this article, Moore does not endorse seeing law as a functional kind. I don't think law is a functional kind either, but this isn't a reason to neglect the importance of functions for explaining the law altogether.

[131] Ibid 121. [132] Ibid 211. [133] See for example Green, 'Functions of Law.'

[134] See Perlman, 'The Modern Philosophical Resurrection of Teleology' 34; see also the discussion of phantom functions in Preston, 'Philosophical Theories of Artifact Function' 217.

social utility of the artifact unappreciated by the participants (e.g. "social cohesion").

With law, however, it is unlikely that individual laws have express proper purposes that are impossible to meet. It is possible, but would have to remain rare, lest continual failure undermine the social respect that is necessary for any law to be effective.

Sociologists could see some function or group of functions that are not reflected in the intended purposes of laws as envisioned by drafters or employed by users. While I think we must be open to this possibility, the likelihood that there are fundamental functions divorced from any intentions of drafters and users is small. Among other things this is because, as a profession, there are not sharp boundaries between legal practitioners and legal scholars and sociologists. Hence discoveries in legal sociology are likely to be reported very quickly in law journals, then to be read by law students, lawyers, judges, and legislators alike. While there might be some distinction between what the legislator and judge are intending and what the sociologist is discovering, it is more likely that there will be feedback between the internal and external perspectives such that it is not too far off the mark to expect that the functions of law in general will be a generalization or aggregation of the functions of those individual retail laws and legal decisions.

I have noted the possibility that some laws have unintended (beneficial) consequences. But if these are to be understood as functions at all, they must rise to the level that they help to explain the persistence of the laws with the unintended consequences. If they are to be proper functions rather than merely use functions, their beneficial consequences must be understood and intentionally adopted widely by relevant officials or others subject to the law.

When we think of law's relation to its function by seeing it as a kind of artifact, we generally expect that it is the intention of a creator that assigns artifacts their functions.[135] But then the question becomes whether the intention is that of the creator of the genre or the prototype, or of each token. Sometimes that isn't very important, as the token will not differ too much from the prototype. However, with law and other kinds of artifacts where each instance will have a different function from the genre as a whole (or the original instance of the genre), the question for understanding law in terms of its function will be whether we do so with the original exemplar or genre in mind or with each later token. I am open personally to the idea that

[135] Remember again that to say that the intention of a creator assigns artifacts their functions is not to imply a specific interpretive strategy when we understand law as a kind of artifact. We are here engaged in understanding the nature of law and not discussing the best way for law to be applied once formulated.

the function of law might change over time as we learn more about human behavior and psychology, although we will be adapting our concept of law as we do so. As a result, I think there must be a greater emphasis on what is done with law at the moment than what was done with law in the beginning. I expect there must be a relation between these two in that modern instances of law will bear some similarities to ancient instances, and some of those similarities are likely to be in terms of law's function. But a complete picture of law's function must include new functions that are imagined by modern legislators.

We also need to be careful here to distinguish a methodology that seeks to explain law by investigating its functions from a methodology sometimes called "functionalism," which was more in vogue in the first half of the twentieth century. The most philosophically subtle legal realist of his day, Felix Cohen did not think that it was useful to explain law in terms of its function, even as he embraced a methodology he called "functionalism." This arose from his desideratum that a definition of law be neutral as to law's function.[136] While he was thinking of what he was providing as a definition, his criterion for evaluation of definitions was whether the definition was useful, not whether it was correct.[137] Hence it might be more apt to think of what he provided as a kind of explanation that was geared to be useful to a specific subset of the population: lawyers.[138]

What made Cohen a realist was his view that law was a "pattern" of judicial decision, in which rules are "probabilities," not norms.[139] Cohen's methodological functionalism was a form of pragmatism, in which "a thing *is* its manifestations, its effects, and its relation with other things."[140] His realism arises out of this method, understanding "'law' as a 'function' of judicial decisions...."[141] For Cohen, then, functionalism as a method meant only that to understand something one must understand how it worked, not what purposes it serves.[142] "Functioning" is therefore understood as "working," operating according to specifications, without necessarily having a clear picture of

[136] Martin P. Golding, 'Realism and Functionalism in the Legal Thought of Felix S. Cohen' (1981) 66 *Cornell Law Review* 1032–57, 1035–36, citing Felix S. Cohen, *The Legal Conscience, Selected Papers* (Yale University Press 1960) 29.

[137] Golding, 'Realism and Functionalism in Cohen' 1039.

[138] Ibid 1035.

[139] Ibid 1039–40, quoting Felix S. Cohen, *Ethical Systems and Legal Ideals: An Essay on the Foundations of Legal Criticism* (Falcon Press 1933) 12, 254.

[140] Felix S. Cohen, 'The Problems of a Functional Jurisprudence' (1937) 1 *Modern Law Review* 5–26, 7, see also Golding, 'Realism and Functionalism in Cohen' 1051.

[141] Golding, 'Realism and Functionalism in Cohen' 1052.

[142] Cohen, 'The Problems of a Functional Jurisprudence' 8. See also Kincaid, 'Assessing Functional Explanation in the Social Sciences' 417, "Functionalism sometimes simply involves no more than identifying the causal roles or functions [that is, effects] of social institutions."

what ends the thing is working towards. Martin Golding argues that Cohen's functionalism led him to a nominalist position about legal rules (which we can see as one form of a realist's characteristic skepticism about legal normativity).[143] If there was a function to be teased out of the legal realist picture, it would be based on the observation that legal rules were used by judges as *post facto* rationalizations for the decisions they had already reached.

There are a few important points to note here, however. One is that this form of functionalism is about meaning, not law per se. In fact, it is this that led Cohen to reject any explanation of law that tended to hone in on a specific function or set of functions that law performs. Law is a set of social processes that is merely descriptive and doesn't itself carry any normative meaning for those who engage with it (here lawyers and judges).

To be fair, the question Cohen says functionalism treats is: "What is the human meaning of law?" (By "meaning" he intends "significance," and hence the question is one of value). This is opposed to the question asked by "analytical jurists," "What is the nature or structure of law?"[144] When examining this question in contexts internal to law, the result is realism: "legal concepts, rules, and institutions [are understood] in terms of judicial decisions or other acts of state-force." When examining it in wider contexts of human behavior, the result is "sociological jurisprudence."[145]

It is here that we can see a glimmer of overlap between the legal realists' notion of functionalism and that of analytic jurisprudence. While realists would eventually see the value in sociological investigations of law to be found in discovering the patterns created by judicial decision-making, analytic jurisprudents can turn the insights of legal positivism into marching orders for sociologists. They are to report back the wider socially valued impacts of law, ultimately (so I argue) to be understood as the functions which explain it. American Legal Realists would marshall the social patterns they discover to the end of improving upon the consistency of the law through the uniform rules movement.

Functionalism as a methodology therefore originally developed (according to Cohen) as a response to formalism (what Cohen calls "the traditional view"), the view that the law describes its own operation accurately[146] (with judges merely rule-following instruments in that operation). Function, in this sense, is meant as the true representation of how the law works: its functioning as opposed to the purposes it serves. In this, legal realism's functionalism is closer to what Leslie Green calls an "instrumentalist conception of

143 Golding, 'Realism and Functionalism in Cohen' 1054.

144 Cohen, 'The Problems of a Functional Jurisprudence' 6–7.

145 Ibid 8.

146 Ibid 9.

law,"[147] in that what is distinctive about it is the means by which it operates rather than the ends it serves.

On this view, Holmes' notion of the bad man represents its functionality. This is the idea that law is to be understood from the point of view of one who is seeking a prediction of how officials will react to contemplated courses of action, rather than from the point of view of one who is seeking to be guided by the law understood as giving reasons.[148] But to develop these considerations more fully, we need to begin our story of the role of functions in contemporary philosophy of law.

[147] Green, 'Law as a Means' 171–73.

[148] Cohen, 'The Problems of a Functional Jurisprudence' 14, quoting Oliver Wendell Holmes, 'The Path of the Law' (1897) 10 *Harvard Law Review* 457–78, 459–61.

3

Dworkin

Justifying Force and the Right Answer

Ronald Dworkin placed his understanding of law's function at the center of his theory. He thought it relatively uncontroversial that

> the most abstract and fundamental point of legal practice is to guide and constrain the power of government in the following way. Law insists that force not be used or withheld, no matter how useful that would be to ends in view, no matter how beneficial or noble these ends, except as licensed or required by individual rights and responsibilities flowing from past political decisions about when collective force is justified.[1]

The formation and interpretation of law is therefore an accretion of such justifications, themselves articulations and applications of the developing moral and political commitments of the community. Since law is an articulation of what justifies the use or withholding of the coercive power of the state, it clearly must invoke the fundamental moral and political principles of the community governed by that state. Otherwise, it couldn't serve as a justification. That is, since the use of force is itself a moral issue in that it involves the potential use of violence and physical restrictions to be placed on non-consenting individuals, it requires moral justification.

Furthermore, refraining from its use risks leaving intact a state of affairs that might itself be morally undesirable. So it similarly requires a moral justification to refrain from its use. Hence any justifications offered for a decision on its use must be made by using moral principles. Since the justification is

[1] Ronald Dworkin, *Law's Empire* (Belknap Press 1986) 93. While Dworkin did claim that his arguments do not depend upon finding a description of law's function (ibid), it is clear that much of his theory can be derived from a certain way of thinking about the function he does adduce. Hence, it is not incorrect to say that his theory depends more upon this description of law's function than perhaps he realized. Furthermore, he introduced this claimed function by saying that our existing jurisprudential discussions actually assume this to be the fundamental purpose of law. Finally, this articulation of law's function can be understood as a refinement of one Dworkin made earlier in what he called the "rights thesis," that judicial decisions justify existing political rights. Ronald Dworkin, 'Hard Cases' (1975) 88 *Harvard Law Review* 1057, 1063–1064.

being offered to members of the community and such moral justifications generally operate by appealing to shared values, they must be put in terms of moral and political principles that the community embraces.

In order to appreciate this fully, consider that appellate court decisions (and some trial court decisions) can usually be divided into the holding—what the court mandates should be done; and the rationale—the justifications offered for that mandate. We can say that the holding is what the apparatus of the government is prepared to enforce. If you are subject to the holding by the court and do not comply with the holding, then you will generally be forced to do so by whatever enforcement mechanism is applicable to your situation in the jurisdiction.

Under Dworkin's theory, the rationale is the reasoning behind threatening you with force in order to make sure you comply with the holding. Since many holdings of appellate courts are merely directions issued to the lower courts from which the appeal came, we can then combine the eventual holding of a lower court complying with those directions and the appellate court's rationale, seeing the latter, and the complex web of other cited authorities, offered as a justification for the former.

While the main focus is on court decisions, statutes and administrative decisions can be seen as policy preferences and choices embraced through democratic processes (in democratic states), which then form the grounds for some of the justifications offered in courts' rationales. That is, statutes themselves are justificatory of court decisions in that they are the policies embraced collectively by the people through their elected representatives (or at least are the choices of a legislature endorsed by a sovereign of some kind, which we can imagine as articulating the values of that political community).[2]

Imagine a moral space of possible commitments of a given community. You may believe that this space consists of all objective moral truths, or perhaps you believe it consists only in whatever opinions about morality individual community members have or might come to have. This metaethical distinction is not important at the moment (and would be rejected by Dworkin anyway.[3]) That community adopts a subset of those commitments, developing and altering those chosen commitments over time.

[2] Believing legal philosophy itself to be a project of interpreting law, Dworkin did not believe in the possibility of a general jurisprudence that was independent of moral and political judgments. Those moral and political judgments are necessarily going to reflect in some way the principles of the philosopher's moral community. He therefore elected to focus on democratic legal institutions in his own work and not make explicit claims about how widely applicable his theory of law might be. Ronald Dworkin, 'Hart's Postscript and the Character of Political Philosophy' (2004) 24 *Oxford Journal of Legal Studies* 1–37, 2–3.

[3] Ronald Dworkin, 'Objectivity and Truth: You'd Better Believe It' (1996) 25 *Philosophy and Public Affairs* 87–139.

If we assume that the community is also committed to the validity and mutual consistency of the principles they adopt (and it is very difficult to see how any person or group can make a moral commitment without also being committed to this), then any given articulated justification for the use or withholding of force either does or does not accurately reflect the proper weighing and balancing of that community's commitments at the time the justification is articulated. This is Dworkin's right-answer thesis.[4] Even if we were to assume the existence of an objective critical morality, we can never be sure that our moral decisions properly reflect that critical morality. The critical morality still allows us to say that our moral choices are correct or incorrect, even if we can never be totally sure of which.

Similarly, if the community has chosen a set of weighted moral commitments from a critical menu, then there is a right answer about whether any given legal decision is consistent with that admittedly still moving target. The articulated legal justifications are attempts to capture the correct balance of the community's moral and political commitments as applied to the case at hand.

Those attempts are more or less successful, as would be seen from the community's chosen subset of objective, critical moral principles, were they epistemically available. That is, any given decision is an attempt to capture the community's principles as they apply to the situation before the court. The decision is more successful if it accurately captures the morally correct commitments of the community regarding that situation and less successful if it is less accurate. Yet any offered justification also carries the necessary implication that the person offering it believes it to be the closest possible justification to the one dictated by critical morality.[5] It is therefore an interpretation of the community's moral commitments.

Since the law itself is the correct chosen set of commitments that justifies the state's use of force, legal validity (in the sense of which laws count as valid members of the system) itself is an interpretive concept about which reasonable people can disagree, but about which there is a right answer. If a given legal enactment or interpretation is in keeping with those moral and political commitments, then it is legally valid. And if the enactment or interpretation is not in keeping with those commitments, then it is not

[4] Dworkin, 'Hard Cases'; 'No Right Answer?' (1978) 53 *New York University Law Review* 1–32; *Law's Empire* 260–63, 'On Gaps in the Law' in P. Amselek and N. MacCormick (eds), *Controversies About Law's Ontology* (Edinburgh University Press 1991).

[5] See generally Dworkin, 'Objectivity and Truth' (and, for criticism of his views there, Paul Bloomfield, 'Archimedeanianism and Why Metaethics Matters' in Russ Shafer-Landau (ed.), *Oxford Studies in Metaethics Vol. 4* (Oxford University Press 2009) 283–302 and my 'Archimedian Metaethics Defended' (2008) 39 *Metaphilosophy* 508–29).

legally valid. But since that question is actually one of critical morality, the highest empowered interpreters can get it wrong. Hence, legal validity is always an epistemically open question, but one about which there is always a right answer.

It should be noted here, however, that since the commitments are also shifting, it is possible for wrong decisions to become right in the future. This is because some wrong decisions may also be a contribution to the ongoing development of the set of moral commitments of the community. I say "some wrong decisions" because it is also likely that some other wrong decisions are beyond the pale of any critical morality.

Just as a more traditional natural law view would hold that what the natural law (as a kind of perfect set of laws) dictates for a given community depends at least partially on the circumstances of that community, an interpretivist view like Dworkin's must accommodate the possibility of moral and political commitments shifting over time as mores and circumstances change. This does not threaten the timelessness of certain principles, of course. Most who believe in a critical morality would probably say that slavery was always wrong, even when a majority of the country thought it was permissible. But they would probably also agree that the ethics of communication have changed considerably to reflect the technologically induced rapidity with which we now communicate. (For example, waiting for a day before drafting a reply to an important message was probably not an egregious slight in an era when such replies took weeks to reach their destinations.)

One of the most important theoretical implications of the right-answer thesis is that there are no gaps in the law.[6] That is, given a system such as ours, with a closure principle like *nulla poena sine lege*, or more generally "everything that is not expressly forbidden by law is allowed,"[7] there will always be a truth value for every possible legal proposition at a given time (even if that truth value is not epistemically accessible).

More precisely, the idea that *every* legal proposition has a truth value doesn't follow directly from the closure principle, since there are legal propositions that are not about duties or rights. If a proposition isn't about prohibitions or permissions, then it would fall outside the closure principle. It might seem then that some of those propositions could lack truth values. However, Dworkin's claim that the function of law is to justify the use or withholding

[6] See for example Dworkin, 'On Gaps in the Law'; 'Indeterminacy and Law' in Stephen Guest (ed.), *Positivism Today* (Dartmouth 1996) 1–9.

[7] A similar argument is made for a (hopefully merely) hypothetical system in which everything not expressly permitted by law is forbidden.

of force along with the right-answer thesis still closes this gap as well. Since performance of that function is necessary for something to be considered law, legal propositions that cannot contribute to such justifications are false, while legal propositions that can contribute to such justifications are true (although their contributions might still be very minor).

Since every supposedly hard question of law has a right answer that a court is trying to uncover, there are no gaps even before the decision of the court is handed down. If you approach the city park on your battery-operated Segway-brand self-balancing two-wheeled personal transport device, there is already a fact of the matter about whether or not you are legally allowed in. This is so before any official has confronted the question and notwithstanding the doubts you will likely experience upon encountering the ubiquitous "no vehicles in the park" sign.[8]

A supposed advantage of this view is that you can have no good reason for complaint when the judge fines you for being the first person to get caught riding your Segway through the park, even though you didn't believe it was a vehicle. In other words, the right-answer thesis explains why the judge's application of the law to your new technology is not a retroactive application of the law; the entire complex web of moral and political principles as articulated in law yields a correct answer about whether or not the Segway is a vehicle for park entrance purposes, before any duly empowered official actually makes that determination. So you are on notice that your Segway either is or is not allowed, even though you have no way of knowing what that notice is supposedly telling you.

It might be a bit unfair to say that you were on notice of something epistemically inaccessible. But if we have the principle that ignorance of the law is no excuse, then we can say that you had sufficient notice given that the judge's interpretation that the law applied to you was open to you as a legal interpreter in your own right. That is, the right-answer thesis solves the apparent problem of the retroactive application of law to hard cases or cases of first impression.

While the judge's interpretation is open to dispute, the system at least provisionally treats it as the right interpretation of the law regarding your situation. Since there is a right interpretation "out there," the system accords the judge's decision that status. And since it is the right interpretation, institutionally speaking, then from that same perspective, it is not unfair to say that you should be held to account under it. Since the right interpretation *is*

[8] See H. L. A. Hart, *The Concept of Law* (Penelope A. Bulloch and Joseph Raz eds, 2nd edn, Clarendon Press 1994 (1961)) 125–27; Frederick Schauer, 'A Critical Guide to Vehicles in the Park' (2008) 83 *New York University Law Review* 1109–34.

the law, and ignorance of the law is no excuse, you have no excuse for failing to know that your Segway was or was not allowed in the park before any competent official has expressly made the determination about whether it is allowed.[9]

A. No Justification Function without Gaps

Many others have argued that the function that Dworkin adduces for law is inadequate for an explanation of law. One reason often given is that a society would need law even where force was never required to ensure compliance.[10] I would like to suggest that Dworkin's application of this function to his argument fails by its own terms. That is, a correct understanding of the use to which Dworkin puts the justification of force function precludes the conclusions he draws that there is always a right answer and that the law has no gaps.

The problem with the right-answer thesis and the inevitable conclusion that the law has no gaps is that they carry the implication that the law is conceptually incapable of failing to perform its function. Recall from the previous chapter that a conceptual necessity for any functional explanation is that the explanandum is capable of failing in the performance of its function.[11] If the explanandum is always perfectly performing its task, we would never conceptually separate the ends and means sufficiently for us to conceive of the thing in functional terms.

For Dworkin, interpretations of law that fail to justify the state's use or withholding of force from the perspective of critical morality are not valid legal interpretations or applications.[12] This is because there would always be a better justification, which represents a better and hence more correct interpretation of the law. Legal validity is always an open question precisely because there can be an argument that there is a better interpretation of law available (and because the criteria of legal validity themselves are open

[9] At the very least, we might say that you assumed the risk of the fine since you knew enough about the law to be aware of the possibility that a judge would hold that your Segway is a vehicle for park entrance purposes.

[10] John Gardner, 'Law's Aims in *Law's Empire*' in Scott Hershovitz (ed.), *Exploring Law's Empire* (Oxford University Press 2006) 207–24, 209, citing H. L. A. Hart, *The Concept of Law* (Clarendon Press 1961) 195; Joseph Raz, *Practical Reason and Norms* (Hutchinson 1975) 159; Finnis, *Natural Law and Natural Rights* (Clarendon Press 1980) 266–67.

[11] Gardner, 'Law's Aims in *Law's Empire*' 216.

[12] See Andrei Marmor, 'The Nature of Law' (2001) *The Stanford Encyclopedia of Philosophy*, Edward N. Zalta (ed.) §1 <http://plato.stanford.edu/archives/win2011/entries/lawphil-nature/>, citing Dworkin, *Law's Empire* 224.

to interpretation). However, interpretations that fail to justify the state's use or withholding of force are necessarily invalid since there will always be another interpretation available that does a better job at justification. So, while validity is a matter of moral judgment for Dworkin, in such a failure case we are already presuming the interpretation is deficient and hence invalid. Since every individual law is itself an interpretation of the legal practice of the community, individual laws are only candidates for legal validity if they are possible best interpretations of the practice. This means that individual laws must themselves contribute to the overall function of law, the justification of the use or withholding of force, in order to be legally valid.

In any possible legal dispute, the state would have to either enforce the status quo or require a change. However, the right answer as to which the state should do is already a matter of critical morality. If the answer given by a given court is wrong, then the best justification for the other choice is the correct interpretation of the law. If the answer given is correct but the justification articulated by the court is wrong, then there is still a better justification that represents the correct interpretation of the law. Since every political and moral value that is embraced by the community is available for use in such justifications, they are already usable as authoritative grounds for legal decisions. If there is a better balance of those values that could be struck, then that is already what the law requires.

At first blush this might seem to solve the problem before it gets off the ground: defective laws are legal interpretations that fail to justify the use or withholding of force, so it would seem possible for law to fail its task. The very notion of a defective law is one that is failing to perform its function.

But the right-answer thesis, with its implication that legal interpretations which are defective in this way are not legally valid, also implies that true law cannot fail to perform its function. Since defective interpretations are not legally valid, they are not law for that community (although they may be treated as law). Hence the law of any given community must be successful at performing the function of providing a correct justification of the state's use or withholding of force. It is conceptually impossible for something to be valid law and to fail to justify the state's use of force.

There are four possible routes out of this conundrum. One could say that legal validity and non-defectiveness come apart, allowing that there are valid laws which fail to perform their function. The second solution is to say that legal validity and membership in the class of law come apart. A third option is to say that law is not to be understood in terms of its function. The fourth route would be to allow that the law has gaps. Each of these would allow for the conceptual possibility that the law fails to perform its function. None of these routes are really open to Dworkin, but we will examine them briefly as they will become important later.

Under the first solution, legal validity is a positivistic notion, while the standards for what makes the law defective can come from non-legal sources, critical morality being a prime candidate. That is, the standards or criteria of validity are set within the legal system by those making and applying the laws. These standards are distinct from whatever makes a law defective, defectiveness being determined by the law's function rather than posited criteria of validity. This allows for the possibility that law is understood in terms of its function but is still capable of failure since what makes something a valid member of the class of law is independent of the purpose it serves, where that purpose is identifiable in a non-legal way.[13] This is the path taken by most modern natural law scholars and will be dealt with in the chapter on natural law.

For Dworkin, however, this option is not open, since legal validity is part and parcel of the justificatory process.[14] Anything that fails to justify the state's use or withholding of force cannot ultimately be valid. The idea that legal validity is a positivistic notion divorced from the political morality of the community runs contrary to Dworkin's basic picture of law.

One might think that Dworkin could have two conceptions of legal validity in play. One is akin to the positivistic notion of membership according to the merely factual pedigree of the legal enactment; the other is the normatively pregnant notion of when a given legal interpretation is morally justified according to the community's standards. However, this option isn't open to Dworkin precisely because of his respect for the language of judicial decisions, in which judges speak of discovering a law's validity status. That is, judges and the rest of the system generally treat invalid laws as invalid retroactively, as if they never had any force. This means that, from their perspective—which Dworkin adopts—the deficient law was never a member of their legal system. Hence the conditions for legal validity in the merely factual, positivistic/pedigree sense are swamped by the (continuously debatable) validity conditions in the normatively justified sense.

[13] This caveat might not seem necessary in that valid laws could aim at a purpose they fail to achieve, even if that purpose was only legally identifiable. The worry, however, is that if the purpose is only identifiable within the law itself, then it is hard to imagine a conceptual separation between the success and validity conditions. That is, if one has to use legal concepts to identify the law's purpose then it would be hard to conceive of a purpose that all valid laws would nonetheless fail, since one would need some paradigm instances of law to articulate that purpose. Our usual candidates for functions of law are all articulated in extra-legal ways. Generating and maintaining order, solving coordination problems, even justifying the state's use or withholding of force; all are described without reference to law.

[14] Dworkin, 'Hart's Postscript' 2.

The second solution is related to the first. This would be to say that legal validity is tied to the function of law but not to membership in the class of law. Under this view, we would say that any law that fails to perform its justificatory function is legally invalid but is still a law. It is therefore still possible for laws to fail to perform their function conceptually.

This appears to be close to what Jules Coleman suggests in defending his brand of inclusive legal positivism against the critiques of exclusive positivists, where he distinguishes between "criteria of identification" and "criteria of validity."[15] I will return to this view in the chapter on legal positivism. For now, keep in mind that Joseph Raz (against whom Coleman is arguing) claims that it makes no sense to speak of legal rules that cannot be valid in any jurisdiction.[16] The idea is that we cannot identify a norm as legal if it cannot be seen as valid within some legal system, since membership of a norm in a legal system is precisely what makes the norm a legal one.

Applying this worry to Dworkin's view, we need only remind ourselves that in Dworkin's picture of the justificatory function of law, the function is both unique and necessary. That is, something cannot be law without performing the function, and only law performs that function in society (in that anything that justifies the state's use of force is usable by judges in articulating an interpretation and therefore already a part of the legal system). Given that, it would not be possible for Dworkin to identify something as law without its functional aspect validating it.

The other two routes are that one must either deny that the law is something to be understood in terms of a function that its users have for it, or one must admit that the law has gaps. The first option is one against which I argue in many places in this book, and would not be adopted by Dworkin as it would undermine his central contention that law is an interpretive enterprise. To perform an interpretation of something for Dworkin is to see it in its best light, which is to put it to a purposive use. Hence, to say that the law is an interpretive enterprise is to say that it is best understood in terms of the purposive uses to which it is put. Dworkin would have been much quicker to jettison the force-justification function he adduced for law than he would have been to give up on the central pillar of his theory—that the law is an interpretive enterprise.

We do have to exercise some caution with this claim, however. Dworkin's contention that the law is an interpretive enterprise may imply that it is best

[15] Jules L. Coleman, 'Negative and Positive Positivism' (1982) 11 *Journal of Legal Studies* 139, 'Constraints on the Criteria of Legality' (2000) 6 *Legal Theory* 171–83, 179.

[16] Joseph Raz, 'Legal Validity' (1977) 63 *Archiv für Rechts und Sozialphilosophie* 339, 339. See also Wilfrid J. Waluchow, 'Legality, Morality, and the Guiding Function of Law' in Claire Grant and others (eds), *The Legacy of H. L. A. Hart, Legal, Political, and Moral Philosophy* (Oxford University Press 2008) 85–98 at 87 n. 2.

understood in terms of its function, but not the converse. It does not thereby imply that any claim that the law is best understood in terms of its characteristic functions leads one to say that it is an interpretive enterprise (and even if it did, it would certainly not require us to agree that it is an interpretive enterprise in Dworkin's sense). Claiming that the law is fundamentally interpretive is sufficient, but not necessary, for saying that it is best understood functionally.

I would be remiss if I did not mention that one might interpret Dworkin in such a way as to give him this way out, which is precisely what Scott Shapiro does in a footnote of his paper 'On Hart's Way Out'.[17] On Shapiro's interpretation, since the rules of law are akin to rules of morality for Dworkin, it doesn't make sense to ask what their function is, just as we wouldn't ask what the point of a moral rule against random killing would be. Hence rules of law may express justificatory principles for Dworkin, but they do not have any function since they simply are the principles they express. Shapiro does recognize the importance to Dworkin's theory of the justification of state coercion, but he sees any functional advantage as secured by that coercion itself, not the justification, and therefore characterizes Dworkin's theory as "nonfunctionalist."

There are two problems with this way of interpreting Dworkin, however. For one, it might make sense to say under this view that individual laws do not have functions, but it still doesn't avoid the idea that the law as a whole is understood in terms of its justificatory function. It may be the case that the social benefits we might otherwise associate with law are here secured by the state's use or withholding of force. (Although we might also think that a mechanism for public justification for that force has its own social benefit in addition to the force itself.) But to say that law is the social mechanism for justifying that use or withholding is still to say that it is understood as a whole in terms of that function.

Again, to say that a social practice is interpretive for Dworkin is to interpret it in terms of ascribing a purpose to it. Evidence for this can be found in Dworkin's caricature of legal positivism (which he calls "conventionalism"), understood to be an interpretation of law in which the essential function is to protect expectations about how the state will act in response to any private action or inaction.[18] More generally, one aspect of any interpretation for Dworkin is that the interpretation shows the interpreted practice in its best light, which is to say that the function of interpretations themselves is justificatory.[19] So even if Shapiro could be right in saying that according to

[17] Scott J. Shapiro, 'On Hart's Way Out' (1998) 4 *Legal Theory* 469–507, 505 n. 67.

[18] Dworkin, *Law's Empire* 114f.

[19] Ibid 65–68.

Dworkin individual laws do not have functions, it is hard to avoid the conclusion that for him, law itself (as a whole) has the justificatory function.

Furthermore, even those individual laws are aspects of how the law performs that justificatory function. While it may be the case, as Shapiro notes, that they do not have a behavior guidance function and hence need not make the practical difference that Shapiro is in the midst of exploring with regard to Hart's theory, individual laws do still have the functional role of serving as the means to the overall justification of the state's use or withholding of force. So we are back with the original conundrum: either Dworkin must give up the right-answer thesis (so that the law can conceptually fail to perform its function) and admit that the law has gaps, or he must give up the claim that the law is an interpretive enterprise, which would be to abandon the central pillar of his theory.

The only option left is to admit that the law has gaps. If the function of law is as Dworkin describes, but the law also has gaps, then we have opened up conceptual space for the law to fail its purpose. If there are legal propositions about which there is not yet any truth value—if some actions are neither legally required, permitted, nor prohibited—then in those gaps the law is not providing any justification for the state's use of force regarding those actions or propositions. That is, if we imagine adopting Dworkin's theory except with the amendment that the law has gaps in which legal propositions ("Legally, X is required/permitted/prohibited") have no truth value, then the function adduced by the theory fails inside those gaps. If there is no fact of the matter about whether the action is legally allowed, required, or forbidden, then regarding that action there can be no justification for any use or withholding of force. The justificatory principles do not come to bear or do not offer a specific solution.

Granted, once an articulation is made by a competent official, that articulation may present a slight alteration to the moral and political principles that are embraced by the community and come to be a sufficient justification for the state's use of force regarding that situation. Since each step in the evolution of a legal principle is a slight amendment to the community's political morality, then filling a gap is an alteration to the set of justificatory principles.

The problem is that this solution would run seriously afoul of Dworkin's picture of law, in that it allows judges to legislate from the bench whenever they are confronted with a "hard case."[20] Dworkin denied the significance (or even reality) of hard cases precisely because there was always a right answer,

[20] See for example Ronald Dworkin, 'Judicial Discretion' (1963) 60 *The Journal of Philosophy* 624–38.

and so judges are not legislating from the bench when they reach decisions. Admitting the law has gaps necessarily entails a rejection of the right-answer thesis, since the whole idea of a gap in the law is that there is a legal question that doesn't yet have a correct answer. Without a right answer, judges who interpret law to fill those gaps are necessarily "legislating" (in Dworkin's sense) new law and we are back to the positivist picture of law in which judges must create new law where there is no fact of the matter about what the law requires of them.[21] Hence, Dworkin would not have been able to accommodate a picture of law that allows for gaps lest his entire theory begin to unravel.

Another angle on this same difficulty with Dworkin's view can be seen by thinking about the relation between his notion of interpretation and the function of law. Assuming again that the function is as Dworkin claims—the justification of the state's use or withholding of force in line with past political decisions—the notion of law itself is an interpretive practice with this purpose in view. That interpretive practice consists in articulating applications of law to new situations which fit with those past practices and highlight the interpretive enterprise in its best light. It is this "best light" dimension that performs the justificatory purpose of the law.

However, if we assume, in line with the right-answer thesis, that nothing which both fits and shows law in its best light can fail to justify the state's use or withholding of force, then we have the same problem we've already seen: the law, understood this way, is conceptually incapable of failing to perform its function.[22]

[21] For an illuminating discussion of all the differences positivists actually see between legislation and what judges do in hard cases, see John Gardner, *Some Types of Law* in *Law as a Leap of Faith: Essays on Law in General* (Oxford University Press 2012) 54–88.

[22] It might be thought that Dworkin could simply distinguish between the normative sense of law with the function of justifying states' use of force and the practice of a state interpreting its own past actions and interpretations, having the same function. Then at least the practice of interpretation as it has actually played out might fail to fulfill its function even if the normative sense could not. The problem with this solution is that there is no way for Dworkin to claim the mere factual, historical, and interpretive practices of the community count as law in his sense of the term. Law requires the normative dimension that would then be left out. So even if there is something that could fail to fulfill its function on this model, it wouldn't be law, and hence he is left with the same difficulty.

Immediately below I also discuss the difficulty of reconciling the recognition of an evil regime as having law with trying to see the force-justification function within the pre-interpretive data about law. This would be another way of understanding the reply here. The data about past practices might be law in a pre-interpretive sense, and it might also fail the force-justification function. But since that function only arises in an interpretive stage along with all of the concomitant normative judgments, the function only arises along with the normative baggage that would make it impossible to fail.

One wrinkle in this analysis is that Dworkin did not claim to give us a theory of law everywhere. Hence there is a "pre-interpretive" sense in which abhorrent legal systems are still legal systems even though they are clearly failing to perform their function from our point of view.[23] The pre-interpretive stage is where one gathers data about what will go into an eventual interpretation without yet making any normative interpretive judgments about what fits or shows the practice in its best light.

The answer to this potential reply is to ask whether the force-justifying function of law is a part of the pre-interpretive data on which all understandings of law are based, or if it is rather an element of the interpretive enterprise itself. If Dworkin believed that the force-justification function was true of all law everywhere and hence was a part of the pre-intepretive data, then it does appear that there is conceptual room for the law to fail to perform its function. On the other hand, if the force-justification function is rather an element of the particular conception (theory/interpretation) of law that Dworkin is advancing against other conceptions, then it is a mark against that theory that it leaves no conceptual room for the law to fail to perform its function.

Think again about the question of whether an evil regime has law. Dworkin's claim was that it is not an illuminating question precisely because there is one sense in which it does have law and another in which it doesn't. The sense in which it does have law is the pre-interpretive sense in which we can recognize facets of that system as elements of the concept of law which are provisionally a part of every imaginable conception. The sense in which the evil regime doesn't have law is the one in which Dworkin's favored theory doesn't allow room for us to see an evil regime as fitting with our notion of law and showing it in its best light. Why exactly does it not fit or show it in its best light? It is precisely because from our perspective we cannot see it fulfilling its function of justifying the state's use or withholding of force. That is, the vast majority of the evil regime's putative laws are not good examples (seen from our perspective) of moral justifications for the use of force in the way that regime does use its force. Hence, it seems clear that the function of law is not merely part of the pre-interpretive data of facts that are likely to be true of every conception of law.

Dworkin's view that the function he adduces is uncontroversial might at first be taken to be a good reason for consigning his notion of the force-justification function to the pre-interpretive data. But if that were the case, we would not even pre-interpretively be able to say that the evil regime has law. So rather than solve the problem, this move actually highlights it: before

[23] See Dworkin, *Law's Empire* 65–66.

we can apply Dworkin's favored function to the notion of law, we can say that the evil regime has law, although we can still anticipate that it will be defective in some way. But after the theory itself tells us what the function of law is, we are left seeing no room for a defective legal system; the fact that the system is failing to perform its function is a reason for seeing it as not a member of the class of law. Hence Dworkin's conception of law, the theory he advances, suffers from the inability to accommodate the conceptual possibility of a legal system that fails to perform its function.

The point of this chapter was not simply to explain where Dworkin's theory fails in its use of law's function as an explanatory method. The lesson we are trying to learn from this failure is that a theorist who seeks to explain law in terms of its function must account for the possibility of the law failing to perform that function. This need provides two criteria of success for any general jurisprudential theory: it limits which functions may be adduced for law by the explanation to those in which the law might fail; it also limits the way in which a theorist may seek to use law's functions to explain it. In the next chapter, we will explore a theory that is more subtle in choosing functions in pursuit of which the law can clearly fail. The problems arise instead in the way the theory explains law via those functions.

4

Natural Law

Natural law is a theory that puts a great emphasis on law's function. Its fundamental tenet is that there is some necessary relation between rationality (or morality)[1] and legality such that laws that are deficient in the former are necessarily deficient in the latter. Hence, most natural law theorists hold that the function of law is to reproduce and precisify the requirements of reason or morality (in pursuit of the common good) for a given community.

Some forms, such as Lon Fuller's[2] and what admittedly might be a positivist caricature of Thomas Aquinas',[3] employ their views of law's function in a strong methodological role that leaves it open to similar arguments to the ones I made against Dworkin's theory. They run the risk of being unable to accommodate defective members of the class, seeing a failure of law to perform its function as rendering the token not-law. That is, laws which do not reproduce or precisify the requirements of reason (in that they are unreasonable laws, either because they demand the unreasonable of their subjects or in that they lead their subjects away from a collective common good) are not truly legal.

Granted, for Fuller, this is a matter of finesse and of degree, as only laws or systems that fail miserably in at least one of his eight desiderata are thereby considered to be sufficiently defective as not to constitute law.[4] Yet there is

[1] Earlier versions of natural law tended to focus on morality (Divinely ordained) as the standard that positive (human-created) law is trying to capture, reproduce, or precisify for the circumstantial demands and challenges of a particular community. Later versions have tended to broaden this to rationality more generally (though still tending to see morality as a subset of rationality, reflecting a strongly moral realist view).

[2] Fuller's view is also distinctive in that he sees the function of law to subject human conduct to the governance of rules, without stipulating that such must be in the pursuit of the common good: Lon L. Fuller, *The Morality of Law* (revised edn, Yale University Press 1969 (1964)) 146. As we will see, this view of law's function is much closer to the one generally contemplated by legal positivists. On this see also John Gardner, *Law as a Leap of Faith: Essays on Law in General* (Oxford University Press 2012) 205–11, arguing that this shared view is more modal than functional.

[3] John Finnis, *Natural Law and Natural Rights* (Clarendon Press 1980) 359.

[4] Fuller, *The Morality of Law* 39. The eight desiderata are that rules must be general, public, not overly retroactive, understandable, not contradictory with other rules, within the capabilities of those subject to them, not subject to overly frequent change, and applied according to their terms.

still some tendency with Fuller and what Mark Murphy calls the "strong reading of the natural law thesis"[5] to say that a law which fails in its function is not a law.

This is the view ridiculed by legal positivists as incoherent in that it appears to state a contradiction: "An unjust law is not a law." A single statement cannot assert both that something is and is not a law, whatever properties one might be attaching to it. Against this Murphy has advanced an interesting and compelling argument that certain terms can function as alienans, distinguishing certain tokens from their putative types. Just as "fake" or "counterfeit" are always alienans, "decoy" is an alienans for ducks, and "glass" is an alienans for diamonds, perhaps "unjust" or "irrational" is one for law.[6] Under this view, the strong reading of the natural law thesis might not be self-contradictory.

There could be two ways of interpreting this view. Under one, the alienans "unjust" or "irrational" fully removes the putative token from the class of law; any membership in the class of law is merely apparent. Another interpretation is that the alienans merely denies legal validity to irrational laws, rather than necessarily removing them from the class of law.[7] That is, under this view the strong natural lawyer is not saying that irrational laws are not members of the class of law, but rather merely that they cannot be legally valid in any legal system. Such a view would introduce its own problems, such as how to make sense of a law that cannot be valid in any possible legal system.

Notwithstanding these considerations, Murphy thinks that there are compelling reasons to side with what he terms the "weak interpretation [or "reading"] of the natural law thesis,"[8] or simply the "weak natural law thesis,"[9] identifying it with the view of John Finnis. Since Murphy and Finnis are the contemporary standard-bearers of the natural law tradition and since they both appear to agree on what Murphy calls the weak reading, we will focus on that as the target for our discussion.

[5] Mark C. Murphy, *Natural Law in Jurisprudence and Politics* (Cambridge University Press 2006) 10–11.

[6] Mark C. Murphy, 'Natural Law Jurisprudence' (2003) 9 *Legal Theory* 241–67, 246. See also Norman Kretzmann, 'Lex Iniusta Non Est Lex – Laws on Trial in Aquinas' Court of Conscience' (1988) 33 *American Journal of Jurisprudence* 99–122, 105, critiquing David Lyons, *Ethics and the Rule of Law* (Cambridge University Press 1984) 62–63 for failing to distinguish counterfeit instances from perverted instances (with thanks to Norv Richards for the reference).

[7] See, for example Norman Kretzmann, 'Lex Iniusta Non est Lex—Laws on Trial in Aquinas' Court of Conscience' (1988) 33 *American Journal of Jurisprudence* 99–122, 105f, calling this a failure of the "evaluative" but not of the "non-evaluative" conditions for inclusion in the class.

[8] Murphy, 'Natural Law Jurisprudence' 260.

[9] Murphy, *Natural Law in Jurisprudence and Politics* 25; 'The Explanatory Role of the Weak Natural Law Thesis' in W. J. Waluchow and S. Sciaraffa (eds), *Philosophical Foundations of the Nature of Law* (Oxford 2013) 3–21.

A. Deficiency and Necessity in the Weak Reading

According to Murphy, the natural law thesis is: "necessarily, law is a rational standard for conduct."[10] The strong reading is to see this necessity as applying to every token of the kind, such that any non-rational standard of conduct cannot be a valid member of the class of law.[11] The weak reading is to see this necessity as applying to the type rather than the token, such that laws which fail to perform their functions are defective members of the class,[12] rather than losing their legal validity or being excluded from the class altogether. This is akin to the difference between saying "necessarily, dogs are mammals" and saying "necessarily, dogs have four legs." In the former, as a taxonomic class superset comprising numerous species, each member of the species must also be a member of the class. In the latter, as a common and expected characteristic of the species, we are referring to a property of the species that might not be found in every member.

Now this example might appear immediately problematic, as we generally would simply say that the latter statement is false. It is simply not necessary for dogs to have four legs, for cheetahs to be fast runners,[13] or for ducks to be good swimmers.[14] One way around this problem would be to put the natural law thesis in a way that does not employ a claim of necessity, for example "law is backed by decisive reasons for compliance."[15]

But even if we were to retain a formulation of the thesis that centers on the claim of necessity, we are generally much more comfortable making such necessity claims when using them to attach functions to types than

[10] Mark C. Murphy, 'Natural Law Theory' in Martin P. Golding and William A. Edmundson (eds), *The Blackwell Guide to the Philosophy of Law and Legal Theory* (Blackwell Publishing 2005) 15–28 at 15.

[11] Saying that irrational tokens cannot be "valid" members of the class is here purposely ambiguous between the implication that they are not members of the class at all and merely saying that they are members but cannot be legally valid in any legal system. Some views of legal validity may collapse this distinction with the claim that for something to be a member of the class of law it must be valid in at least one existing legal system. But it may be useful to keep this distinction in mind in order to appreciate the nuances of the weak natural law thesis.

[12] "Failure" here and for now implies that either the law was intrinsically unable to accomplish what it was designed to do, or that contingent facts arose preventing an otherwise well-designed law from accomplishing its task. In either case, the law is not what reason required of the situation (even if we would have had no way of knowing what reason required). As our default understanding is to see functions as proper functions, as explained above, laws that "fail" merely because they are not used as intended (or at all) are not thereby considered defective (although any such misuse would be considered a defective instance).

[13] Murphy, 'Natural Law Theory' 21.

[14] Murphy, *Natural Law in Jurisprudence and Politics* 10–11.

[15] Ibid 10; see also Murphy, 'The Explanatory Role of the Weak Natural Law Thesis' 5.

we are when discussing many other properties. Since we are talking about purposes rather than inherent characteristics of a type that we expect to see in every member of the class, we can make claims of necessity without expecting to see every token fulfill (or even be designed to meet) the type's purpose.

Consider the difference between saying "necessarily, dogs have four legs" and "necessarily, hammers are for driving nails." Even if we come across a hammer that will only ever serve the purpose of a doorstop, we don't think we have thereby proven false the claim that hammers are necessarily for driving nails. This is due to the fact that its maker designed the object in such a way as to clearly place it within a class of objects that share the nail-driving function, even if she did so with the knowledge that some tokens (perhaps even this one) would never serve that purpose.[16]

Of course there is the phenomenon of artifacts designed to mimic the form of something that is understood to have one function while having a completely distinct function. Good examples of this abound in the Restoration Hardware catalog of vintage repurposed home furnishings, many tokens of which are now created for their "re"purpose.[17] (Think, for example, of doors serving as tables, which then become so popular that the company begins manufacturing a line of door-tables.) If these items still belong to the class of things whose characteristic purpose they were never truly intended to have (but only to mimic their form), then we might be reluctant to agree to claims of necessity linking functions with their types.

Nevertheless, to the degree that we still think the necessity claim is accurate (perhaps in the absence of such counterexamples for law), we do so based on the idea that tokens need not be successfully performing these functions in order to maintain their membership in the class being functionally described. The weak reading of the natural law thesis is therefore saying only that, once we settle on a function that captures and explains the nature of law, tokens which fail to perform that function are deficient members of the class, and that their deficiency is determined by that failure. Under this reading, we apparently cannot complain that the natural law theorist is leaving open no conceptual possibility of failure. Defective members of the class are as easily accommodated as broken chairs.[18]

[16] See the discussion of "pure" ends, which no one desires or intends to achieve, in Peter Achinstein, 'Function Statements' (1977) 44 *Philosophy of Science* 341–67, 360–61.

[17] As noted earlier, Preston would call this "recycling." Preston, 'Philosophical Theories of Artifact Function' in A. Meijers (ed.), *Philosophy of Technology and Engineering Sciences* (Elsevier 2009) 213–34, 215–16.

[18] Remember that misuse or non-use do not necessarily imply that the law itself is defective, although it might be a defective application of it.

The weak reading captures Finnis' analysis of the "central case" of the concept, seeing failures to perform as deficient members rather than counterexamples, a strategy also employed by legal positivists such as H. L. A. Hart and Joseph Raz.[19] By focusing on core examples or paradigms, we are encouraged to focus on what features are central to the notion being explained, seeing counterexamples as outliers. "[A] paradigm or central case is simply the case that shows how the other cases – including those supposed counterexamples – ought to be."[20]

One of the main advantages of this approach is that it maintains the inclusion of non-standard exemplars in the class of law. This is important precisely because we might learn a lot about the nature of law by examining outliers and what makes them outliers. Of course we also wish to delineate law and distinguish it from other similar social activities and institutions, so there is somewhat of a fine line to walk between inclusion and exclusion. As we flesh out this approach, we need to insure that it is maintaining the advantage of allowing us to include and learn from outliers (without including too much).

This is all well and good so far. The problem arises in Murphy's defense of seeing non-performers as deficient examples rather than counterexamples. That defense depends upon a background condition in which humans are rational and hence the law is functioning properly when giving good, decisive reasons to humans that act on those reasons.[21] Non-performers are then aberrations from this background condition. This in turn depends upon a number of moves that are themselves open to doubt and introduce a further doubt on their own.

One problem is that Murphy introduces the notion of "characteristic activity" to flesh out the functional explanation so as to avoid the problem that many other things might perform law's function.[22] This move itself was motivated by the recognition that, without it, law could not be a functional kind (in which performance of the function is sufficient for membership in the class).[23] Since so many other institutions and areas of human belief and activity tend to perform similar functions to ones that are frequently adduced for law (morality, religion, private promising, etiquette, etc.), relying on law's function alone will not distinguish it from other institutions or areas

[19] Finnis, *Natural Law and Natural Rights* 10–12.

[20] John Gardner, 'Nearly Natural Law' (2007) 52 *American Journal of Jurisprudence* 1–23, 3.

[21] Murphy, *Natural Law in Jurisprudence and Politics* 35.

[22] Ibid 32. See also Allan Beever, 'The Law's Function and the Judicial Function' (2003) 20 *New Zealand Universities Law Review* 299, using the phrase "performative functions" to refer to characteristic activities and preferring that notion to "purposive functions."

[23] Murphy, *Natural Law in Jurisprudence and Politics* 32. This corresponds to Gardner's notion of a "distinguishing function": 'Law's Aims in *Law's Empire*' in S. Hershovitz (ed.), *Exploring Law's Empire* (Oxford University Press 2006) 207–24, 207.

of behavior.[24] So if we understand a thing's function to include its characteristic activity, then we have more hope of providing a functional explanation that can serve to distinguish the explanandum from other entities. That is, in order to provide a function the performance of which is sufficient for membership in the class one is trying to explain, Murphy bundles the thing's characteristic activity with its purpose to make the explanans explanatorily unique.

The problem with this move by Murphy is that it incorporates characteristic activity[25] into the notion of function itself. This is problematic because it resurrects the difficulty of non-standard instances getting excluded from the class. Consider Murphy's own example from these considerations that the heart's characteristic activity is pumping blood: "while the end of the heart is to circulate the blood, it is clear that only objects whose characteristic activity is that of *pumping* can be classified as hearts."[26] While he can still easily say that a stopped heart is still a heart,[27] he believes it needs to employ a pumping mechanism when operational in order to count as a heart. Putting aside for the moment my admonition that we are better served focusing on artifactual examples rather than biological ones, it seems to me that this is the kind of intuitive claim that is a result of Murphy already being committed to his theoretical structure. I fail to see any good reason why artificial hearts (or even natural ones in some as yet undiscovered species) could not perform their tasks through some means other than pumping, such as the use of propeller structures.

To the contrary, while using a functional explanation commits one to saying that the explanandum is a means to the accomplishment of some end, it does not commit one to saying that the explanandum must perform its role in a specific paradigmatic way.[28] The inclusion of characteristic activities in the description of functions themselves artificially narrows the class of what can be included in the description to the point that we are in danger of excluding useful and informative exemplars.

[24] This is not to say that natural lawyers in general require that law's function be distinctive. Rather, it only means that Murphy hopes to show that law is a functional kind, which is misguided precisely because it is not necessary for law's function to be distinctive in order for its function to be explanatorily essential.

[25] Following Leslie Green, characteristic activities can be understood as formal or modal elements: 'The Functions of Law' (1998) 12 *Cogito* 117–24, 121; 'Law as a Means' in P. Cane (ed.), *The Hart-Fuller Debate in the Twenty-First Century* (Hart Publishing 2010) 169–88, 170.

[26] Murphy, *Natural Law in Jurisprudence and Politics* 31, emphasis in original.

[27] While he could say this, in correspondence he claimed to side with Aristotle's view that a severed hand is no longer a hand.

[28] "Although functional talk involves both the idea of a means and an end[,] what makes such talk teleological is the commitment not to a means but to an end." Achinstein, 'Function Statements' 362.

This is clear if we limit ourselves to consideration of functional kinds (where everything that performs the function is considered to be a member of the class), although I reiterate that law is not a functional kind. If "leader" is a functional kind in that everyone who leads is a leader,[29] this says nothing about characteristic activity. Some lead by giving orders, some by setting an example, some by doing. While to explain something in functional terms is to say that it is a means to some end, it is not to say that it operates in a specific way in the pursuit of that end. If we came across a posited normative system that guided behavior through some means other than the legislation of rules and/or threats of force, we shouldn't thereby exclude it from the class of law *ab initio* (although we may eventually decide to do so for other reasons).

This problem for Murphy arose from the need to distinguish law from other social institutions or normative systems that apparently perform the same functions. Clearly, many of the functions commonly adduced to explain law are performed by other conventions, normative systems, or institutions. The problem comes from demanding too much from the functions one uses to explain law, believing that in order for a functional explanation to be successful, it must maintain that the explanandum is a functional kind, that its function sets it apart from everything else. Hence (for Murphy) the characteristic activity must be made part of the function in order to accomplish that task.

While we might agree that a complete explanation of law (or anything else) gives us the ability to differentiate it from other similar systems, it is not the case that the differentiation must come through the function itself. Adequate explanations of hospitals and universities must make reference to their functions, even though other social institutions perform the same functions. Hence, although means are important in a functional explanation of law (or other institutions), we shouldn't see those means as part and parcel of the function such that we are still seeking a set of sufficient conditions for membership in the class within the ambit of functions alone. Differentiation from other institutions may come through a particular combination of functional and modal characteristics. More importantly, this differentiation is a requirement of the theory as a whole, not each part of the theory. So we shouldn't necessarily expect to see a distinguishing function for law, nor should we agree with claims that it is a functional kind.

It is the inclusion of characteristic activities within the notion of function that leads Murphy to claim that the law is better understood akin

[29] The example is from Green, 'Functions of Law' 109.

to biological systems rather than artifactual ones. He is led to that claim because he cannot ecumenically identify a creator or inventor to whom we can appeal in order to attach the function to the object, which is what we do for artifacts.[30] So in order to be able to say that exemplars which fail to perform their function are not counterexamples to the functional explanation, he turns to biological systems and their supposed characteristic activities. As long as they perform those activities they are members of the class, even if they don't succeed in fulfilling their function.

This leads him to agree with Michael Moore that functional kinds have equilibrium states and that functional ascriptions take place in the context of larger systems of which they are a part and to whose equilibrium states they contribute. (We have been following Ruth Millikan in calling these "Cummins functions," and have seen that they are not the best to use in this kind of explanation.) From this we get claims like the claim that the function of the human body is physical health[31] and that the "privileged background" equilibrium state is for humans to be rational beings,[32] both of which rankle a pre-theoretic ear.

While Murphy takes issue with Moore's overly restrictive notion of functional kinds, preferring to broaden them to include characteristic activities, he is still buying into the idea that law is a functional kind—any performance of its broadened function (to include its characteristic activity) is sufficient for membership in the class of law. He also accepts Moore's adoption of Cummins functions, that a thing's function must be the effect it has as a member of a larger system that has a goal to which the explanandum contributes (hence the insistence upon equilibrium states). Moore was also led to this desideratum by the inability to rely upon designer's or user's intentions, since those cannot be identified for biological systems, which clearly (to him) still are explained using functions.[33]

We have already seen that the analysis of biological functions and artifactual functions are (generally) distinct. Hence if we confine ourselves to seeing the law as an artifact, we can help ourselves to the less problematic notions of function that are attendant upon artifacts. Most artifact types are not functional kinds[34] in that we have many tools for the same

[30] Murphy, *Natural Law in Jurisprudence and Politics* 34.

[31] Moore, 'Law as a Functional Kind' 210–11.

[32] Murphy, *Natural Law in Jurisprudence and Politics* 35.

[33] M. S. Moore, 'Law as a Functional Kind' in R. P. George (ed.), *Natural Law Theory: Contemporary Essays* (Clarendon Press 1992) 188–242, 210.

[34] We may conceive of some artifact-types as functional kinds. An example might be "timepiece," referring to any artifact that is used to tell time, although I remain unsure about whether a sundial is a timepiece and hence whether even this example is really a functional kind. If we think

job:[35] staples and paper clips, hammers and nail guns, universities and liberal arts colleges. Admittedly, many artifacts have complex or multiple functions that make them distinguishable from other artifacts which perform some but not all of those functions. Yet we cannot in principle say that they are functional kinds, that anything which performs the function is necessarily a member of the class.

Equilibrium states and privileged backgrounds are only ever relevant when trying to accommodate the problems of functional ascriptions in biological systems. Since functions only make sense in terms of some goal for the sake of which the function is to be performed, once we dispense with an intelligent designer (whose purpose, while ultimately inscrutable, at least generally includes the flourishing of the creation as a whole), we are left grasping for goals to serve as substitutes. Within the context of evolution by natural selection, we at least have a kind of systemic goal, the survival and reproduction of the species, which purpose individual biological systems (such as particular organs) can be said to serve. (Of course, while quite common, this kind of thinking is not actually what the theory warrants. The most we can say of any given biological sub-system is that it conferred *no more* of a reproductive *disadvantage* than other systems performing similar functions, which happened to have also historically appeared through mutation. The mistake is in inferring from the presence of a trait to its survival advantage. This is especially important in considering traits that do not tend to appear in the organism until after it has completed all of its expected reproductive tasks, where the organism does not itself present a threat to its own offspring.)

The notion of the relation of function to equilibrium state is then a way of capturing the benefit that a given biological subsystem provides to the organism as a whole (and possibly also the benefit the organism provides to the survival of the species). But where goals and purposes are less problematically assigned, less sense can be made of the necessary relationship between function and equilibrium state, and still less of the utility of the notion of equilibrium states to the functional explanans. This is manifestly clear in the case of artifacts. Take the example of an automatic smoke detector alarm. Is the equilibrium state that of readiness to sound where smoke is not present, that of sounding where smoke is present, or both? Is a unit without batteries in some other kind of equilibrium state even though it is incapable of

that a characteristic mechanism is necessary for something to be a timepiece (e.g. clockworks), then I would argue that the notion is not that of a functional kind for the same reasons I previously argued against characteristic activities.

[35] This is Preston's notion of multiple realizability. Preston, 'Philosophical Theories of Artifact Function' 214–15.

functioning? Even if we could answer these questions, it is not clear what this notion of the equilibrium state is adding to the basic explanation of what the smoke detector is for: alerting people to the risk of fire in the presence of smoke.

The focus on the need to identify equilibrium states also leads theorists such as Murphy and Moore to argue for necessary harmonies within functionally explained systems. While it allows them to say that parts in disharmony are necessarily malfunctioning, it further leads them to claim that elements which are necessary for the proper functioning of the system are parts of that system. Hence the driver on a riding mower is a part of the mower,[36] and people (as legal subjects) are parts of the legal system.[37] Murphy's solution to this problem is to say that people, as "natural objects," have functions independent and prior to those of the legal system. The system is therefore adapted to the proper functioning of its parts and its privileged background equilibrium state is that of the fully rational human being.[38]

While the problem that motivated these moves is the need for an inventor or creator, in artifactual explanations this is not quite as problematic as Murphy and Moore seem to have envisioned.[39] It may be unlikely that we can identify a specific person or group as the inventor of law. But we can certainly more easily do so for particular legal decisions and pieces of legislation. Even if, as in many systems, laws are compromises among a wide variety of competing interests and are authored, passed, and implemented by a large number of different people with different intentions, it is also the case that they tend to develop as reactions to specific social problems or conflicts (or, at the very least, as a manifestation of a need or desire of a lawmaker or group able to dictate their needs or desires to the lawmaker).

As for the notion of law in general, our inability to identify a creator is no more problematic than that of an anthropologist discovering an ancient artifact in need of explanation. Consider the case of the Antikythera mechanism, pieces of which were found in 1900 in an ancient shipwreck. Without prior knowledge of the object, researchers needed to investigate the artifact itself in order to determine its function, which, as with most any artifact, is essential to determining what it is. Through painstaking reconstruction of its operation, researchers theorized that it was an analog computer for predicting eclipses and the movements of heavenly bodies over time.

[36] Moore, 'Law as a Functional Kind' 207. Moore's example comes from *In Re Erickson* 815 F.2d 1090 (7th Cir., 1987).

[37] Murphy, *Natural Law in Jurisprudence and Politics* 35–36.

[38] Ibid 36.

[39] On this point see also Achinstein, 'Function Statements' 350.

Note that while the process of investigation involved re-creating its operation (i.e. its modal or formal characteristics), researchers cannot claim to have understood what it was until they have figured out what it was for. While there have been some attempts at identifying an inventor, this is not necessary in order to arrive at reasonable theories about its function and hence its identity. Similarly for law, we do not need to identify a first law-giver in order to theorize about the functions of law. We need only to investigate its effects and how it is used and adapted by other people and institutions.

The relation between law and the rationality of human beings, so central to Murphy and other natural lawyers, is also far from unproblematic. While it may be the case that we would need law even if we were perfectly rational (although perhaps without the need for enforcement), in the real world it is not clear how much the law assumes its subjects to be rational. On the one hand, we could envision law as merely providing information that rational individuals would not otherwise have about the proper way to act. That is, if everyone was perfectly rational, the only thing standing in the way of perfectly rational behavior would be information about what the correct balance of reasons requires in any given situation. Sometimes this may be as simple as making one solution to a coordination problem more salient than others (e.g. by mandating that everyone drive on a given side of the road). But the law also may be a corrective on our somewhat irrational behavior, in which case giving us standards backed by decisive reasons may not be an adequate way of characterizing what law is doing.

Let's say that someone is slightly irrational in that he is over-valuing his own prudential reasons in situations in which he actually has better (moral?) reasons to prefer the wellbeing of others. This person is actually very rational in assessing his own prudential reasons, just not so good at weighing them against reasons he has to promote the welfare of others. It seems as though this is precisely the kind of person that the law is attempting to accommodate in providing sanctions to back up its dictates. After all, if the law was dealing with perfectly rational individuals (and doing so perfectly), there would be no need for sanctions, since it would correctly be reproducing what reason requires of everyone and they would correctly see that it was doing so. So sanctions are based on both a baseline of expected rationality (in that potential violators will see that it is not in their interest to violate the law) and expected irrationality (in that potential violators are not already motivated to conform merely on the assumption that the law is reproducing what reason already requires).

If the function of law is to foster the common good by providing decisive reasons to act in promotion of that good, then it is not clear how those reasons are being provided. While it may be fairly straightforward to say that law does what it does by manipulating the reasons people have to behave in given ways, it is another step to say that it operates by providing "decisive reasons."[40]

If my discussion of the advantages of seeing the law as an artifact for the purposes of its explanation is correct, it also counts as an additional point in favor of positivism and against natural law. For a natural lawyer who agrees that the best notion of function to employ is that of an artifact, the most she can say about its application to law is either that it should be employed somewhat metaphorically (in that there is an element of legality that is beyond its positive, artifactual, aspects) or she must continue to maintain with her intellectual forebears that law is an artifact designed by God. The positivist can claim instead that the law is an artifact without having to qualify this claim with metaphorical or divine elaborations. Natural lawyers are correct to embrace the use of functionality in their explanations, but are pushed to natural (i.e. biological) or Aristotelian[41] interpretations of the role of that functionality, perhaps partially by the fact that an artifactual approach lends itself more to positivism.

B. What Separates the Weak Reading and Legal Positivism?

Some have suggested that the weak natural law thesis is not sufficiently distinct from legal positivism, or even that positivism can embrace the weak natural law thesis as Murphy envisions it.[42] If the weak natural law thesis is

[40] Murphy, *Natural Law in Jurisprudence and Politics* 10.

[41] While Murphy thinks implausible my interpretation of Aristotle, taking him to exclude from the class anything that fails to perform its function: 'The Explanatory Role of the Weak Natural Law Thesis' 13 n. 24, I believe this is a quite standard interpretation of Aristotle. It is a belief to which he is clearly pushed by his other metaphysical and taxonomical commitments. Nevertheless, I admit this Aristotelian tendency has become so ingrained that we may not have clear ideas about what kinds of failures exclude exemplars from the class. It seems equally correct to say there has never been a perpetual motion machine as to say that all failed attempts at their creation resulted in defective perpetual motion machines. However, this is not captured by Murphy's distinction between the "constitutionally incapable" and the merely "unable": ibid 12–13. *Pace* Murphy, we are not likely to say that a well-conceived pre-Wright brothers design that only just failed to take flight (while clearly still constitutionally unable due to the laws of aerodynamics) is as much or as little a flying machine as two planks nailed together and thrown in the air. There is obviously some vague "open texture" boundary at the edge of any of these sets of artifacts. But that boundary is not captured or clarified by excluding the constitutionally unable and including the mere failures. See also Achinstein, 'Function Statements' 349, showing that artifacts can have impossible functions; Baker, 'The Metaphysics of Malfunction' 84; and Beth Preston's discussion of phantom functions in 'Philosophical Theories of Artifact Function' 217.

[42] See for example Shapiro, *Legality* 36.

merely holding that laws not backed by sufficient reason are defective, then it would appear that legal positivism need not deny this claim, as positivists are certainly of the general opinion that irrational or immoral laws are bad or defective, just so long as they are still law, as the weak natural lawyer admits.

If our collective jurisprudential goal is the clarification of law and an explanation of its nature in some form, this may not be a criticism at all as it suggests that there is a convergence of opinion on some key features of law. Furthermore, if there are still any differences between the positions, it might start to look as though they are merely semantic or otherwise inconsequential.

The weak natural lawyer holds that an understanding of law's functionality leads one to say that irrational laws are defective *qua* law in that they are deficient in a legal way. This is so because law's function is a facet of legality itself. Hence laws that do not perform this function are legally defective. It is this that a legal positivist might still plausibly deny (although, as we are about to see, some might not believe that they still have reason to do so.[43]) Since a positivist might say that the existence of law is entirely a matter of social fact and that its normativity is therefore determined by those facts (in some way yet to be explained,[44]) there cannot be a *legal* standard for judging laws that comes from a non-social source (such as reason or critical morality). Hence a morally or rationally deficient law is deficient but not *legally* deficient for such a positivist, while a natural lawyer maintains that it is.

But this might just be a matter of terminology, with no practical consequences. What does it matter if this kind of defect is considered legal or not, since no one is any longer denying the presence of such a defective law in the class of laws, or necessarily denying it legal validity? Once we see these theories in the light of the ways in which they use claims about law's function, we will see that the differences between the theories still have weight.

Disagreements about the functions that best explain law (and the way those functions explain the law) amount to disagreements about the nature

[43] Ibid; see also generally Gardner, 'Nearly Natural Law.'

[44] There is a brewing debate about whether the legal positivist claim is that legal facts reduce to social facts, are merely grounded upon them, or perhaps supervene upon them. See Andrei Marmor, 'Farewell to Conceptual Analysis (in Jurisprudence)' in Wilfrid J. Waluchow and Stefan Sciaraffa (eds), *Philosophical Foundations of the Nature of Law* (Oxford University Press 2013) 209–29 at 216; David Plunkett, 'A Positivist Route for Explaining How Facts Make Law' (2012) 18 *Legal Theory* 139–207, 151f; George Pavlakos, 'The Metaphysics of Law: From Supervenience to Rational Justification' in Bartosz Brozek, Antonio Rotolo, and Jerzy Stelmach (eds), *Supervenience and Normativity* (Springer forthcoming, 2016); Tomasz Gizbert-Studnicki, 'The Social Sources Thesis and Metaphilosophy' in Tomasz Gizbert-Studnicki, Adam Dyrda, and Pawel Banas (eds), *Metaphilosophy of Law* (Hart Publishing forthcoming 2016). While I am inclined to side with those who think that the relation is one of grounding, I don't believe that the discussion in this book depends upon one or another of these relations being correct. For more on grounding see Shamik Dasgupta, 'On the Plurality of Grounds' (2014) 14 *Philosophers' Imprint* 1–28.

of law. Even if natural lawyers and positivists both admit that positive law is a thorough-going human creation, there is still an open question about whether law itself is such an artifact, whether there is another law beyond what humans make. If there is, then that law sets standards for human law to live up to, and it is in the nature of law to set them and for human-made law to be measured by those standards. It has implications for answering the question of where the normativity of law comes from and how we should expect to judge attempts by human law to capture that normativity, whether we wish to say immediately that anyone who violates a good law has necessarily acted immorally (or irrationally). A positivist can say that there are possible laws which fulfill law's overall functions (as well as those laws' more particular own individual functions), yet which one is not morally or rationally blameworthy in violating.[45] A natural lawyer cannot say this; if a law is fulfilling the overall function of law, then one is at least prima facie blameworthy in violating it.

John Gardner, a legal positivist, has taken an additional step in admitting that immoral laws are legally deficient. If we adopt the central case method that both Finnis and Hart advocated, then it seems fairly clear that in its central case law has a moral aim. Since, following Raz, law purports to impose moral obligations as its means of accomplishing its function, law is only successful when it succeeds in imposing a moral obligation.[46] Hence the central case of law is that of law successfully imposing a moral obligation on its subjects. This is the central case because, when we think about something in terms of its function, the central case is when that thing is successfully performing its function.[47] Hence, the central case of something understood functionally may rarely, if ever, actually be found.

One might very well wonder what is left to separate the two positions once this qualification is made. It does go beyond the distinction I drew earlier between the natural lawyer seeing a morally deficient law as thereby legally deficient and a legal positivist position holding that morally deficient law need not be legally deficient. Gardner understands an implication of Raz's view (with which he agrees) to be that morally deficient laws are thereby legally deficient as well.

It is clear that morally deficient laws lack legitimate authority under Raz's view. If we are saying that morality is a species of rationality and agree with Raz that the function of authority is to get us to comply better with the

[45] This possibility may require that such a good law not be legitimately authoritative for some reason, in order for the positivist to say that one is not blameworthy in violating it.

[46] Gardner, 'Nearly Natural Law' 18, citing Raz, *The Authority of Law: Essays on Law and Morality* (Clarendon Press 1979) 8, 159.

[47] Gardner, 'Nearly Natural Law' 16.

correct balance of reasons,[48] then it is hard to see how a morally deficient law can be legitimately (i.e. morally) authoritative.[49] While such a view does not entitle us to say immediately that morally deficient laws are thereby legally deficient, it is also not an unreasonable conclusion to draw. Raz's idea that law is a paradigm case of legitimate authority[50] does suggest that laws which lack legitimate authority are legally deficient.

The ultimate answer to this question of the proper implications of Raz's view depends upon how closely we wish to tie legal deficiency to legal invalidity. The more we think that legal deficiency of this sort tends to imply that the deficient laws are somehow legally invalid, the less the implication Gardner draws from Raz's views seems viable. But Raz believes both that legally invalid rules cannot be laws[51] and that legal validity is entirely a matter of social fact.[52] Hence, saying that irrational laws are legally deficient in that they cannot be legitimately authoritative is not going to have a direct impact on their legal validity or membership in the class of law. So Gardner's interpretation appears reasonable.

Gardner sees the remaining distinction between weak natural law and legal positivism as resting upon the difference between saying that laws are "defeasibly morally binding" (following Hart) and saying that they are "presumptively morally binding" (as Finnis does).[53] For Gardner, to say that laws are defeasibly morally binding is only to say that laws which are not morally binding are deviant applications of the concept of law; deviant but otherwise unproblematic.

To say that laws are presumptively morally binding is to say we should assume that laws we encounter are morally binding unless and until we see reasons to hold otherwise of those laws. Even if we can say that law is morally binding in the central case, since the central case is one in which its claim to legitimate authority is successful, that does not entitle us to presume that laws are binding, since the central case may rarely or never be encountered.[54] Establishing that non-deviant law is morally binding only establishes that for the central case. It does not do so for all of law, and hence it does not entitle us to make any presumptions.

In effect, Gardner has uncovered a way in which Finnis is still under the sway of seeing successful performance of its function to be a necessary

[48] Joseph Raz, 'The Problem of Authority: Revisiting the Service Conception' (2006) 90 *Minnesota Law Review* 1003–44, 1018.

[49] See for example Raz, *Authority of Law* 235, 'Authority and Justification' (1985) 14 *Philosophy and Public Affairs* 3–29, 6, 'The Problem of Authority' 1012.

[50] Joseph Raz, 'Authority, Law and Morality' (1985) 68 *Monist* 295–323, 300–02.

[51] Raz, 'Legal Validity' 339. [52] Ibid 343–44.

[53] Gardner, 'Nearly Natural Law' 19–20. [54] Ibid 21.

condition for membership in the class of law, although Finnis is not embracing that claim fully. As a weak natural lawyer, it is not strictly necessary, as Finnis and Murphy are quick to allow that deficient laws are still laws. But by reasoning from law's admittedly moral function to a claim that it entitles us to presume law to be morally binding, Finnis is seeing its functional characteristics in the successful case to be presumptively applicable to all instances.[55] To make that presumption is to believe that it is something approaching necessity for membership in the class of law. Sure, there are deviant examples out there, and that deviance undermines any moral bindingness they may have. But to presume that law is morally binding is to see a close connection between the success condition and the criteria for membership in the class. To say instead that the law is only defeasibly morally obligatory is to underscore that its moral function may not be successfully fulfilled.

A focus on the different ways in which things might fail to fulfill their functions also helps to cash out the importance of this distinction in a way that Gardner does not appear to recognize fully. Tools can fail to perform their functions at the token-level and at the type-level. That is, you can have one hammer that fails to drive nails (failing at the token-level), or you can imagine that our notion of hammers was such that their heads were made out of a gelatinous substance so that none of them could drive nails except into the softest of surfaces. At the type-level, we would generally say that the tool was not suited to purpose. So the problem with inferring from the fact that law has a moral aim to the conclusion that it is presumptively morally obligatory is that such an inference implies an assumption that law is well suited to accomplish that moral aim.

Take the example of (non-legal) punishment. We might wish to say that punishment has a moral aim: the correction or prevention of unwanted behavior. We can strengthen this moral aim by saying that only immoral behavior is unwanted and appropriate for punishment. Hence the function of punishment is to minimize immoral behavior. Putting aside for the moment questions about the morality of punishment outside the legal sphere, even if we admit that it has a moral aim, we might be very hesitant to say that it is effective in limiting immoral behavior. Perhaps we might believe that psychology has proven education, mediation, or other forms of intervention to be better methods for minimizing immoral behavior.

What is clear is that many tools or practices can have moral aims without expecting those aims to be satisfied in any general way better than

[55] See for example John Finnis, 'Law and What I Truly Should Decide' (2003) 48 *American Journal of Jurisprudence* 107–30, 114, claiming the "presumptive obligatoriness of posited law is obvious and obviously reasonable," and *Natural Law and Natural Rights* 361.

alternatives. We are not saying that they are "constitutionally" incapable of success. Rather, we are only saying that, given the availability of other superior methods to accomplish those goals, we are doubtful about punishment's fitness to purpose. If we believe (a) that the law has a moral aim and operates towards that aim by purporting to impose obligations (usually accompanying these with threats of force); and if we additionally believe (b) that there are other methods of providing for that moral aim which do a better job than law could, then it seems fairly clear that we should not presume that the law's claims to obligate us are generally (or ever) correct.[56]

In its successful case, it would succeed in imposing that obligation, and so it would be correct to say that it is a defeasible property of law that it imposes moral obligations when successful. Doubts about its fitness to purpose simply underscore the fact that we cannot reason from such defeasibility to a presumption.

Hence it is this that still separates the weak natural lawyer from the legal positivist: the weak natural lawyer seems to require an assumption that the law is the best means we have available for accomplishing its function. This is certainly in keeping with their traditional focus, even after paring away any mistaken implications about unjust laws losing their validity or membership in the class of law. The legal positivist can see law as a tool of human creation for accomplishing the moral goal of providing for the common good, but can nonetheless admit that this tool is as imperfect as the humans that create and use it, that it may not be so well suited to its task as the natural lawyers believe it to be.

[56] Of course a sub-optimal method might still successfully obligate, but only in conjunction with a justification or explanation for the inaccessibility of a better method. If impositions upon people's autonomy in the form of imposed obligations (generally backed by threats of force) are ever to be justified, it must be because they are the morally best accessible means of accomplishing a moral aim. The point here is that sub-optimal methods should never be *presumed* to obligate.

5

Legal Positivism as a Functional Explanation of Law

Legal positivism rests on the belief that law is entirely a human creation. As such, it is reasonable to say that legal positivists hold law to be a kind of artifact.[1] If it is an artifact, then it is entirely appropriate to understand its nature via an exploration of the social functions it performs or is intended to perform by its creators and users.

This last statement might be slightly controversial in the realm of artifacts more broadly. Some put less emphasis on intentionality in the understanding of artifact functions,[2] and some put less emphasis on functionality in the understanding of artifacts.[3] I will argue, however, that these caveats are not necessary for law. For now we will engage with legal positivism on the presumption that if law is a kind of artifact, it is the kind of artifact generally to be understood in terms of its functions, and that the intentions of users or drafters are essential to identifying and understanding those functions.[4]

Modern legal positivism owes its strength and influence primarily to the work of H. L. A. Hart.[5] Hart himself under-emphasized the role of law's

[1] See for example H. L. A. Hart, 'Legal and Moral Obligation' in R. E. Flathman (ed), *Concepts in Social and Political Philosophy* (Macmillan 1973) 187–200, 188; John Gardner, 'The Legality of Law' (2004) 17 *Ratio Juris* 168–81, 171; Gardner, *Law as a Leap of Faith: Essays on Law in General* (Oxford University Press 2012) 54; Leslie Green, 'Law as a Means' in P. Cane (ed.), *The Hart-Fuller Debate in the Twenty-First Century* (Hart Publishing 2010) 169–88, 172; Brian Leiter, 'The Demarcation Problem in Jurisprudence: A New Case for Scepticism' (2011) 31 *Oxford Journal of Legal Studies* 663–77, 666.

[2] For example Beth Preston, 'Why Is a Wing Like a Spoon? A Pluralist Theory of Function' (1998) 95 *The Journal of Philosophy* 215–54; *A Philosophy of Material Culture: Action, Function, and Mind* (Routledge 2013).

[3] Amie L. Thomasson, 'Public Artifacts, Intentions and Norms' in M. Franssen, P. Kroes, T. A. C. Reydon and P. E. Vermaas (eds), *Artefact Kinds: Ontology and the Human-Made World* (Springer 2013) 45–62.

[4] This emphasis on the importance of intentions of users and drafters is not meant to imply or impose a specific interpretive theory for judges to use in making applications of law.

[5] Hart, *Concept of Law* (Penelope A. Bulloch and Joseph Raz (eds), 2nd edn., (Clarendon Press 1994 (1961))), *Essays in Jurisprudence and Philosophy* (Clarendon Press 1983).

functionality in his own work,[6] likely due to his early sparring with Lon Fuller[7] and his later disputes with Ronald Dworkin.[8]

While Fuller and Hart mostly agreed that the function of law was to guide human behavior, Fuller believed that this fact could be used to derive standards inherent in the concept of any enterprise with that purpose. Those standards then served as the internal source of judgments to be made about the efficacy of any legal enterprise. In effect, Fuller claimed that the notion of law's function served as a source of judgments of instrumental value about a given legal system's fitness to purpose.

Fuller extended this claim unjustifiably to the conclusion that systems which failed to be fit for purpose were not "really" law, seeing success as a membership condition for law, a move that Hart rightfully rejected. While not making the same mistake, however, Hart seemed to think that a greater emphasis on law's functionality might lead to the same result, perhaps treating that as a reason not to agree with such an emphasis.[9] As previously detailed, Dworkin then carried this mistake further, leading Hart to distance himself again from appeals to law's functionality.

Nevertheless, Hart does appeal to law's functionality at several key points in his theory, as pointed out by Stephen Perry.[10] At its most basic, Hart's theory is that law is a union of primary and secondary rules validated by a rule of recognition. Primary rules are rules that guide the actions of subjects directly, usually duty-imposing rules. Secondary rules are rules about the primary rules, generally specifying powers and rights of officials and offices, detailing how legal entities are to be formed and considered valid, sometimes also coming in the form of duties of those officials. (The primary and secondary rules can therefore be understood in terms of their social functions within a legal system.) The rule of recognition is a kind of supreme secondary rule, a background practice of those officials that they see as normative for determining which actions of which officials count as valid law for their

[6] See Nicola Lacey, 'Analytical Jurisprudence Versus Descriptive Sociology Revisited' (2006) 84 *Texas Law Review* 944–82, 957.

[7] H. L. A. Hart, 'Positivism and the Separation of Law and Morals' (1958) 71 *Harvard Law Review* 593, 602; Lon L. Fuller, 'Positivism and Fidelity to Law – a Reply to Professor Hart' (1958) 71 *Harvard Law Review* 630.

[8] Dworkin, 'Hart's Postscript,' *Law's Empire* (Hart 1998 (1986)); *Taking Rights Seriously* (Harvard University Press 1978); the postscript to Hart, *Concept of Law* 238–76; 'Comment: Legal Theory and the Problem of Sense' in Ruth Gavison (ed.), *Issues in Contemporary Legal Philosophy* (Clarendon 1987) 35–42.

[9] See Hart, 'Positivism and Separation' 602, favoring an analysis of the concept of law as opposed to a critical approach, grouping an investigation into its "functions" in the latter.

[10] Stephen R. Perry, 'Hart's Methodological Positivism' (1998) 4 *Legal Theory* 427–67, 427, 437–38, 456.

community. The key move in the development of a robust legal system is when a society moves from a system of merely primary rules to the inclusion of secondary rules—the move from what Hart calls a "primitive" legal system to a fully developed municipal legal order.[11]

While the focus on the distinctive means by which law accomplishes its tasks is another indication of his reluctance to engage with law's functionality, there are several places in which Hart's argument depends explicitly on the behavior guidance function of law. One is where he articulates the advantages of moving from a "primitive" legal system to a modern municipal legal system through the addition of secondary rules. While it is important not to over-read his reliance on those advantages,[12] the adaptability and responsiveness of a fully developed legal order are only the functions that are added by the addition of secondary rules. The point is that they are necessary for any reasonably complex society to guide behavior successfully. While it may be fairly clear where Hart came down on the question of the value of such behavior guidance, such an implicit endorsement is not essential to his argument. This fuels his insistence that he was doing "descriptive" (I prefer the term "explanatory") jurisprudence.[13]

The other place that the behavior guidance function shows its importance is in the section where Hart discusses the "minimum content of natural law."[14] There he discusses the need for law to have certain characteristics in order to be capable of fulfilling its purpose, given the kinds of creatures whose behavior is to be guided. In particular, the law needs to have rules against unprovoked violence and certain other invasions for it to be capable of serving as a normative system for creatures like us.

In other words, while he may have believed the behavior guidance function that he articulated for law to be of such generality as not to be of much jurisprudential use, it still served at key points in his theory to explain important

[11] Hart, *Concept of Law* 86.

[12] They are only advantageous for societies with certain characteristics, albeit characteristics it is hard to imagine a society without. Plus they come with their own costs in possibly having a complacent polity replacing its moral judgments with the legal norms that government imposes. Wilfrid J. Waluchow, 'Legality, Morality, and the Guiding Function of Law' in C. Grant, B. Colburn, A. Hatzistavrou, and M. Kramer (eds), *The Legacy of H. L. A. Hart, Legal, Political, and Moral Philosophy* (Oxford University Press 2008) 85–98, 90; Jeremy Waldron, 'All We Like Sheep' (1999) 12 *Canadian Journal of Law and Jurisprudence* 169, 169.

[13] Hart, *Concept of Law* vi. "Descriptive" tends to carry the connotation that one's description is devoid of any normative judgments, while explanations cannot be developed without some normative judgments, such as what is important to include in the explanation. Yet the main focus of an explanation is not to push a normative judgment about the explanandum. On this see generally Julie Dickson, *Evaluation and Legal Theory* (Hart 2001).

[14] Hart, *Concept of Law* 193ff.

aspects of law. It is also entirely possible that, even with that very general articulation of law's function, one value of Hart's theory can be found in helping us to identify key features of legality which then, in turn, help us to further refine our understanding of its functions.

Scott Shapiro makes the argument that Hart also relies on the behavior guidance function in his adoption of what Jules Coleman calls the "practical difference thesis," which is the idea that for law to govern conduct it has to be the legal norms that are guiding conduct, and not any ultimate moral norms that the law may be endorsing.[15] Notwithstanding Hart's apparent de-emphasis, Shapiro notes that almost all of Hart's arguments against his predecessors, such as Austin and Bentham, and contemporaries, such as Fuller (in the original edition of the *Concept of Law*), relied upon the assumption that the proper function of law is to guide behavior.[16] Shapiro goes even further, arguing that Hart's view is deeply functionalist in seeing the existence and particular forms that legal systems take as a result of the functions they serve.[17]

Both Dworkin and Fuller shared the mistake of believing that successful performance of the function they adduced for law serves as a kind of membership condition for putative laws or legal systems. But while Fuller's embrace of this claim was made centrally with his articulation of the eight ways to fail to make law,[18] Dworkin's was somewhat more subtle. As explained earlier, it is not that Dworkin states baldly that anything which cannot justify the state's use or withholding of force cannot be a law. Rather, any interpreter of what the law requires will necessarily see only those principles that justify the state's use or withholding of force to be in the corpus of the legal system being interpreted. In short, Fuller's eight desiderata were structurally necessary conditions for a legal system given his assumption that functional success served as a membership criterion, while for Dworkin it was the interpreter (which for him includes the legal philosopher) who imposes the membership criteria in embracing the principles that the community articulates as its political morality.

[15] Jules L. Coleman, 'Incorporationism, Conventionality, and the Practical Difference Thesis' (1998) 4 *Legal Theory* 381, 383.

[16] Scott J. Shapiro, 'On Hart's Way Out' (1998) 4 *Legal Theory* 469–507 503.

[17] Ibid. See also Jules L. Coleman, 'Methodology' in Jules Coleman and Scott Shapiro (eds), *The Oxford Handbook of Jurisprudence and Philosophy of Law* (Oxford University Press 2002) 311–51 at 342, noting the possibility of understanding Hart as offering a "social-scientific/functionalist explanation of law."

[18] 1. ad hoc orders instead of rules; 2. insufficient publicity; 3. overly retroactive rules; 4. incomprehensible rules; 5. contradictory rules; 6. rules requiring the impossible; 7. overly frequent changes to the rules; 8. failure to apply the rules as publicized: Lon L. Fuller, *The Morality of Law* (revised edn, Yale University Press 1969 (1964)) 39.

The result for Dworkin embeds the exclusion entailed by failure into a notion analogous to legal validity: laws that are seen as failing in the performance of law's wholesale function to justify the use and withholding of force are deemed legally invalid by the interpreter. Interpretations that do not uphold the correct principles justifying the state's use or withholding of force are ruled legally invalid for that very reason. For Fuller, legal validity was more of an afterthought after meeting the eight desiderata; like Hart, a way to pick out which norms get the backing of the state once the system is operating to guide behavior.

Faced with these notions of the relevance of law's function, it is not surprising that Hart believed that he needed to deemphasize it in his thinking. Furthermore, in stripping away any greater detail than guiding human conduct,[19] he refuses to articulate a wider purpose for that guidance, making this function appear to be more of a modal characteristic of the way law does whatever it does. It is on the basis of some of these insights that Leslie Green has developed his position that law is understood not in terms of its purposes but in terms of its methods.

Green understands Hart's difference with Fuller to be a rejection of the latter's emphasis on understanding law in terms of the ends it serves.[20] Instead Hart followed Hans Kelsen in the claim that there is no overarching end that law serves. It is to be understood entirely in terms of the means by which it serves a wide variety of ends. That is, the ends it serves are too variable to be classified and characterized univocally, let alone for those ends to serve as a basis for understanding legal practice in all its complexity.

We will return to Green's arguments here later. Suffice it for now to say that while behavior guidance might not seem to be enough of an end to say that law is best understood in terms of that function, we need not rest with this notion alone. Rather, it can serve as a starting point for more detailed discussions of the varieties of ends that law serves, while seeing this behavior guidance as an organizing principle for that wide variety. It also pays to bear in mind how much jurisprudential work has been done with this notion of law's function, such that arguments to the conclusion that behavior guidance is too thin a notion to provide much of jurisprudential relevance threaten to ignore lots of ink, at least some of which was setting down useful ideas.

A. The Inclusive/Exclusive Debate

At least since the first generation of scholars writing after *The Concept of Law* was published in 1961, there has been an internecine debate among legal

[19] Hart, *Concept of Law* 249. [20] Green, 'Law as a Means' 170.

positivists. Exclusive positivists such as Joseph Raz[21] and Scott Shapiro[22] see the positivist ethos as implying that there can be no legal system that makes moral criteria a robust condition of legal validity. That is, since any true proposition of morality (if such exists) is beyond human epistemic access, and since law—including the criteria by which it is determined whether a given putative legal norm is a member of a given legal system (and thereby provides reasons for those subject to that system)—is fundamentally a human creation, legal validity cannot depend upon moral criteria. What is humanly created and determined through and through cannot depend for its status on something that is not a human creation and is beyond human knowledge.

If propositions of morality have no truth value, all the more reason why the truth of legal propositions—which clearly are frequently true or false—cannot depend upon them. If there is no such thing as true propositions of morality, there would again be no fact of the matter about some questions of legal validity, which would be to place it outside the class of what is humanly determined.

Inclusive legal positivists such as Hart himself, Jules Coleman,[23] and Wil Waluchow[24] take the opposite tack and claim that if human beings wish to create an institution whose validity depends on something of which it is beyond their ability to have concrete knowledge, then although there will be questions of legal validity that cannot be reliably answered, that is their prerogative as creators of the system. This inclusivist position might sound somewhat like Dworkin's right-answer thesis, in that there may be situations in which there can be legally valid laws that everyone considers invalid and legally invalid laws that everyone considers valid. However, the difference between them is that the inclusive legal positivist only holds that there is at least one *possible* legal system that incorporates moral criteria among the criteria of legality, not that they must be included (or that ours is such a system).

This debate can be understood as a debate over the functions of law and what kind of thing the law must be in order to be capable of accomplishing those functions. While I have claimed, with Gardner, that for something to

[21] For example Raz, *Authority of Law*; 'Authority, Law and Morality'; *Ethics in the Public Domain: Essays in the Morality of Law and Politics* (Clarendon Press 1994).

[22] For example Scott J. Shapiro, 'Law, Morality, and the Guidance of Conduct' (2000) 6 *Legal Theory* 127–70; 'Was Inclusive Legal Positivism Founded on a Mistake?' (2009) 22 *Ratio Juris* 326–38.

[23] Jules L. Coleman, 'Negative and Positive Positivism' (1982) 11 *Journal of Legal Studies* 139–64.

[24] Wilfrid J. Waluchow, *Inclusive Legal Positivism* (Clarendon Press 1994).

be understood in terms of its function, it must be conceptually possible for it to fail in the performance of that function,[25] the converse is not the case. It is certainly possible (*pace* Murphy[26]) that something can be understood in terms of its function, even where it cannot succeed in performing that function.

Admittedly, we might be reluctant to characterize a whole class of things in terms of its function where none of the class could ever succeed. However, I think Mark Murphy's example of perpetual motion machines is actually a counterexample to the point he wishes to make with it.[27] We can equally correctly say "There has never been and never will be a perpetual motion machine" and "All perpetual motion machines are doomed to failure." While both are equally correct locutions, I have several reasons for preferring the former (although I admit that these are not entirely dispositive in themselves). For one, it seems to me that the latter is more informative in itself. The former requires the speaker to make more of a qualification in laying out success as an existence condition for such machines. Furthermore, theorists of functional explanations in artifacts generally note the need to accommodate artifacts that have functions which are impossible to meet.[28] The former locution seems to deny this possibility.

Exclusive legal positivists hold that to be a positivist is to see legal norms as posited by human beings and hence to require a social source. This is something the inclusive positivist denies, holding instead that, while still a human creation, we can (if we choose) put a robust moral condition in our society's norms of legal validity and hence make legal validity something that is not epistemically accessible. They thus deny the need for a social source to every legal norm, although every legal norm must still ultimately be *authorized* by a social source.[29]

[25] John Gardner, 'Law's Aims in *Law's Empire*' in S. Hershovitz (ed.), *Exploring Law's Empire* (Oxford University Press 2006) 207–24, 216.

[26] M. C. Murphy, 'The Explanatory Role of the Weak Natural Law Thesis' in W. J. Waluchow and S. Sciaraffa (eds), *Philosophical Foundations of the Nature of Law* (Oxford University Press 2013) 3–21 12–13.

[27] Ibid 13.

[28] See for example Achinstein, 'Function Statements' (1977) 44 *Philosophy of Science* 341–67, 349, using the example of a divining rod to show that artifacts can have functions that are impossible for them to perform; Baker, 'The Metaphysics of Malfunction' (2009) 13 *Techne* 82–92, 84; and Preston, 'Philosophical Theories of Artifact Function' in A. Meijers (ed.), *Philosophy of Technology and Engineering Sciences* (Elsevier 2009) 213–34, 217, noting that "phantom functions" (ones that artifacts are supposed to perform but are never capable of doing so) are a common and expected phenomenon that any theory of artifact function needs to account for.

[29] This discussion somewhat papers over a more subtle distinction pointed out by Coleman, 'Incorporationism, Conventionality, and the Practical Difference Thesis,' and Matthew Kramer, 'How Moral Principles Can Enter into the Law' (2000) 6 *Legal Theory* 83–108.

Exclusive positivists use a function-based argument to attack inclusive positivism, saying that allowing robust moral criteria into the grounds of legal validity (thereby putting legal validity potentially beyond what is epistemically accessible) renders law unable to perform its function of guiding behavior. The idea is that if an essential or fundamental function which law is supposed to perform is guiding behavior, then agents must in principle be able to access the guidance that law provides. Making legality depend on morality requires those agents to determine for themselves what morality requires as a means of determining what guidance the law provides. That is, they cannot determine what the law is telling them to do without first determining what morality requires, which would generally trump any guidance the law offered anyway. This either obviates the law's authority, since agents are being left to their own devices to determine what to do,[30] or means that the law is not making any practical difference in what the agent is to do, since what morality requires would determine what is to be done on its own.[31] In setting forth this latter claim that law must be capable of making a practical difference, Shapiro explicitly argues that it is required by any view that sees a behavior guidance function to legal rules.[32]

As mentioned earlier,[33] Coleman's inclusivist answer is to distinguish between "criteria of identification" and "criteria of validity."[34] In doing so, he argues that the function-based argument of exclusive positivists only establishes that the law be identified by its social sources, not that its legal validity must be determined by its social sources.[35] If this distinction is tenable, it introduces the possibility that membership in the class of law comes apart from legal validity: that there are legally invalid laws that are still members of the class of law.

However, it is not so clear that these two come apart in the right way. It may be the case that those laws which meet the socially sourced criteria of identification are merely a subset of those which meet the not necessarily socially sourced criteria of validity (in which case all members of the class of law would still be legally valid). This would be in keeping with Coleman's

[30] Joseph Raz, *Ethics in the Public Domain: Essays in the Morality of Law and Politics* (Clarendon Press 1994) 210–37.

[31] Shapiro, 'On Hart's Way Out'; 'Law, Morality, and the Guidance of Conduct.'

[32] Shapiro, 'On Hart's Way Out' 502–05; 'Law, Morality, and the Guidance of Conduct' 167–69.

[33] This was discussed as one possible exit for Dworkin's theory from the problem of seeing successful performance as a membership condition for law.

[34] Coleman, 'Negative and Positive Positivism'; 'Constraints on the Criteria of Legality' (2000) 6 *Legal Theory* 171–83, 179.

[35] Coleman, 'Constraints on the Criteria of Legality' 179.

usage since the point of the distinction was to suggest that legal validity is something that can have criteria beyond epistemic access, while allowing the law still to perform its guidance function. (Only laws that are identifiable can provide guidance.) One way of suggesting that the distinction is more than merely making the legally identifiable a subset of the legally valid is to use examples from ancient or overturned law. These would be candidates for membership in the class but clearly not performing their guidance function, since they would appear no longer to be controlling in a legal decision, and hence not valid.

Wil Waluchow has a slightly different argument against exclusive positivism's appeal to law's function, which shows even more clearly how the internecine debate is a dispute over the law's functionality and how the law is to accomplish its tasks. The issue is over how to interpret the obvious fact that bills of rights and constitutions incorporate the need for moral judgments into the validity criteria they set forth. (In states with a constitution that sets forth the conditions of legal validity explicitly, the rule of recognition is likely to give prominent place to the constitution. I say "likely" because it is always possible to have a constitution that is ignored by officials and the law in such countries, according to a positivist, would be whatever the officials recognize.) Furthermore, laws are frequently and necessarily going to include morally pregnant terms such as "reasonable" or "unconscionable" in generally worded statutes and controlling judicial decisions.

Inclusive positivists claim that moral terms in these places show that legal validity can sometimes depend on conformity with moral norms, thereby partially undermining the sources thesis. Exclusive positivists say that these moral terms simply give more discretion to the officials empowered to make validity declarations, perhaps giving them what Raz calls a "directed power"[36] to make their validity declarations on the basis of their personal moral judgments. (The only restriction the law gives them in using this moral language is to decide on the basis of their own moral judgments.) This, of course, maintains the sources thesis in that the validity of the law depends for the exclusive positivist only on the source of the law.

As mentioned above, the key arguments by exclusive positivists against inclusive positivists involve an emphasis on the idea that it is law's primary function to guide behavior. Shapiro claims that inclusive positivism undermines the guidance function in that the law itself is not guiding behavior since, on the inclusive view, one must appeal to underlying morality in order to determine guidance. The law is supposed to settle what those subject to it

[36] Waluchow, 'Legality, Morality, and the Guiding Function of Law' 88, citing Raz, *Ethics in the Public Domain* 242.

are supposed to do. But if one needs to consult the underlying morality to determine what that is, then it is not making a difference in what one is supposed to be doing. That is, the law fails to make a practical difference in the subjects' conduct.[37] On Raz's view, the idea that the validity criteria could include a robust moral requirement (as opposed to merely purporting to include one, thereby giving officials moral discretion) undermines the law's guidance function by interfering with the law's authority.[38] If the authority of law is legitimated by its ability to get its subjects to comply with reasons that already apply to them, then if the legal validity of its directives is made to depend on morality directly, subjects would need to check the directive against their moral judgments in order to determine whether the law is valid (and only valid laws can be authoritative). While legal subjects might already be well advised to check any legal directive against their own moral judgments, this is generally at the risk of acting contrary to valid law. If that risk was taken away then law's guidance function in getting subjects to comply with the balance of right reasons would be undermined.

Waluchow thinks that these strategies for arguing against inclusive positivism threaten to undermine the arguments in favor of exclusive positivism.[39] The problem exclusivists have with inclusive positivism is that it allows legal validity to depend on the right answer to controversial moral questions. The law cannot guide conduct if its validity and hence its applicability is made to depend on questions that it was supposed to settle. Waluchow claims that any guidance that is sacrificed by inclusive positivism would be missing anyway on the "directed powers" account of the discretion that exclusive positivists think moral terms introduce when included in the validity criteria. Recall some of the disadvantages of moving to a robust legal system with secondary rules: there may be a disconnection between what is legally valid and what will be found morally acceptable by legal subjects (not to mention what might be morally acceptable independent of what subjects believe). Furthermore, there is an inherent tension between generally worded rules and the desideratum of applying these rules in ways that avoid unwanted or absurd results. While laws need to be generally worded in order to provide guidance to the widest possible class of targeted subjects (and to be rules at all), that general wording will always threaten to include instances that would be better left out of the law's ambit. The need for general rules that avoid absurd applications will require the introduction of vague terms and officials to interpret and apply them.

[37] Shapiro, 'Law, Morality, and the Guidance of Conduct' 129.

[38] Raz, *Ethics in the Public Domain* 210.

[39] Waluchow, 'Legality, Morality, and the Guiding Function of Law' 89.

Waluchow claims that all legal systems have to strike a balance between these two requirements: the need for rules that can be interpreted by individual legal subjects so as to guide their behavior directly, and the need to leave certain questions open to later official interpretation lest the rule yield absurd results. Hence any sacrifice in guidance that is made by including a moral requirement among the legal validity conditions will be the same whether this moral term is understood to introduce a robust moral requirement or merely to increase the officials' directed discretion.[40] Therefore, there is no practical difference between inclusive legal positivism and exclusive legal positivism when it comes to what they imply about the law's guidance function. Both will offer guidance to a certain degree and, as a result of the necessarily open texture nature of legal language, both will countenance some sacrifice of its ability to provide that guidance in order to avoid having formalistic style rules that yield absurd results. Any moral terms in the constitution, basic charter, bills of rights, or even among more quotidian laws and judicial decisions will offer the same kind of imprecise guidance to subjects and officials regardless of whether one sees them as thereby offering those officials discretion to alter the law or as providing an antecedent moral requirement that the officials are trying to capture.

Notice, however, that much in this argument collapsing the practical distinction between inclusive and exclusive positivism depends upon focusing on moral acceptability rather than seeing morality as imposing an objective critical standard. This should not be surprising since it is an argument about the practical implications of each theory; practically speaking, critical morality (if it exists) is not epistemically accessible. That is, if we see a moral requirement in a legal system's validity criteria and think that is merely bringing in a requirement of moral acceptability, then there can't really be much difference between the implications of inclusive and exclusive positivism. Hence, as Waluchow notes, this argument only works against the kinds of practical considerations against inclusive positivism that are raised by Shapiro and Raz: that inclusivism undermines the law's guidance function. If we focus on moral acceptability, it doesn't appear to undermine the guidance function any more than exclusive positivism would already allow where there are apparent moral requirements among the legal validity criteria (which exclusive positivists will say simply increase directed discretion for the officials).

Shapiro and Raz would likely reply that if we are only talking about moral acceptability anyway, then much of what they are saying is exactly correct

[40] Ibid 92–93.

and to the point. Their problem with inclusive positivism only arises if the legal validity criteria are understood to include a robust moral norm. The correct interpretation and application of such a norm is necessarily always open to doubt because it is not epistemically accessible. If the supposed moral norm is only one of acceptability, then the validity of the law only depends on the acceptance of the officials making the validity determinations anyway.

If we do limit ourselves to saying that only moral acceptability is implicated by any inclusion of an apparent moral requirement among the criteria of legal validity, the one place the two theories would still diverge is if the requirement is for some acceptability wider than that of the officials themselves. That is, if the validity criteria make it a requirement that the law be morally acceptable to the official making the determination of legal validity herself, then it only gives her the kind of directed discretion that Raz and Waluchow discuss. But if the criterion requires a wider moral acceptability, then the official would ideally have to do some kind of study of social attitudes towards that moral norm.

A very imperfect example might be the U.S. Supreme Court's Eighth Amendment jurisprudence, in which what counts as "cruel and unusual punishment" is interpreted according to the "evolving standards of decency" of the society as a whole.[41] While the Court actually combines its view of this wider acceptability with its own moral sentiments on the matter, one could imagine a court seeking to apply only the existing moral judgments of the community as a whole.[42] In such a situation, the distinction between the implications of inclusive and exclusive legal positivism would come down merely to whether the Court was discovering an already existing condition of legal validity or imposing one with its decision. That is, the exclusive positivist would insist that the official empowered to invalidate a law for non-conformity with a moral requirement among the legal validity criteria is altering the law when making a determination about the law's validity that differed from past decisions or presumptions. An inclusive positivist would say that the community's moral attitudes would render the legal validity in question an antecedent fact that the official is attempting to capture. As far as the guidance offered to individuals attempting to determine what behavior the law requires of them, there is no practical difference as, even on the inclusive account, legal subjects are well advised (legally speaking) to comply

[41] *Trop v. Dulles* 356 U.S. 86, 101 (1958).

[42] Of course legal positivism is not to be seen as recommending any position in favor of or against such an application. I merely mention it as a possible legal conclusion of how to treat apparent moral requirements found among a system's validity conditions.

with the law as officially recognized at the time of the contemplated behavior (unless an imminent change is reasonably expected).[43]

I suspect it is true that there is very little practical difference between inclusive and exclusive positivism. However, that should be far from surprising since positivists generally take pride in the fact that their theories have no practical implications on the way that law is to be practiced. As legal positivism is a theory about legal validity,[44] the difference between them is a theoretical one about the metaphysics of legal validity, yet one that has some wider implications about the theorists' underlying beliefs about law's nature.

Nevertheless, I can see one minor way in which there appears to be a practical difference between the two theories. Although it is minor, given the positivists' view that their theory generally avoids practical implications about how law is to operate, it is somewhat troubling. Take the example of what are called tax protestors or tax deniers. (I prefer the latter term for the sake of clarity in the distinction immediately below.) These are people who deny the constitutionality of the income tax (in the U.S. and Canada) or deny that the statutes enabling the income tax were properly passed. Their argument is that the income tax law is *already* legally invalid, although the officials empowered to make legal validity determinations have not yet appreciated that fact. Compare the tax denier to the tax resister, someone who refuses to pay income tax because of a belief that the government has no moral right to collect it, or as a form of civil disobedience to protest what the government is proposing to do with one's tax remittances. These people do not claim that the income tax is already legally invalid; they say, at most, that it *ought to be* abolished or held legally invalid by officials in the future, once officials appreciate the moral wrongness of the tax.

Generally, the arguments of the tax deniers are laughed out of court, while the tax resisters are not asserting any existing legal right not to pay their income taxes. Yet it appears that the inclusive positivist picture does lend some credence to the style of argument being engaged in by the tax denier. Of course, a prudent lawyer subscribing to an inclusive positivist picture would not advise her clients to make the argument that the tax is unconstitutional, since those arguments have already fallen on deaf ears. Yet it does appear that there is at least a kind of rhetorical practical difference between the two positions, in that one favors legal arguments that emphasize an existing state of legal validity that the official is to discover, while the other emphasizes the authority of the official to make the determination.

43 Waluchow, 'Legality, Morality, and the Guiding Function of Law' 94–95.

44 Gardner, *Law as a Leap of Faith: Essays on Law in General* 33.

This is, of course, an extremely minor difference and it is very likely that two lawyers, each of whom subscribes to an opposing version of legal positivism, would still make exactly the same arguments, tailored perhaps to their understanding of the official's own beliefs or the prevailing political mood. A so-called "activist" court might be more receptive to arguments couched in language emphasizing the court's power to make validity determinations that alter the state of the law, suggesting a more exclusive positivist picture. A court enamored with political promises to exercise "judicial restraint" would likely be somewhat more receptive to arguments made in the inclusive positivist mode that emphasize their role merely to discover the law's pre-existing validity or invalidity.

I say that this is somewhat troubling because it might suggest that the various positivists are taking sides in this particular legal argument over whether the court should be seen as finding legal validity or creating it. True, it does not appear to have any practical implications for any legal question of the proper interpretation or application of a law. But it does seem to have some political connotations, especially as the debate over how to characterize the work of a constitutional court tends to be a sticky one.

One way to smooth this over somewhat is to recognize that inclusive positivists would not deny that judicial decision-making is always a form of lawmaking. Rather, they are merely saying that there can be a state of legal validity that courts are trying to capture when they make those validity determinations.

Nevertheless, this is perhaps a reason to see the metaphysical questions about legal validity to be cutting toward the exclusive positivist camp. The overarching claim of positivists about legal validity is that it is whatever those developing and implementing the legal system want it to be. The question is whether they can include a criterion that is beyond anyone's power to capture and accurately implement. In short, if we see legal validity as an aspect of law's artifactual nature, then it seems difficult to see how it can depend on something that is beyond the power of human beings to have knowledge of. If we are merely talking about moral acceptability then perhaps we can have knowledge of that condition, and so the idea of legal validity depending on a factual state that requires further inquiry and research is not necessarily troubling. But if we are talking about a robust critical moral condition, then questions of legal validity will no longer be truly artifactual because we are not in a position to certify that it conforms to that condition. Hence it does appear that inclusive legal positivists turn their backs on law's artifactual nature in at least this minor way.

Now an inclusive positivist might respond that there is nothing wrong with creating an artifact that is validated by something that is beyond our power to certify. Imagine a clock that is supposed to be aligned to an unobservable astronomical event, perhaps when the moon of a distant planet is at apogee. Imagine as well that because the apogee is always at a point where the moon is obscured by that planet, we can never observe the moon's apogee directly. The clock is supposed to predict that event and is programmed using some complicated calculations based on observations of the planet and its speed, as well as the speed of the moon when it is observable. But, because of the distance, there is always some room for some error to creep into the observations made. Perhaps we know of the existence of unseen sources of distortion but cannot yet precisely measure their effects. Now, it would seem as though the clock is still a perfect example of an artifact even though its reliability cannot be verified. If we can say that this clock can be created and would be verified by measuring the unmeasurable, then it would seem as though we can create laws that are validated by the unknowable.

The answer to this analogical argument is that the analogy doesn't hold between the accuracy of clocks and the validity of law. While I have been at pains to emphasize that successful performance of its function cannot be a membership condition in law as a class, the same cannot be said of legal validity. A law that is nowhere and never valid is not a law in any proper sense. As we've seen before, laws come in systems that are individuated by their validity criteria. Yet a clock of immeasurable imprecision is merely one whose success in performing its function cannot be measured. That is, the analogy breaks down because legal validity is not an element of law's proper functionality. (Although it does determine the granting of *status* functions within legal institutions, we have seen that status functions are akin to the mathematical notion of function in mapping value and are not the proper functions we are discussing.) Invalid laws can sometimes perform the functions of valid laws. This is not troubling because we are not saying that the law is a functional kind such that performance of the function is sufficient in membership in the class of law.

Instead, legal validity is an aspect of law's institutionality. Institutions carry norms of many kinds. Some of these will purport to determine the behavior of people who interact with the institution. Others will set forth criteria for determining which aspects or instances of the institution count as member norms. These are the institution's validity criteria and determine which putative instances or applications are robust and which are counterfeit.[45]

[45] John R. Searle, *Construction of Social Reality* (Free Press 1995) 88–89, and, for example, *Making the Social World* 98.

This can be seen in institutions such as organized sports, where to be capable of making an official determination as an umpire or referee requires being appointed to the office by the procedures countenanced by the organization. One cannot simply walk onto the field wearing the appropriate uniform and expect one's calls to be recorded for official play. It is similarly visible within law, not only with the obvious examples such as legal currency, but also in setting forth the conditions necessary for certain documents to have official recognition and legal effect. Legal validity is simply the same notion applied to legislation and government actions themselves.

B. Legal Validity, Morality, and Membership Conditions

To provide an overview of where we are, let us lay out the spectrum of positions on the relation of legal validity to morality and see how this spectrum tracks understandings of the notion of law's function and its best role in explaining law. At one end of the spectrum would be exclusive legal positivism (ELP), with its claim that there can be no dependence of legal validity upon moral criteria. Next would come inclusive positivism (ILP), with its claim that there is at least one possible legal system in which legal validity depends at least partially on morality. Next would come Murphy and Finnis' weak natural law (WNL) thesis, which claims that irrational (under their view a superset of, if not a synonym for, immoral) laws are deficient *qua* law. Next would come Dworkin's interpretivism (ITP), the view that there is a right interpretation of a community's chosen moral standards which determines legal validity, even though that interpretation many not be fully reflected in any extant opinion. This makes legal validity more dependent upon morality in that immoral interpretations cannot be correct, yet it is still the community's specific selection of moral principles that the law reflects. Next would come Lon Fuller's view (PNL for "procedural natural law," an unfortunate moniker but one that is common in the literature) that there is a specific set of norms constituting an internal morality of law, which must be a facet of legal validity such that complete failure in any one norm (and some less complete failures of multiple norms) prevents membership in the class of law. This makes legal validity more dependent upon morality than interpretivism in that deeply immoral rules are not even candidates for inclusion in the class of law and the moral principles that serve as criteria are universal and not chosen by the community, yet the morality that tests law is an internal and circumscribed set of principles. Finally would be a strong natural law thesis (SNL), under which adherence to relevant principles of an external morality is a necessary condition of legality and hence present in all systems' criteria of legal validity.

Less ← Dependence of legal validity on morality → More

ELP – ILP – WNL – ITP – PNL – SNL

In terms of the explanatory role of law's function, the (right-hand) three theories that see greater dependence of legality on morality all hold some form of the claim that success in performance of the function is a necessary condition for membership in the class of law. This runs afoul of the view that something can only be characterized by its function where there is the conceptual possibility of failure, and it introduces the difficulty associated with saying that deficient instances are not members of the class (which really amount to the same problem). The three theories that see less dependency of legality on morality (where they recognize the importance of law's function for understanding it) see its function as explaining the nature of law and its operation, without seeing that function as setting forth a necessary condition for membership in the class of law.

What this shows is that while legal validity itself is not an aspect of law's functionality, the relation a theorist holds of it to morality has an implication for how the theorist conceives the role played by law's function in setting membership conditions. This is not surprising since legal validity itself is a kind of membership condition. Invalid laws are not members of the legal system in which they are invalid. (As Raz pointed out, it is possible for valid legal norms not to be members of the system in which they are valid since legal systems can and frequently do have long-arm provisions for incorporating foreign legal principles, as well as provisions for recognizing the non-legal norms of other institutions within their jurisdictions.[46]) But the more a theorist makes legal validity depend on morality, the more difficult it is to see laws retain their membership in the class of law when that morality fails them.

C. Social Plans vs Institutionalized Abstract Artifacts[*]

One important recent contribution to the positivist literature is Scott Shapiro's planning theory of law.[47] In many ways, the theory is quite sympathetic to many of the methodological and metaphysical points I am making here.[48]

[*] An earlier version of much of this section was accepted for publication as 'Law as Plan and Artifact' (2016, forthcoming) 7 *Jurisprudence*.

[46] Joseph Raz, *Practical Reason and Norms* (2nd edn, Princeton University Press 1990 (1975)) 152–53.

[47] Scott J. Shapiro, 'Law, Plans, and Practical Reason' (2002) 8 *Legal Theory* 387, *Legality* (Harvard University Press 2011), 'Massively Shared Agency' in Manuel Varga and Gideon Yaffe (eds), *Rational and Social Agency* (Oxford University Press 2014) 257–93.

[48] See Bigelow and Pargetter, 'Functions' (1987) 84 *Journal of Philosophy* 181–96, 185, noting that a representational theory of functions in which a plan for future effects is what guides the

It sees law as a tool of human creation and as such understands law in terms of the social functions it performs. According to the planning theory, legal activity is "social planning [that] is shared, official, institutional, compulsory, self-certifying [and] whose aim is to solve those moral problems that cannot be solved, or solved as well, through alternative forms of social ordering."[49] But there are two difficulties in Shapiro's theory, an examination of which will support the claims I am making in this book and show why, though it is undoubtedly true, seeing law ontologically as a form of social planning is not quite enough to solve the jurisprudential problems at hand.

The first is an older jurisprudential problem that is not adequately solved by the planning theory as it stands. That is the problem of the persistence of the law: the fact that the validity and normativity of a law tends to extend beyond the tenure of the authority that created it. Shapiro's focus on plans leads him to say that the law persists only so long as the relevant community members share the plan. For him, this answers the question of how the normativity of law can extend beyond the creating authority. Yet we should still be uneasy with our sense that the law is not quite as ephemeral as suggested by considering its ontology to consist in a shared social plan. Of course the law is an instance of social planning and we can learn a lot about it by focusing on that. But it is also something more that makes it take on a life beyond the plan itself. This problem can be solved by a re-emphasis on, and greater understanding of, what it means to say that the plan is an institutional one.

The other is a new problem raised by Shapiro's focus on self-certification. Self-certification is the fact that a legal system gets a presumption of validity from any superior jurisdictions. He uses this idea in an attempt to solve the "Identity Question": how to differentiate law from other forms of social planning.[50] Hence, adding self-certification to the other aspects of the planning theory is supposed to allow the elements of the theory to be jointly sufficient conditions for law, rather than merely necessary conditions. The problem I see with self-certification is that it is an arbitrary solution to the identity problem which threatens circularity. This is especially true when we see that Shapiro himself gives hints at its weakness by mentioning the fact that self-certification is a matter of degree.[51] Beyond that, however, we can imagine legal systems that do not self-certify at all (for example a municipality that must obtain certification for any new legislation from its superior jurisdiction, perhaps after an insurrection), and self-certifying institutions that are not legal systems (certain contractual arrangements).

development of the explanandum is particularly well suited for artifacts, citing Andrew Woodfield, *Teleology* (Cambridge University Press 1976).

[49] Shapiro, *Legality* 225. [50] Ibid 8–9. [51] Ibid 224.

My suggestion that we see laws as institutionalized abstract artifacts is not to deny that they are plans. As plans, laws are tools for solving certain kinds of social problems.[52] But their institutionalization gives them a greater permanence and identity beyond the plans themselves. This is not in opposition to Shapiro's theory, since he embraces the institutional nature of law, and to look at plans as kinds of tools gives them most of the properties of artifacts. (He explicitly refers to shared plans as "abstract entities."[53]) Yet Searle's use of status functions in explaining institutions can solve the identity problem without the need to rely on self-certification. Law is differentiated from other social institutions and shared plans because it is given that status as distinctive in its creation and conceptualization.

Shapiro points out that what is special about institutions is that institutionalized plans can operate independently of the intentions of the participants.[54] It is therefore the institutionality of a plan that can also help contribute to its permanence and existence beyond the mental states of those who create and use them.

Recall that Searle distinguishes social facts, which are mind-dependent, from brute facts, which are not. That a given object is made of wood and metal is a brute fact; that it is a hammer is a social fact, dependent on collective intention at some level. Institutional facts (which are usually facts about or created by institutions, although it is possible to have institutional facts without pre-existing institutions[55]) are a subset of social facts, and one of the important advantages of institutions, as Shapiro mentions, is that they allow for relations, rights, and duties among people that do not depend directly upon the intentions of those people. It might therefore seem there is a misfit between Shapiro's notion of institutions and Searle's. As will become important shortly, however, Shapiro is quick to admit that "the institutionality of law is ultimately grounded in intentions"[56] as the normativity of law depends on master plans that are endorsed by officials. So intentionality is important, just not the particular intentions of the immediate participants.

We've seen that what distinguishes institutional facts from other social facts is that there is a collectively intended assignment of a status that carries deontic powers to something such as a person, event, practice, object, or other social phenomenon, via a constitutive rule.[57] One key feature of institutions, which is brought out in the conveyance of deontic powers with the

[52] Ibid 173. [53] Ibid 190. [54] Ibid 210.

[55] Searle's example of this is the line of stones, the remnant of an ancient wall that comes to be treated as a boundary. Searle, *Making the Social World: The Structure of Human Civilization* (Oxford University Press 2010) 94.

[56] Shapiro, *Legality* 211. [57] Searle, *Construction of Social Reality* 23–26, 40–45.

assignment of status, is the fact that institutions can create desire-independent reasons for action.[58] That is, one key purpose of institutions generally is the creation of new rights and obligations where they did not exist previously.[59] This clearly echoes Shapiro's catalog of the advantages of institutions.

There is one more piece to the picture: the constitutive rules are generally "codified" allowing for the conferral of status upon a *type* of object rather than a *token* object.[60] This provides for the possibility of iteration: many different people can hold the same office; many pieces of specially described paper can be the same unit of currency; many different actions can constitute the same crime; many different ceremonies can create a legal marriage. Each of these examples requires only one rule to create the status rather than conferring the status on token events, entities, or practices. "Codification specifies the features a token must have in order to be an instance of the type...."[61]

While Searle is never very explicit about what must take place for codification, it is clear that legal codification is one paradigm example. But we should not limit his notion to the legal one, as there are clearly non-legal institutions that provide for some kind of official application of statuses to types. Nor should we expect a "sharp dividing line between social facts in general and the special subclass of institutional facts."[62] There are informal institutions which are not codified, where status is conferred on tokens only. The advantages of leaving the institution informal, of not codifying, are that the application of the status it conveys can remain "flexible, spontaneous, and informal."[63] But, as Shapiro notes, these aspects can be serious disadvantages in contexts in which coordination of action is at a premium, or where there are other disagreements that must be solved for the community to function. So the very situations that call for a common general plan are those that call for some kind of codified institution.

It seems fairly straightforward that Shapiro's planning theory and Searle's theory of institutions are broadly compatible. The planning aspects are captured by the collectively intended assignment of status and the purposes for which that assignment is made.

While I won't delve into this in any detail here, it seems that the planning theory can even help close a loophole in Searle's theory that he has been at pains to address. The general formula for a status function is "X counts as Y in context C," the characteristic form of a constitutive rule.[64] We can

58 Searle, *Making the Social World* 23. 59 Ibid 91.
60 Searle, *Construction of Social Reality* 53; *Making the Social World* 91.
61 Searle, *Construction of Social Reality* 53. 62 Ibid 88. 63 Ibid.
64 Searle, *Making the Social World* 10.

immediately see that much, if not most, of the content of legislation takes this form, as does that of administrative regulations. Even court decisions can frequently be reinterpreted this way if they are not explicitly formulated to follow the formula.

The issue that bothered Searle for a while was the issue of "freestanding Y terms," instances in which status appears to be conveyed without a pre-existing entity that receives the status.[65] Examples of this are seen in the creation of corporations and in electronic money. (An outstanding example of the latter was seen in the bank bailout in the U.S. Troubled Asset Relief Program of 2008–09, in which no new currency was actually printed in order to provide the banks with $70 billion in additional capital to cover their bad loans.)

Searle's answer to the problem of the freestanding Y term is to say that a person that fits a given, institutionally set description can create a status by declaration.[66] This operation is Searle's paradigm of law: "The law is a Declaration that authorizes other Declarations."[67] But any who are left with a bit of metaphysical doubt about this solution can turn to Shapiro and say that the X term in the case of the apparently freestanding Y term is actually the social plan that sets the function that the new status is to fulfill. In effect, the Declaration sets out the plan. So a declaration of the form "We make it the case by declaration that the XYZ Corporation exists" can be reinterpreted as "The social plan to create the XYZ Corporation counts as the creation of the XYZ Corporation when the specified legal conditions are met to interpret the plan as a legally effective declaration."

This is also my aim in characterizing law as an institutionalized abstract artifact: its institutional nature is captured by Searle's theory; its abstract nature is captured by Shapiro's claim that law is a plan and hence an abstract entity; and seeing it as an artifact is meant to call up more clearly the notion that the law is a tool created by human beings to address specific tasks so it is to be understood and identified in terms of its functions. This also captures the sense that the law has a life of its own beyond those who create and use it. And it shows why legal positivists should embrace analyzing the law in terms of its functionality, a point endorsed by Shapiro.[68] So perhaps

[65] Ibid 20, citing Barry Smith, 'John Searle: From Speech Acts to Social Reality' in Barry Smith (ed.), *John Searle* (Cambridge University Press 2003) 1–33.

[66] Searle, *Making the Social World* 99.

[67] Ibid 100. Searle capitalizes "Declaration" to note that it is a specific speech act, but doesn't require actual vocalization or written recording as it can be accomplished using any system of symbols. Ibid 11.

[68] Shapiro, *Legality* 213–14.

the theories can help each other out, but let us return to focus on Shapiro's theory.

Shapiro mentions that one of the great advances of Hart over the previous forms of legal positivism is that Hart provides for the persistence of law, while theorists such as Austin, who analyze legal obligation as "a habit of obedience" to a sovereign, could not give a satisfactory account of why law persists beyond the lives of individual sovereigns or the habits of their subjects.[69] Hart's advance was to analyze the law in terms of rules rather than habits.[70] Rules of change and of recognition provide for the continuity of the lawmaking power from sovereign to sovereign and the validity of laws made by previous administrations.[71]

The problem is that rules of change and recognition, as fundamental rules, are described by Hart as social practices, which Shapiro claims shows Hart committed a category mistake in their characterization. Rules are a different kind of thing from practices.[72] What's more, by focusing on practices rather than habits, we have not advanced from the psychological dependence of the habit theory, further jeopardizing Hart's advances in explaining persistence. While one of Hart's key theoretical advantages was to focus on the distinction between the normative state of being under an obligation and the psychological state of being obliged, by explaining legal obligation in a way that ultimately rests on practice theory rules, we are still left with a psychological state at the bottom: the disposition to engage in the practice.[73] This is further magnified by Hart's insistence that officials internally accept the law as reason-giving, a view which Shapiro shares.[74] So while we have an advancement over the notion of habits in that we can explain the persistence and presence of law where people have not yet developed any habits, the law is still no more permanent or stable than any other social practice (some of which, admittedly, can last for quite while).

Instead for Shapiro, the fundamental rules of a legal system are plans, and this is supposed to solve (among other things) the problem of persistence.[75] The solution comes in the form of a master plan that is adopted and gives certain people the authority to create sub-plans that provide solutions to particular problems. Once a hierarchical arrangement is accepted by community

[69] Ibid 74. [70] Ibid 87. [71] Ibid, citing Hart, *Concept of Law* 57–61.

[72] Shapiro, *Legality* 103–04, emphasizing that rules are abstract objects.

[73] See generally Stephen Perry, 'Hart on Social Rules and the Foundations of Law: Liberating the Internal Point of View' (2006) 75 *Fordham Law Review* 1171–1210.

[74] Hart, *Concept of Law* 89; Shapiro, *Legality* 183. For a critical examination of this facet of the theories see my 'The Anarchist Official: A Problem for Legal Positivism' (2011) 36 *Australian Journal of Legal Philosophy* 89–113.

[75] Shapiro, *Legality* 119.

members, then there is a shared plan for further social planning.[76] This is a master plan for those tasked with social planning, authorizing them to make further plans. When the right person makes a determination of right or obligation under the master plan, her determination is binding simply because it is an aspect of the master plan.[77] Persistence is supposed to arise from these facets. "As long as they are approved in accordance with the requirements of the shared plan, the [sub-]plans will be deemed binding, both by the planners and the [subjects] generally, and followed accordingly."[78] Since the shared master plan and various sub-plans dictate that "the planning of past inhabitants" continue to be valid, those plans persist though time, perhaps even beyond the lives of original planners and community members.[79]

It still must be the case, however, that the group members accept at least the basic plan. Notice in the quotation above that Shapiro is focusing on the fact that the sub-plans "will be *deemed* binding" and "followed." We are still in the realm of seeing the persistence of law as strongly psychologically dependent. While shared plans are not practices in that they are abstract entities, as plans they still must be accepted and be the objects of the group members' intentions.[80] Of course, there is a social practice at the base of law in what the officials will deem to be valid, but that practice is "structured by a shared plan." That shared plan "must be practiced by that group if it is to exist. They must accept it and it must dispose them to act accordingly."[81]

There are strong reasons for a legal positivist to emphasize the dependence of law on the acceptance of the community. We do not believe that the law is mandated by something outside of the practices and beliefs of the community. Furthermore, there are good reasons for sharing the intuition that if everyone wakes up tomorrow believing themselves no longer bound by the legal system, it has ceased to exist.

On the other hand, I would argue that institutions don't just cease to exist quite so easily. We usually think they must be *dismantled*. If everyone woke up tomorrow with that belief, we would still want some form of official declaration that the legal system has ceased to have effect, notwithstanding the problem that we would no longer believe the officials had any official capacity. This isn't just because of worries about enforcement. (Imagine we know that everyone, including the police, shares this new belief.) Rather, it must be that we think our institution has changed the world in some way, even as we no longer believe that change to be holding its characteristic impositions upon us. We would likely want a declaration, another institutional act, to unmake the institution.

[76] Ibid 165. [77] Ibid 166. [78] Ibid. [79] Ibid 189. [80] Ibid 190.
[81] Ibid.

It may be that there is something irrational in this desire. If we do not think the institution holds any further deontic power, then it is hard to see any sense in a further institutional act or its power to alter reality. But we can also see this problem arise on the level of sub-plans, in individual laws. This is the issue of laws "on the books" that are no longer enforced or of which we may not even be aware. Shapiro would say that these laws can still be valid if they would be picked out as valid by officials following the master plan dictating their determinations of validity. However, take some law that would be deemed obviously absurd and invalidated on that basis by an empowered official whose interpretive theory includes a prohibition on seeing absurd laws as remaining valid. On that basis, there is little difference between this as yet unattended-to antediluvian law and the law of a foreign jurisdiction. Once considered, it would be deemed not to be a valid member of this particular legal system. Yet there is one important difference between the two. Foreign laws don't have the right pedigree to be considered members of this legal system, while this law clearly has the correct pedigree. Before it is actually pronounced invalid, it is still a member of this legal system (with the potential for being at the root of jurisprudential conflicts).

Again, Shapiro might explain this with the notion of it being a sub-plan of a master plan that we do accept. But without denying the notion of it being a plan, I want to suggest that it makes more sense to explain this particular facet of legal systems as owing to their institutionality rather than to their nature as plans. That institutionality confers a greater endurance on these plans than is the case with more simple social plans. If you'll forgive a metaphor, they have become stitched into the fabric of social reality, rather than simply ironed on.

(Although they are synonyms, I switch here to referring to the "endurance" of the law rather than its "persistence" to highlight that we are no longer dealing with the exact problems raised with the habit theory: persistence between sovereigns and beyond subjects' habits. Rather, we are now worried instead about the endurance of the law beyond its utility to community members.)

There is no doubt that law is dependent on intentionality for its existence as a creation of human beings. But it is not quite so dependent on human psychological states for its endurance. Searle's theory helps to capture this. Since the deontic powers conveyed in the creation of institutions are something that parties to those institutions come to expect and rely upon, there needs to be an equally formal way of altering them, even if those with them and subject to them no longer see any utility in them. That is, they have become part of the way in which members of the relevant community conceptualize and carve up the world, part of the background assumptions with which they deal with each other.[82] This is still true where the particular rights and duties no longer have any use. When we encounter someone with whom we have a contract, even where we both know that neither of us has any further use for the contract, we also know that the other person *could* choose to exercise her rights under it until we dissolve it.

This aspect of institutionality also helps to respond to a worry that Shapiro has raised about these thoughts.[83] His reply was that if a nuclear bomb exploded over a small country such as Belgium, wiping out all its inhabitants, we wouldn't think there was a continuing need to dismantle its legal system. While I do wonder about the possibility that Belgians happening to be abroad at the time might need some sort of official procedure, it is nonetheless clear that an institution still depends upon the people involved with it and their beliefs for its continuing existence. If the people of Belgium woke up tomorrow having amnesia about their own legal system and believing themselves instead to be a province of Luxembourg, there would be no need for any dismantling of the Belgian legal system so long as the Luxembourgians and the rest of the world are willing to go along with these beliefs. So I cannot claim to have completely eliminated the psychological dependence of the legal system. Rather, the claim is that the existence of the institution (which is still psychologically dependent) can be separated from some of the beliefs in the norms and other deontic powers that it represents. I say "some" of those beliefs since there is still a strong sense in which the institution is identical with the deontic powers that are conveyed with its creation. When we stop seeing the utility of that particular system of deontic powers, we still have the worry that others *could* claim their right to employ them (even if we know that those others also currently see no utility in them). This is likely why we still need an official reassurance that the institution has ceased to exist in the form of a new declaration to that effect.

It's not that Shapiro's theory cannot accommodate the endurance of law. Rather, I suggest that the focus on the planning nature of law rather than its institutional nature can tend to distract us from this fact. This is especially true when Shapiro discusses legal authority. For Shapiro, being granted authority by a master plan is necessary but not sufficient to obtain that authority.[84] The subjects must also be disposed to follow the directives of those putative authorities since those authorities are makers of plans for others.[85] Hence

[82] This is not intended as a reference to Searle's concept of the "Background," "the set of nonintentional or preintentional capacities that enable intentional states of function": Searle, *Construction of Social Reality* 129.

[83] These replies were made verbally by Shapiro at the Second Jurisprudence Workshop at the University of Antwerp, May 31, 2012.

[84] Shapiro, *Legality* 179. [85] Ibid.

general acceptance of the ability of the putative authorities to plan for others is another necessary condition for legitimate authority (which, when combined with the condition that they are authorized by the master plan to plan for others, makes them jointly sufficient). This is needed to avoid situations where, for example, a splinter group declares independence and jurisdiction over a given community. The group shares a plan authorizing them to issue directives for the community, but they can't dispose the rest of the community to comply.

However, just as we might want to prevent cases like the splinter group from being considered instances of legitimate authority, we might want to look at aspects that suggest the continuation of authority where the same hallmarks are present. Recognizing that the distinction between these kinds of cases is murky, take Raz's example of the legitimate government of Poland, in exile in London during the Second World War.[86] The authorities were authorized by a shared plan that then lapsed as a result of military conflict. Let us imagine a general collaboration of the Poles still resident in Poland with the Nazis, such that the exiled government is no longer able to dispose its subjects to comply with its directives (assuming they can still communicate those directives). To say that this government in exile is still the legitimate government of Poland is to call into doubt Shapiro's "general acceptance" condition.

Of course, it is possible to analyze this situation as an interregnum, or to say that there was a gap in the legitimacy of the planning authority for Poland from the time the Nazis invaded until the time the government was reinstated. But that would be to say that nothing they did while in London had any legal effect until they later ratified those actions (admittedly complicated by the fact that they did not relinquish their claim to authority until the fall of the communist government in 1990). Granted, these are not the "normal conditions" to which Shapiro points as part of his condition that subjects be motivated to comply. But they exemplify the problem I am highlighting: that institutionality gives more endurance to the plans than its makers and subjects psychologically need to accept.

All this is not to say that laws or legal systems live on forever, beyond the communities that use them. Clearly, entire systems are rendered invalid with something as simple as a declaration by an official of a superseding system. The point is that it generally takes some institutional act, even if one not contemplated by the pre-existing legal institutions, to unmake a legal system.

This is important for replying to another point Shapiro raised,[87] that the Articles of Confederation, the original constitution of the United States, were

[86] Joseph Raz, *Between Authority and Interpretation: On the Theory of Law and Practical Reason* (Oxford University Press 2009) 128.

[87] Also at the workshop in Antwerp.

abrogated by official actions that would not have been deemed valid under the Articles' own terms. Since the Articles required unanimous consent of the states in order to abrogate them, there is a good case to be made that the current U.S. Constitution (which required only nine of thirteen states to ratify it before it became valid) was illegal and invalid at its inception, at least until Rhode Island ratified it in 1790.

The point I am making here is not that the official action altering or abrogating the institution must be one that is contemplated by that institution itself. Rather, it simply must be official and institutional, and come to be generally accepted. (Admittedly, there may be a considerable period of doubt where it is not clear which system is governing, especially during revolutions, military conquests, coups d'état, or even the peaceful election of a party of radical reform.)

Nor should we say that internal acceptance of the plan and the intentions and psychological states of officials and subjects are unimportant. Plans must be made; people must collectively intend the conveyance of deontic powers with the declaration of a constitutive rule that conveys status. The advantage of seeing the law as an institutionalized abstract artifact is that it can help to explain better our sense that the law endures beyond the use of its officials and subjects. The law can still be a plan, but a special kind of plan that can continue to exist after participants cease to be willing participants.

The other issue I mentioned with Shapiro's theory was his reliance on self-certification to answer the Identity Question. The Identity Question is the problem of how to differentiate law from other forms of social organization and guidance that share many of the same characteristics.[88] The law, for Shapiro, is unlike other "shared, official, institutional, compulsory" instances of shared planning with moral aims in that it gets a presumption of validity from any hierarchically superior shared plan.[89] This seemed necessary to Shapiro in order to explain why other social organizations that have official, institutional, compulsory authorities with moral aims are not legal systems.

His example is a condominium board that has the power to set rules for the behavior of residents.[90] The key difference between the condo board and a legal system is that "*federal law automatically presumes that state law complies with federal law*,"[91] while the condo board gets no such presumption: it cannot enforce its rules unless and until it convinces a superior legal official that its actions are valid. But subordinate legal officials generally need not make any such demonstration.

While this is certainly generally true in the U.S. and many other modern legal systems, it also seems like it might just be an arbitrary feature that

[88] Shapiro, *Legality* 8. [89] Ibid 220–21. [90] Ibid 218–19.
[91] Ibid 220, emphasis in original.

happens to be common among legal systems at the moment. Furthermore, it is not so clear that non-legal institutions don't frequently share this property of self-certification.

Let us start by looking more closely at Shapiro's example. He compares the situation where the state in which the condo is located passes a law outlawing "skinny dipping in any pool, public or private" with one in which the condo board passes a rule for their condo area that skinny dipping not be allowed in their pool.[92] What seems clear is that, in the first case, the police "can simply yank the skinny-dipper out of the pool and charge him with the crime of skinny dipping."[93] They don't need approval of a superior official to do so. On the other hand, in the latter case, the condo board cannot physically remove him without contacting the police.

> For Florida, like many other legal systems, does not permit owners to enforce their property rights (as opposed to their right not to be physically harmed) through this form of self-help. Rather, they must call the police and hope that the police agree that the skinny dipper is trespassing on their property. Furthermore, they are not permitted to change the locks on the resident's condominium.[94]

Notice that this analysis depends on the fact that Florida law does not permit the owners to exercise self-help. But it could have done so.

Of course, to that Shapiro might respond that the key is that the condo board would need legal authorization to exercise self-help, while the police do not need legal authorization for their actions to be presumed valid. The police themselves are authorized by a general plan that sets out their duties and responsibilities in their official role. The law *happens* to give them a presumption of legal validity for their actions.

We could just as easily imagine the situation is reversed: imagine we live in a hyper-libertarian state where property rights trump even rights over bodily integrity, but suspicion of government power runs deep. In such a state, the law could easily be that acts of forcible ejection from private property are presumed valid until proven otherwise, while police actions must all be pre-authorized by judicial review (as we do now with warrants for searches and arrests of those not caught red-handed).

Even the case of the skinny-dipper might not be typical for our system. Many actions of condo boards do get presumptions of validity; they are allowed to enforce their rules within certain legally prescribed limits. The reason the board does not get a presumption of validity for forcible removals is simply that such cases involve the imposition upon a right we consider to be particularly precious: that of bodily integrity. If the condo board had a rule that specified the

[92] Ibid. [93] Ibid. [94] Ibid.

television in the common room may not be played after 11 p.m. without special arrangement, they would not need prior legal approval to cut the power to the common room after 11 p.m. when a resident's screening party has run long.

Shapiro defines self-certification as a planning organization's freedom "to enforce its rules without first demonstrating to a superior (if one exists) that its rules are valid."[95] But I worry that he is here limiting his conceptualization of enforcement to cases of interference with bodily integrity. (This would be uncharacteristic, since elsewhere he is mindful that there are many means of enforcement.) Since it is common, but by no means unique, for legal systems today to have a monopoly on the use of force,[96] conceptualizing enforcement in this way can easily be confused for self-certification. Shapiro himself notes that the power of enforcement does not need to be unlimited.[97] So some systems simply have even greater limits in that they may not use force.

When we realize that many rules don't require "force" for enforcement and many planning organizations do not require any prior authorization for enforcement of their rules so long as they don't need to interfere with bodily integrity to do so, the self-certification of legal systems seems much less unique to them. Many, if not most, private contractual arrangements provide for enforcement by one party denying access to the benefits of the bargain to the breaching party. While such enforcements are subject to validation by the courts, the need to bring court action in order to challenge the validity of enforcement indicates that it carries the presumption of validity.[98]

Furthermore, it is not so clear that legal systems are quite so self-certifying. One example is the case of the hyper-libertarian system. For another, consider a municipality that had recently been in rebellion and is now required to pre-certify all of their legal activities by a state control board. This is common today in cases of financial mismanagement for any expenditures by financially strapped municipalities. The kind of oversight that undermines self-certification even seems built in (conceptually if not practically) to some Commonwealth countries' system of government, in which all acts of Parliament must be approved by the Governor General (as the representative of the monarch) before becoming law.

Shapiro has replied to these considerations[99] by suggesting that, in cases where the system does not enjoy the presumption of validity from a hierarchically superior jurisdiction, the system is simply a subsidiary of that superior jurisdiction rather than a distinct legal system. Hence, where the Governor

[95] Ibid 221. [96] Ibid 219. [97] Ibid 223.

[98] Shapiro himself cites a presumption that is rebuttable in the courts as evidence of self-certification: ibid.

[99] Verbally, at the discussion in Antwerp on May 31, 2012.

General's approval is simply pro-forma, we can call the former colony's legal system separate. But where the Governor General exercises real authority to withhold Crown approval, the system is simply a sub-part of the British legal system. (However, after the Balfour Declaration of 1926 and for those dominions it covered, the Governor General was to be seen as the representative of the Crown as head of state for that country, and in no way connected to the British government.)

Putting aside these complexities, however, it is not clear what Shapiro sees as the defining mark of a sub-system as opposed to a distinct system. He clearly sees state law as a distinct system, while arguing that colonies with powerful Governors General are merely subsidiaries. When pressed, it appears that the only way to draw this distinction rests upon whether or not the system exhibits self-certification. But that is manifestly circular: non-self-certifying systems are not counterexamples because they are merely subsidiary systems. Yet the only thing we can point to showing that they are subsidiary rather than independent systems is that they are not self-certifying.

By way of a better reply, Shapiro might wish to remind us that self-certification is a matter of degree and hence legality itself may also be.[100] The condo board that can turn off the power to the television room has less self-certification than the state police, which has less than the state legislature, which has less than the federal government. As long as the organization is "*almost*" always free to enforce without certification, we should feel comfortable in calling it a legal system.[101]

There are two problems with this move, however. One is exemplified by the hyper-libertarian example, in which it begins to appear that the condo board is more of a legal system than the municipality with its limited police force. The other comes with a reminder of what work this aspect of legality was supposed to do: answer the Identity Question. If the point of including this characteristic in our analysis of legality was to differentiate law from other forms of social planning, then the more it is open to matters of degree, the less it can accomplish this task. Since Shapiro is adding self-certification in order to answer the Identity Question, it is not clear that he can fall back upon the fact that self-certification is a matter of degree and still have it be enough of a necessary and jointly sufficient condition to meet the task.

In support of the claim that legality might be a matter of degree, Shapiro cites this passage from Raz:

> The attempt to characterize legal systems by the spheres of activity which they regulate or claim authority to regulate cannot be a very precise one. The general traits

[100] Shapiro, *Legality* 224. [101] Ibid 223, emphasis in original.

which mark a system as a legal one are several and each of them admits, in principle, of various degrees. ... It would be arbitrary and pointless to try and fix a precise borderline between normative systems which are legal systems and those which are not. When faced with borderline cases it is best to admit their problematic credentials, to enumerate their similarities and dissimilarities to the typical cases, and leave it at that.[102]

Notice that the context of this passage from Raz is where we are attempting to answer what Shapiro calls the Identity Question by investigating characteristic "spheres of activity" that legal systems regulate. This is not the project in which Shapiro is engaged. He is leaving the spheres of activity wide open and instead engaged in characterizing legality as a specific sub-type of a common human activity, that of planning.

Notice also that Raz claims it is "arbitrary and pointless" to seek a fixed borderline between legal and other normative systems. But by trying to answer the Identity Question, Shapiro has given us a point in doing so. Given that many facets of legal systems are shared by other planning systems, it will certainly seem a bit arbitrary to fix a clearer line between the legal and the non-legal. However, the point was to answer the Identity Question, to see what places the law apart from those other systems. Self-certification doesn't seem to fit the bill, even admitting it is a matter of degree. We simply cannot say that systems which exhibit a lower degree of self-certification are borderline cases and leave it at that because many of those systems are paradigmatic cases of law. And there are too many possible systems with a high degree of self-certification that appear to be similarly far from the borderline, into the space of systems that are clearly non-legal.

Rather than throw up our hands at the possibility of answering the Identity Question, I suggest again that we turn to the notion that the particular kind of plan that law represents is an institutionalized abstract artifact. Let's start with the artifact aspect. Consider what it is that makes a hammer what it is, while a rock you use for driving nails is not a hammer. Both are used to perform the same task, yet the hammer was designed and developed to perform that task. It is a tool created by a human being to perform a function, while the rock is only accidentally performing that function as a result of the human's usage. So a hammer is something that gains that identity as a tool designed and created for that purpose. It is differentiated from other things that can be used to drive nails merely because of the fact that it has an artifactual nature that was self-consciously designed.

[102] Raz, *Practical Reason and Norms* 150.

If all we have is the rock when we need to drive a nail, we might be tempted to call the rock "my hammer." But the use of the possessive pronoun in this context marks it as a hammer in a merely nominal way. I couldn't ask a friend who has just arrived to "hand me the hammer" (and even asking for "my hammer" would require explaining the special context).

Instead, the inventor of the hammer created a tool with the function of driving nails, and subsequent manufacturers of hammers have followed a pattern and improved upon it based on an understanding of that function and that the tool they were making was designed for that purpose. In this way we developed the concept hammer as referring to tools created for this purpose and distinguishing them from other objects that happen to be useful for the same purpose. If someone asks us the Identity Question about hammers,: what separates them from other objects that can be used for the same purpose, we simply give the answer that it is a tool expressly created for that purpose and designed to be identified as that particular type of artifact.

It is clear that whatever functions law performs, other social arrangements can also perform some or even all of them. Shapiro focuses on solving the moral problems associated with the conditions of legality. Other normative systems can solve many of those problems, although many often not as completely or as well. Rocks also frequently won't do as good a job hammering as a hammer, although sometimes they will admittedly do better, just as sometimes customs, religion, or etiquette can do a better job than law. What sets law apart from those other systems of social planning is that it is expressly designed for the purpose of solving those problems and designed to be recognized as such. Those other systems might not be expressly designed at all, or might be designed primarily for some other purpose and only happen to also be useful for solving some of the same problems, or might not be a planning system.

Put in Searlean terms, law is a specifically created status that provides for the institutional creation and assignment of other statuses. So there is some truth to the statement that something is law because we call it "law." It is a creation of fiat, via Searle's "Declaration." This is the arbitrary aspect of what is suggested by Raz in the quote above. Any attempt to draw a sharp line among borderline examples of legal systems will be arbitrary because distinctions on the border will come down simply to what participants tend to consider to be legal activity. But like the hammer, there is some limitation on the kinds of social plans that are candidates for legal plans, set both by the methods by which they are created and adopted, and the purposes to which they are put.

The upshot of this is that legality is not really a matter of degree, even though the aspects of law that demarcate it from other normative systems and institutions are themselves matters of degree. This is necessary in order to see that the Identity Question is still answerable despite the fact that aspects of the answer are matters of degree. Otherwise, once we admit that the facets of law which demarcate it from other institutions and systems are matters of degree, we would have to give up on answering the Identity Question with any reasonable amount of specificity.

Once we see that the law is an expressly designed social institution for solving those pesky social problems, we should be less worried about the Identity Question. What sets the law apart is that we make it special when we make it. We make it special by making it an institution with a special status, conferred when appropriately sourced norms are used to solve for the conditions of legality. When we realize this, we should see that we don't need to focus on self-certification as a hallmark of legality because that is not what makes it special.

This has not been to deny that law is a form of social planning. Rather, my point was to show that it is not *just* a form of social planning; that its institutionality, properly considered, can enhance the planning theory to provide a better answer to law's endurance and help avoid the temptation to see local contingencies like self-certification as essential to law.

6

Metaphysics then Method

While I've stated that I favor a legal positivist picture of law, Gardner has noted that legal positivism is a theory about legal validity and not a theory about law's nature more broadly.[1] Hence legal positivism is compatible with a variety of views about law's nature and what the best way to investigate that nature might be. These are questions of metaphysics and methodology, respectively.

At first glance it might appear that issues of methodology must be settled first in order to then perform the investigation that will illuminate law's nature. But I believe this to be somewhat backwards. Rather, the method of investigation must be determined at a basic level by a picture one already has of law's ontology. That is, in order to determine what methods will best yield a deeper understanding of the subject matter, one must already have at least a basic understanding of what type of thing law is. One uses that basic understanding to settle upon a method for gaining greater insight into the particulars of law's nature. In other words, metaphysics must come before methodology, telling us some general truths about law's nature. Then we use that to determine a method for further specification, which in turn can be used to determine what is interesting and unique about law.

One implication of this is that we don't start with arguments about what makes law unique or different from other social practices or institutions. That question has proven difficult to answer precisely because there hasn't been sufficient clarity on law's ontology such that the differentiation question yields plausible answers.

The problem has been that much of what law does can and has been done by other social practices or normative systems. This is true both of the ends that law serves and of the means by which it pursues those ends. Plenty of other aspects of society involve the positing of rules, the interpretation and application of those rules to new situations, social pressure to conform to

[1] John Gardner, *Law as a Leap of Faith: Essays on Law in General* (Oxford University Press 2012) 33.

those rules, and the imposition of consequences for failures to conform to those rules. Examples such as social clubs, governing bodies for certain sporting or gaming activities, organized religions, residential communities, institutions of higher education, workplaces, and even families exhibit many of the same structural and functional features as legal systems. While one might counter that they get their status through authorization by the legal system, this is certainly not true of all of them, and any of them could exist and operate in a similar fashion without a municipal legal system to recognize it.

When we ask what individuates something, we are asking a metaphysical question. What is a feature of its ontology that sets it apart from everything else? Hence the best chance of answering the question of what differentiates law from these other phenomena will come from first answering more clearly what kind of thing law is, and then developing a methodology to investigate what differentiates it.

I believe that such an investigation must remain open to the usefulness of empirical evidence, while the preliminary metaphysical work to fix law's genus will be more philosophical and universal. So what I propose here is a deeper understanding of law's metaphysics and to see how that leads to a methodology. The exercise of that methodology will then be a collaboration of philosophers and empirical social scientists. The primary idea, developed throughout this book, is that law is a kind of institutionalized abstract artifact and the method it leads to is what I will call jurisprudence as modest joining.

To say that law is a kind of institutionalized abstract artifact is to suggest that we pay special attention to three features of law in discussing its nature. It is to say that it is something made with purpose by human beings and to be understood in terms of that purpose. However, unlike many other artifacts, it is not a physical object. But its abstraction should not be understood to suggest something unimportant or ephemeral. This is where its institutionality is a defining factor. As an institution, it is created with a view to a certain kind of permanence. At the same time, as an institution, it is created in order to alter the norms that apply to people who are parts of it or subject to it.

Now, there are institutionalized abstract artifacts other than the law. It is likely that most, if not all, institutions themselves are abstract artifacts after a kind. This is because, as we have seen, formal institutions generally are fixed by type rather than token in that they follow a set of codified rules for determining which instances are bona fide members of the institution. But let us first investigate further reasons for understanding law as a kind of artifact.

As already summarized, Beth Preston sets out five phenomena that are commonly seen in the relation between an artifact and its function. I submit that law's display of these phenomena, when it comes to particular laws but also with regard to law as type of artifact, is further evidence that law is properly understood as an artifact.

First is the fact that artifact functions are generally "multiply realizable." This means that functions characteristic of the type can be fulfilled via a variety of methods, some of which will be identified as the same artifact while some may be seen as different types of artifacts.[2] That is, there are many differing examples of a given artifact type, and there are many different types of artifacts that perform the same function. There are many forms a hammer can take (claw, ball-peen, framing, etc.) and some of the hammer's characteristic functions can be performed by other artifacts (e.g. nail guns).

Multiple realizability can be seen in legal contexts in both ways and is important for answering claims that law is a functional kind or that its failure to display a function unique to it vitiates the whole project of understanding it in terms of its function. In the first form we can see an example in the different ways in which the law operates to incentivize behavior or to disincentivize unwanted behavior. Sometimes it might impose a tax; sometimes it might impose a monetary penalty; sometimes it might impose a social penalty (like shaming); sometimes it might have a more serious punishment. Clearly these operate in very different ways and might have different communicative purposes behind the choice of one or another method for disincentivizing unwanted behavior. As we will see, the difference between communicative functions of these different options within the over-arching context of incentivizing behavior is another characteristic feature of artifacts, as members of the same artifact type will display some different features with different sub-functions.

The other side of this feature is that we usually expect a variety of different artifacts to serve the same function. Hence, the fact that there are other social institutions and practices that serve some of the same functions as law is not a point against seeing it as best understood in terms of its function. Once we see it as a genre of artifact, and that many different artifacts can perform the same function and yet are still understood in terms of that function, we can say the same of law.

We do not expect to see a function that only law can perform and which sets it off from every other social institution or practice. Not only is this a point against seeing law as a functional kind; this also shows that artifactual kinds are not generally functional kinds.[3] Hence, to the extent that artifacts

[2] Beth Preston, 'Philosophical Theories of Artifact Function' in A. Meijers (ed.), *Philosophy of Technology and Engineering Sciences* (Elsevier 2009) 213–34, 214–15.

[3] As mentioned in note 34 of Chapter 4, I am of two minds about an example like the kind "timepiece." If it refers as well to sundials, then it gets close to being a functional kind (although

are still best understood in terms of their functions, the argument that law is not a functional kind is not itself an argument against seeing the importance of function for an adequate explanatory theory of law.

One problem with claiming that law is an artifact is that, as we've seen, artifacts generally have creators or authors. This might mean that to characterize law as a kind of institutionalized abstract artifact is to invite trouble from customary laws, which don't appear to have an author.

I think that the solution to this problem can be found by investigating the distinction between a customary rule and a customary law. Rules are abstractions, but they need not be artifacts. It seems a stretch, for example, to refer to moral rules as artifacts unless one is particularly strident in one's belief that moral systems are merely creations of a powerful elite in order to keep the masses in order, or of an otherwise powerless minority seeking to displace the values of their betters.

Another possible solution can be found in the tradition of theorizing about artifacts that allows for non-intentional creation.[4] But since we are going to be thinking of artifacts as providing reasons through communicated intentions, we will have to stick to the idea that law is the kind of artifact intentionally created.[5]

To the extent that a customary rule arises without the conscious intention of an individual or group, it does so as a practice that comes to be seen as normative.[6] Rules about the placement of silverware when setting the table are likely an example of this kind. Somehow the practice of where to put the fork and where to put the spoon and knife became fairly regular and, at a certain point, people began criticizing each other for not placing the silverware where others expected. While it is possible that there was a specific person who originated the critical reaction to others' misplacement of silverware, thereby suggesting this common practice be understood as normative, we don't have to assume there was such a single person.

A customary law, however, implies something more than merely that a customary rule is in place. It implies a collective disposition to resort to some

a glance at the sun's position in the sky can also be used to tell the time, and that certainly isn't an artifact).

4 Preston's is a strong version of this view: Preston, *A Philosophy of Material Culture: Action, Function, and Mind* (Routledge 2013). But see as well Ruth Garrett Millikan, 'Wings, Spoons, Pills and Quills: A Pluralist Theory of Function' (1999) 96 *Journal of Philosophy* 191–206; Paul E. Griffiths, 'Functional Analysis and Proper Functions' (1993) 44 *The British Journal for the Philosophy of Science* 409–22, 418–19.

5 See also note 39 of this chapter.

6 This is not to say that it is normative merely because it is a practice, as Hart says is possible with some rules: H. L. A. Hart, *The Concept of Law* (Clarendon Press 1961) 54.

kind of official or collective response to violations of the rule (or that the exercise of powers it confers will be officially or collectively supported). That is, where we merely have a customary rule in place, violations are generally met with individual disapprobation and censure. Where we have a customary law in place, we expect a more organized response on the part of the rest of the community. This could come in the form of a mere expectation that the community will stand behind an individual exercising self-help in the protection of, or compensation for, his customary rights. Nevertheless, it is that expectation that confers a level of official imprimatur on the responses to violations.

This facet is also related to the need for a customary law to be a part of a system of norms if it is to be a law rather than merely a rule. It is that system which validates the communal response to violations of the rule. Even if it's possible that there is no mechanism for deciding disputes over the applicability of the customary law,[7] its norms must still be a part of a wider system for it to have the character of law.

So there is no problem in saying that a customary law is institutionalized[8] and abstract. The only issue is with calling it an artifact, since on our analysis that seems to imply an author.[9] But even with that there should be no real issue since, once we rise to the level of intentionality required for official or communal response, we can imagine there was some person or group who originally self-consciously decided to raise the level of the customary rule to the point of seeing it appropriately officially or communally enforced.

That law can incentivize behavior via multiple means, each of which has a slightly different sub-function (expressing disapproval or blame, raising revenue, etc.), is an example of another phenomenon Preston associates with artifact functions: they are "multiply utilizable." This means that we frequently see artifacts designed to perform more than one function at a time. An example she cites is a uniform, which serves the general clothing function but also serves to identify the wearer as belonging to a specific social group.[10] Criminal law serves to disincentivize unwanted behavior but also to communicate disapproval or blame in a way that taxes do not. That communication might be a method of disincentivization, but it might also serve its own distinctive ends such as giving victims a sense of justice being done.

[7] But see Joseph Raz, *Practical Reason and Norms* (Oxford University Press 1999 (1975)) 132–38.

[8] In Searle's framework, it is more likely that customary laws are informal institutions to the extent that there is no official codification. Searle, *The Construction of Social Reality* (Free Press 1995) 53, 87–88, *Making the Social World: The Structure of Human Civilization* (Oxford University Press 2010) 91.

[9] Again, there are plenty of theorists who deny the need for intentionality in the creation of artifacts and thereby deny the need for an author. See note 4 of this chapter.

[10] Preston, 'Philosophical Theories of Artifact Function' 215.

Again we see this reflected at both the level of specific laws and the level of law as a type or genre of artifact. Plenty of particular laws are designed and/or used to perform more than one function (e.g. a tax used to increase revenue as well as disincentivize behavior, or a driver licensing law designed to ensure drivers have a minimum amount of safety training that also provides for a government-issued identity card to facilitate the authenticity of personal identification). There is clearly a wide variety of functions that law performs as a whole as well, if we understand them as generalized descriptions of all of the ends to which individual laws are put.

More importantly, this helps to deflect the criticism that law's functions in general are too diverse to be jurisprudentially helpful or interesting. If law is a type of artifact, then since artifacts are often multiply utilizable, the fact that law performs many functions is not itself a reason against seeing the importance of those functions to understanding it. Admittedly, if the functions prove to be overly numerous and diverse, our project might be a very complicated and difficult one. But even within the context of multiple utilizability, we can hope to see some similarities and patterns among the diverse functions we uncover. Inculcating desirable behavior, providing an authoritative settlement of disputes, coordinating the actions of people with distinctive individual plans, and providing for social order are not very far apart from each other.

A related worry might be that such unified descriptions of law's functions are so general as to be trivial. This is certainly something to contend with when we are arriving at our generalized descriptions. However, we should also keep in mind just how much jurisprudential utility has been made from something as trivial as saying the function is to "guide behavior."

Multiple utilizability is related to another aspect frequently seen with artifact functions, "recycling." This is where the artifact is used for a wholly different purpose than the one originally intended or to which it was initially put.[11] One example would be the door repurposed as a table. This phenomenon is seen in law wherein an old and disused statute is "dusted off" for new purposes distinctive to the ones it was originally designed for. This might involve a reinterpretation of some of the key terms in the statute. Or it might just be a situation in which a creative lawyer realizes that the original application set was needlessly limited to cases or persons no longer seen, or that the law can be used in novel ways. An example here might be a statute designed to fight organized crime being used to prosecute corporate fraud or corruption.

The creativity sometimes involved with recycling brings up another important phenomenon of artifact function that is also ubiquitous with law, "reproduction with variation." This is the fact that artifacts are almost always

[11] Ibid 215–16.

viewed as multiple members of a given type, where those members change somewhat over time as innovation leads designers to new designs that better serve their functions.[12] The evolution of the bicycle is a great example here. This facet can be easily seen across legal systems and within legal systems. As new legal systems are developed after new governments are formed or political power changes hands, many officials will look to other legal systems for guidance in how to better design their own system, reproducing the valuable aspects of that foreign system while adapting it to the particularities of the community for which it is being drafted.

Where there are multiple jurisdictions within an overarching system, such as in the United States, we can see examples of this aspect in the uniform rule movement. The goal of the movement is to reproduce core "best practices" for a wide variety of legal subjects, yet each jurisdiction may tinker slightly with the rules for their own implementation. Within a system one can point to formal aspects of certain rules that are refined over time for many different statutes. In the realm of judicial opinion, this process is even more obvious with rules of precedent forcing a continual reproduction of existing norms, just as the drift of interpretation and the application of existing norms to novel situations induce variation.

"Malfunction" occurs where, because of mistaken usage, manufacturing or design defect, accident, or normal wear and tear, the structures designed to serve the function cannot perform it.[13] This is to be contrasted with cases where there is something wrong with the end being served itself, such as seeing that end as a disvalue. In law, malfunction happens any time we see a new enactment not accomplishing its task, or an old enactment that no longer is capable of doing so. Sometimes a law designed to decrease homelessness will actually increase it. Perhaps a law whose purpose is to increase the availability of medical insurance coverage has no effect on rates of insurance coverage.

This phenomenon serves both to underscore further the appropriateness of seeing the law as an abstract artifact and to reinforce the ideas discussed in previous chapters about the need to accommodate failure in any functional theory—not to see failure as a reason for immediate exclusion from the class being explained. We do not think of artifact function without acknowledging at least the conceptual possibility of failure. Hence theories that do not allow for that conceptual possibility—either because they see failure as a reason to remove the failing example from the class of law, or (in what amounts

[12] Ibid 216–17.

[13] Ibid 217. See also Wright, 'Functions' 146, noting that where the artifact was designed to accomplish the result, malfunction does not threaten the claim that the failed result is the artifact's function, and generally Baker, 'The Metaphysics of Malfunction.'

to the same thing) because they define away the possibility of failure by making successful performance a necessary condition for inclusion within the ambit of the theory—are at the very least precluded from seeing law along artifactual lines. As I've also argued, they are not even being true to the functional analyses they espouse.

One might worry here that the status functions we see in institutions are created by fiat or declaration and are not capable of failure. For example, laws that create a legal right or impose a legal duty might be said to have the function of creating that right or duty and yet to be incapable of failing at it. (We can understand legal rights and duties as instances of institutionally created statuses in that they are products of the legal system.) As an initial reply, remember that the creation of legal rights and duties are a *means* by which law might perform other functions, rather than being functions themselves. If we imagine the preambles of such enactments, it is hard to imagine them saying the purpose of the law is to create a right or duty and nothing more. Rather, the creation of the right or imposition of the duty would be articulated as a means of accomplishing some other goal or solving some social problem. Put more generally, status functions create statuses within the institution as a means of accomplishing the institution's purposes. Once again, status functions are akin to the mathematical notion of function (mapping one value onto another) and are not to be confused with the proper functions we are using in our explanations of law.

Furthermore, there are a number of ways in which such laws can still fail even to create the right or duty. First, the law itself could fail to be a valid member of the system in which it was enacted for a number of reasons. If the law is invalid, the rights or duties it purports to create would not be recognized within the legal system. Of course, in that case the supposed law is not a member of the system and therefore not a law at all, so this doesn't really answer the problem. Second, the target audience of that law could fail to recognize those rights or duties. That is, even if the law is deemed a valid member of the system, it could lack sufficient collective respect for that particular law for it to be effective. One might say here that the legal rights or duties are still created and so the law is successful even if not respected. However, one measure of the efficacy of any institution is the level of acceptance that its status impositions get. Since these are ultimately social facts, widespread lack of acceptance means that these entities won't have the powers that are claimed for them within the institution. Lastly, we might follow Raz in saying that legal rights and duties are *claims* to impose moral rights and duties.[14] Those

[14] Raz, *Authority of Law* 153–57, 'The Obligation to Obey: Revision and Tradition' (1984) 1 *Notre Dame Journal of Ethics and Public Policy* 139, *Practical Reason and Norms* 123–29, 162–77;

claims are false where those laws are not legitimately authoritative, although they may still be legally valid. On this view, a legally valid right or duty might still fail to create a moral right or duty. But one implication of saying that it is not legitimately authoritative is that people will generally not have any good reason to respect the law creating that right or duty. Hence, even if we could understand the function of the law to be simply to create that right or duty, it can fail to do so by failing to bring about the robust moral rights and duties the law purports to create.

Finally, there is a related phenomenon which Preston calls "phantom function," wherein an artifact type is produced to serve a function that no artifact has ever been able to accomplish.[15] Now, because this phenomenon relates to artifacts by type (as opposed to malfunction),[16] we don't expect to see it present with every type of artifact. Examples here are divining rods, amulets (assuming the falsity of the superstitions on which they are based), and my favorite from above: the perpetual motion machine.

At the token level of law, it is entirely possible that individual laws have functions that they are incapable of successfully performing. Perhaps some kinds of goals are just not open to law as a means of accomplishing them, such as making everyone happy. At the type level, if as I argue law has a set of characteristic functions, then it is clear that they are not phantoms, since many laws do accomplish their purposes. But the point of Preston's catalog was to show the phenomena that a theory of artifact functionality must accommodate, not that every artifact (or every artifact type) must exhibit all of these phenomena.

The phantom function phenomenon is strong ammunition in my argument against Mark Murphy.[17] You will recall that Murphy argues that anything constitutionally unable to perform its function cannot be a member of the class explained by that function. While he allows for defective members of a given type that is understood in terms of its function, this is not the case for any kind of thing that is more fundamentally doomed to failure by a constitutional inability. Hence, for him there has never been a perpetual motion

see also Matthew H. Kramer, 'Legal and Moral Obligation' in Martin P. Golding and William A. Edmundson (eds), *The Blackwell Guide to the Philosophy of Law and Legal Theory* (Blackwell Publishing 2005) 179–90 at 181–82.

[15] Preston, 'Philosophical Theories of Artifact Function' 217. See also Peter Achinstein, 'Function Statements' (1977) 44 *Philosophy of Science* 341–67, 349.

[16] See also L. R. Baker, 'The Metaphysics of Malfunction' (2009) 13 *Techne* 82–92, 84, making the distinction without reference to token/type.

[17] See Chapter 4, note 41 and Mark C. Murphy, 'The Explanatory Role of the Weak Natural Law Thesis' in W. J. Waluchow and S. Sciaraffa (eds), *Philosophical Foundations of the Nature of Law* (Oxford University Press 2013) 3–21, 12–13.

machine. But if phantom function is a phenomenon we expect to see from time to time among artifact types, then we should not be uncomfortable saying instead that all perpetual motion machines are doomed to failure.[18]

So by seeing that law exhibits the properties that Preston lays out for artifacts to be understood in terms of their functions, we have additional evidence both that law is a type of artifact and that it is one best seen in terms of its functions. This is not dispositive of the claim, since these properties could also be exhibited by entities that aren't artifacts. It does, however, lend some strong support that law tracks these characteristics so well.

A. Instrumentalism and Law's Function

As already discussed, many legal positivists, including Hart, do not appreciate the need to understand law in terms of its function, notwithstanding their embrace of law as an artifact. Leslie Green argues that law is best understood in terms of the means by which it accomplishes the wide variety of ends it serves.[19] He opposes this to viewing the law as an end in itself. Following Hans Kelsen, he defends a version of the "instrumentalist thesis," according to which law can only be identified as a means and not as an end. He also associates this view with Hart, especially in his dispute with Fuller,[20] arguing that Hart followed Kelsen as well in rejecting the idea that law as a whole served some identifiable purpose.

As an initial matter it should be clear that the three propositions rejected by Green are not the same, a point he acknowledges. To say that law is an end is different than to say that law can be identified by its ends, which in turn is different than to say that there is an end or purpose that is served by law as a whole. To say that law is an end is to say that it is something for the sake of which we might act or aim our decisions. If we see law as a valuable form of governance, then we might be willing to say that it is (or can serve as) an end. That is to say that humans can or do adopt law as a goal in their actions.

It actually seems fairly uncontroversial that this is sometimes true. When a group of legislators assemble to vote on a piece of legislation, we can easily say that law is their end in the sense that their goal is the creation of a particular law.[21] We might be more reluctant to say that law in general is their end.

[18] See Baker, 'The Metaphysics of Malfunction' 84, using precisely this example.

[19] Leslie Green, 'Law as a Means' in P. Cane (ed.), *The Hart-Fuller Debate in the Twenty-First Century* (Hart Publishing 2010) 169–88. See also Green, *The Authority of the State* (Clarendon Press 1988) 68–71.

[20] Green, 'Law as a Means' 170.

[21] Green himself makes this point: ibid 173.

While we might more generally say that a law can be the reason for someone's action, for example when stopping at a red light in a deserted area, doing so is not to see law as an end of action. (Avoiding a violation of law might here be the goal of the action.) Perhaps it makes more sense to say that a group of officials drafting a constitution for a newly independent nation have the goal or end of law. But even there, it seems more precise to say that their end is the creation of a legal system. One other possibility is that if we identify law with the more normatively pregnant notion of the rule of law, we can say more easily that government by law (that is, consistent with rule of law principles) is an end for which many strive.

Nevertheless, we more often distinguish the notion of law as a system of rules from the value that is brought to society when that system is both in place and conforms to a set of formal criteria, perhaps akin to those set forth by Fuller. When we do make that more common distinction, it is more difficult to say that law *simpliciter* is or constitutes an end in itself.

To say that law can be identified by its ends, however, is different from saying that it serves as an end. That it can be identified by its ends is actually inconsistent with the view that it is or serves as an end itself. To say that it can be identified by its ends is to say that its ends are distinctive. That is, the ends at which it aims are distinctive. This suggests that it is a functional kind in that possession of those ends is sufficient for anything to be law.

This is compatible with the view that the law itself is primarily or wholly a means towards those ends. It is not identifying the law *with* those ends but rather *by* them. To say that law is aiming at them is to make a distinction between law and that at which it aims. After all, if there were no distinction between a thing and its ends, having the thing would be all one would need to have accomplished those ends.[22]

As I have already mentioned, however, one who embraces the importance of law's function to understanding it does not thereby have to claim that the ends it serves are distinctive. Recall the distinction between the hammer and the nail gun. One cannot understand either one without understanding the end they both serve of driving nails. Yet it is not the end that distinguishes one from the other.

If we agree that law is an artifact, as Green himself appears to,[23] then, as with most other artifacts, we are led to say that one cannot completely understand the law without understanding its functions, even though those

[22] As we have seen, this is one reason for acknowledging that in order to give an explanation of something in terms of its functions, one must admit the possibility of it failing to perform those functions.

[23] Green, 'Law as a Means' 172.

functions do not serve to differentiate it from other artifacts that serve the same purposes. Remember that differentiating the explanandum from other phenomena is a requirement of the explanation as a whole and not a specific part of that explanation. It is not a requirement that the differentiation be done by the functions alone. To say that knowing something's function is a key facet of any adequate explanation of it does not entail that its function must be what sets it apart from other things. While a complete explanation of something will allow one to differentiate those things from others to which they might be similar, for things requiring a functional explanation, it might still be the unique way in which means and ends (or modality and function) are combined that differentiates those things from others.

If law did have a function that distinguished it from everything else, then it would be a functional kind. However, the fact that its function does not distinguish it from other forms of human activity and other kinds of social institutions does not mean that we should therefore conclude it is more of a modal kind, that it is distinguished by what it does rather than its ends.[24] After all, many other institutions and forms of behavior operate according to the positing and interpretation of rules, and the imposition of penalties for non-compliance.

Finally, neither the view that it is identified by its ends nor that it serves as an end are the same as the claim that the law serves a specific purpose or has a neatly explainable end. If it is an artifact that serves many purposes, then our job is simply made more complex by this fact; it is not in itself a reason to abandon the method of searching out its functions.

Green compares the law to a Swiss Army knife.[25] But of the Swiss Army knife we do not say that its functions are irrelevant to understanding it simply because it has so many different possible uses. Nor do we say that its designer's intention that it be useful for a myriad of purposes means that the intention is irrelevant. Rather, all of these uses can come to be characterized in a general way. For the Swiss Army knife, perhaps it is to provide a lightweight and easily accessible means to manipulate or adapt one's environment in small ways.

The danger in applying this to law, as Green notes, is that such a general characterization may be so vague as to be jurisprudentially useless.[26] If such a characterization does prove too vague to be much use, then we must leave the possible ends as varied and say they are all relevant to understanding the tool. Another explanation of the Swiss Army knife is that it is an artifact that is designed as a combination of other tools (exhibiting both "multiple

[24] Ibid 180, admitting at n. 6 that this is not a sharp distinction.
[25] Ibid 184.
[26] Ibid.

utilizability" and "reproduction with variation," in Preston's terminology.[27]) So it carries the functions of all of those other tools as a set. With law, it may very well be that some of the myriad functions can be grouped together under a general description, while some cannot. The law would then be a kind of Swiss Army knife, with some general tools and some specific ones. But we would still need to understand as many of those functions as possible in order to get a sense of what it was.

Green claims that thinkers as diverse as Aquinas, Bentham, Fuller, and Hart all "share an instrumental conception of law" wherein the law is understood as an instrument for accomplishing ends, whatever they may be.[28] Where they diverge is over the "instrumentalist *thesis*," that law can only be identified by its means. It is this thesis to which he hopes to give qualified support. He does not argue that the thesis entails that law can only have instrumental value (acknowledging, as noted above, that it is possible for it to serve as an end in certain circumstances). The goal is rather to make it "harder to doubt" that "law's means contribute more to the identification of law than do its ends...."[29]

One question is then a methodological one of explanations: is identification in the sense of differentiating the explanandum from other things (what Shapiro calls the "Identity Question"[30]) the primary occupation of explanation? It is certainly beyond doubt that identification is an important aspect of explanation, especially where what one hopes for is a kind of field guide for the tourist unfamiliar with the explanandum. But it strikes me that this limited an explanation, even for such a tourist, would leave rather a lot out. The better tour books try to give insight into the culture of the place and what the locals do with their lives that gives those lives value and interest to them. In other words, we want to understand not just what makes the explanandum different from similar entities, but what is important about the explanandum to those that engage with it, its significance in the wider culture in which it appears.

Note that such a more complete explanation does not require an endorsement of the explanandum, what it is for, or the way that people are using it, a caveat with which Green also agrees. To understand law is therefore to understand why it is useful to those who use it, which includes an understanding of how it is used by them, but doesn't necessarily commit the tourist to valuing it in the same way its users do.

Imagine unearthing a very distinctive item from an archeological dig. It has a unique shape and markings and, with more digging, a few more items

[27] Preston, 'Philosophical Theories of Artifact Function' 215–17.

[28] Green, 'Law as a Means' 173. [29] Ibid 188. [30] Shapiro, *Legality* 8–9.

of similar shape and markings are found. As the dig progresses, all of the artifacts unearthed during the dig are kept in a special room on shelves. Imagine that they are not yet sorted in any way other than by the dig location and date they were found. The lead researcher on the dig now asks a graduate assistant to bring all of those specially shaped and marked artifacts to her for closer examination. The student has all he needs to identify which artifacts the researcher is requesting. That is, we have enough information to differentiate one artifact from another merely by the location and date of discovery. Yet neither the student nor the researcher understand anything about what the artifacts were used for, which is necessary to identify them in the sense of knowing what kind of thing they are.

This is why providing the means to identify an institution simply to distinguish it from other social phenomena is not enough of an explanation for a complete understanding of the topic. A theory that hopes to explain what the thing is must confront what the item is used for, in order to explain the features it has. Modal features are only understandable in the context of an understanding of the ends those features serve. Its surface features may very well be quite distinctive, and it may very well be differentiated from other items primarily by those surface features. But that cannot be a sufficiently detailed understanding of it to say that one has a complete theory of the item. Additionally, whatever it was used for might also be an end that other artifacts were capable of achieving. Nonetheless, the ends of the artifact are needed in order to understand the significance of the distinctive surface features and how the artifact was used.

B. Thomasson on Artifacts and Signaling Functions

Green's argument about law being identified more by its modal or structural features than its functions mirrors a similar argument made about artifacts more generally by Amie Thomasson.[31] However, we can use her argument to underscore the centrality of functions to understanding law. Thomasson tries to show that artifacts do not need a required function, and when they have one, it need not play an essential role in the classification of that artifact. The main purpose of her argument is to allow for works of art still to be understood as artifacts, even though they arguably sometimes do not have any intended function. This is important because when we look at the argument

[31] Amie L. Thomasson, 'Public Artifacts, Intentions and Norms' in M. Franssen, P. Kroes, T. A. C. Reydon, and P. E. Vermaas (eds), *Artefact Kinds: Ontology and the Human-Made World* (Springer 2013) 45–62.

in greater detail, we can see that with this goal it might make sense to say that certain types of artifacts (like artworks) can be understood without reference to any functions, but other kinds of artifacts (perhaps like law) will still need reference to function for a complete understanding.

She begins by noting that there are three commonly held views about artifacts: that they must have an intended function;[32] that it is this intended function that determines what kind of artifact it is ("functional individuation"); and thus that artifacts are mind-dependent in that their identity depends on an intention. She argues instead that they don't have to have intended functions; that when they do have them, such functions are neither necessary nor sufficient for their classification or identification; and that it is their intended features that are important for classification, not their functions.[33] The focus will again be on public artifacts, which depend for their identity on public norms.

First we must remind ourselves of the important distinction between artifact-kind and artifact-token. The availability of artifact tokens that may lack functions (as some works of art arguably do) suggests there may also be artifact kinds that are not individuated through functions. Even though some works of art have functions (e.g. to raise political awareness, to advertise a product, etc.), the assumption that some might not means that the artifact kind "work of art" as a whole does not get its distinction from other kinds of artifact via a function that all members must perform or aim at.

Also, even if we are talking about an artifact kind that is understood by a proper function, not every member needs to be intended to serve that function. (Think of the doors that are designed to be used as tables and more generally of Preston's notion of multiple utilizability, the idea that many artifacts can be used to serve a wide variety of ends.)[34] Hence neither having, being intended to perform, nor being used to perform the function, let alone succeeding in performing it, is necessary or sufficient for membership in the class picked out by the artifact kind.

Instead, Thomasson argues, what individuates artifacts is their intended features "which may or may not include an intended function."[35] This shows that on her view, the function of an artifact kind *might* still be an intended feature. So if Green's argument that law is to be understood in terms of its characteristic features is understood to mirror Thomasson's, that in itself would not necessarily be an argument against seeing function as the key

[32] But see Beth Preston, 'Why Is a Wing Like a Spoon? A Pluralist Theory of Function,' (1998) 95 *The Journal of Philosophy* 215–54; *A Philosophy of Material Culture: Action, Function, and Mind* (Routledge 2013) 176–77.

[33] Thomasson, 'Public Artifacts, Intentions and Norms' 46.

[34] Preston, 'Philosophical Theories of Artifact Function' 215.

[35] Thomasson, 'Public Artifacts, Intentions and Norms' 48.

feature for understanding law. Law might be the kind of artifact that has function(s) as individuating intended features.

Recall that Thomasson's argument is about artifacts in general, broadening the identifying criteria to intended features more widely in order to accommodate artworks. Some artifact kinds are still best to be understood in terms of intended (or, more broadly, proper) functions.[36] Whether or not it is best to use functions or some other intended feature of the artifact will depend on other aspects of the artifact kind in question.

Thomasson provides an analysis of whether a token is a member of what she calls an "essentially artifactual kind"[37] (understood as a kind all of whose exemplars are necessarily artifacts):

> Something is a member of an essentially artifactual kind K only if it is product of a largely successfully executed intention to make a K, where the maker must have a substantive concept of the nature of Ks that largely matches that of some prior K makers (if any) and intend to realize that concept by making an object with K-relevant features.[38]

On this view, the K-relevant features can vary from kind to kind. Hence some kinds are best understood in terms of intended function, others in terms of other features.

The question for our dispute with Green is then whether law falls into one of the kinds that is still understood in terms of function or not. Applying this analysis and saying that law's functions are the intended features that explain it appears to allow for mistakes in the content of law, but not in the creation of law. This seems to respect our pre-theoretic intuitions about the relation of law to its function and where problems arise. It would allow for a lawmaker to err in the content of the law being made, perhaps through a wording problem, an issue with vague language, or even perhaps a printing error. But it would not allow someone to make law accidentally.[39]

[36] Ibid. See also Thomasson, 'Artifacts and Human Concepts' in E. Margolis and S. Laurence (eds), *Creations of the Mind: Theories of Artifacts and their Representation* (Oxford University Press 2007) 52–73, 56–57, arguing that artifact functions are to be understood as intended proper functions. In conversation, Thomasson confirmed that law is likely in this category.

[37] Thomasson, 'Realism and Human Kinds' (2003) 67 *Philosophy and Phenomenological Research* 580–609, 593, crediting Risto Hilpinen with the term. See also Thomasson, 'Artifacts and Human Concepts' 58, contrasting essentially artifactual kinds with the example of gold spheres for which it is only a contingent fact that all exemplars are artifacts.

[38] Thomasson, 'Public Artifacts, Intentions and Norms' 48–49, referencing Thomasson, 'Realism and Human Kinds' 599–600.

[39] It is fairly difficult to imagine someone making law accidentally. Three possible cases come to mind, only one of which seems to present serious difficulty. One might think of a kind of sleepwalking legislator empowered to make law on his own, who accidentally creates a law while asleep. Intuitions might differ on whether any such activity is void *ab initio* or only voidable (and

Notice also that it does not require someone making a token of K (here a law) to have a concept of Ks that includes a well-understood notion of K's overall function, even if the feature that individuates Ks happens to be their function. Rather, the important thing is that the maker has enough of an understanding of what a K is to match her intentions to what other makers (if any) previously intended.[40] So it is entirely possible that the features that a lawmaker has in mind when drafting or legislating are not the functions shared by all laws, even if the kind is itself still to be best understood in terms of those functions. It is only needed that the lawmaker is sufficiently matching important intentions of prior lawmakers, which might be merely token functions, or might even be merely non-functional structural features.

Thomasson's point that echoes Green here is that the key notion is how the object is to be used or treated, what she calls "receptive" features.[41] This allows that public artifacts have, among other things, a purpose to communicate something to other possible users. Hence public artifacts must be intended to be recognizable as artifacts of that kind and this includes a norm of treatment.

In order to understand her point and its implication for law, we have to remember that many artifacts are members of multiple kinds and have

answers may vary by each legal system that confronts the issue), but it seems to be a very open question whether such an activity would create a valid legal norm at its inception. We might be more comfortable saying that when the accident is discovered, it would need to be reaffirmed in order to maintain any validity. That reaffirmation could then be seen as the moment of intention, allowing merely that the intention and the creation be separated in time, but otherwise thereby conforming to Thomasson's analysis. One might also think about sole legislators being mind-controlled or hypnotized so as to create a law without intention. But such cases are likely more easily dealt with as akin to a coup d'état. Perhaps the biggest threat here is that one might think of customary law as a kind of accidental law, or at the very least as non-intentionally created law. That is, perhaps someone began whatever practice was to count eventually as a customary law. But in beginning that practice, the person did not have the intent to create a law. Of course, customary law has presented a problem for many legal theorists and we have already discussed some of those issues at length. The best way to address it may be to see it as a vestigial counterexample to the notion of law as a full-fledged artifact, putting customary laws instead in the category of instruments or tools, to borrow Dipert's taxonomy: Randall R. Dipert, *Artifacts, Art Works, and Agency* (Temple University Press 1993) 27–30.

[40] If she is making a novel prototype, then things are a bit more complicated. But almost every invention can be understood to be some kind of improvement upon a previous artifact type (back to the first stone flint cutting tool designed to be recognized as such, which itself was an improvement upon objects used as instruments in their natural states), with a more specific or different functionality. See Preston, *A Philosophy of Material Culture: Action, Function, and Mind* 164–77. Thomasson does not rely so heavily upon the notion of improvement upon prior artifacts, allowing inventors to create new artifactual kinds by intending to match an imagined design and its effects. Thomasson, 'Artifacts and Human Concepts' 60–62.

[41] Thomasson, 'Public Artifacts, Intentions and Norms' in M. Franssen, P. Kroes, T. A. C. Reydon, and P. E. Vermaas (eds), *Artefact Kinds: Ontology and the Human-Made World* (Springer 2013) 45–62, 49.

features or sub-systems that can have distinctive purposes from the artifact as a whole. So, for example, a dinner jacket is an article of clothing and shares the functions of other clothes, but also is recognizable and distinguishable from other kinds of clothes by distinctive features that govern how or where it is to be worn. Thomasson's point is that these features may have no other purpose than to signal those interacting with the artifact about the norms of behavior that are in play with regard to the artifact.

Here is where Green's argument about the identification of law by what it does rather than the aims it may serve comes in, but also shows that Thomasson's and even Green's views are still conducive to a functional explanation of law. If those "receptive" features are there to signal to those interacting with the artifact of the norms in play, then that is precisely one of the functions of those receptive features. This point is of particular significance: one key function of law is precisely to signal to those subject to it that the normative content of specific laws are being singled out for a special kind of social emphasis.

Much of what Green says is distinctive about the law is the way in which it is worded or operates in society. But a key feature of the way it operates is to signal to those within its jurisdiction that it is conveying a norm of behavior, one that gets a special kind of social and governmental backing. Hence, the structural or modal features that Green emphasizes as distinctive for law are still functional in that they are performing this signaling function. In effect, Green's focus on identifying and differentiating the law from other social phenomena is itself providing the function that explains those features of law: they are to call attention to the fact that a given rule is legal in character and therefore demands a certain kind of treatment and behavior in response.[42]

We can also use this to see how Green's methodological preoccupation with the identification question leads him to his emphasis on structural

[42] Green might wish to reply that this is still a modal feature: the way that law accomplishes its functions is to signal that the norms it creates and deploys are to get special treatment. I suspect there can be no answer to the question of whether an intermediate goal that is instrumental for the sake of a more ultimate goal is best thought of as an end or merely as a means. Suffice it here to say that explaining things in terms of their functions is to orient the explanans to both ends and means where those means happen to be integral to the accomplishment of the ultimate ends and can serve as the motivating reason for those creating or interacting with the explanandum. One might think here of my claim that the creation and manipulation of statuses is generally a means rather than an end of institutions. Why isn't the signaling that law does similar to the marshalling of statuses? My answer is that signaling the special treatment we wish to give certain norms can be appealed to as a reason for elevating or recording a given standard as a law (even if it is still usually an intermediary end). However, the mere creation of a new status cannot generally be given as a reason for its own creation.

features. It is precisely those structural features whose function it is to provide that identification, making the law recognizable and distinct from other institutions and social practices, if only by marking out its special status. So if your goal is to discover what sets law apart from other entities, you are understandably drawn to those structural features that do the setting-apart.

Now, this does not here say anything against Green's argument that the law's overall function is either too general or too myriad to be jurisprudentially useful. Rather, it shows that by focusing instead on the modal or structural characteristics, Thomasson's point can be used to say that they are themselves understood in terms of the very identification purpose that Green argues for them (even though Thomasson's is more generally an argument that artifacts need not be identified by their functions). They are to be understood in terms of that function: to identify law as law.

In order to include art in the class of public artifacts, Thomasson argues that the key to understanding public artifacts more generally is that they are intentionally created with certain "intended features that may, but need not, include an intended function."[43] She claims an advantage of her view is that it provides in one metaphysical theory a way to account for functional, religious, and art artifacts. "If we take the relevant intended features unifying artifacts into artifactual kinds to be functional, we risk leaving out works of art; if we make them structural or perceptible, we seem to get a poor view of many functional artifact kinds...."[44]

While I am sure that she did not intend this list to be exhaustive of public artifact kinds, notice that the vast majority of public artifacts—perhaps almost everything that isn't primarily artistic—would come under the functional category and be understood primarily in terms of their function. Even the religious artifacts are likely separated because of problems with what Preston calls phantom functions, which, if accounted for in a complete theory of artifacts, would likely bring them back into the functional fold. Whether the religious artifact is to make rain or appease an angry god, it is still understood in terms of its functions, even if we don't believe the objective really exists or that it is possible to be achieved. So this in itself is strongly suggestive that law (which in most modern manifestations is neither essentially artistic nor generally religious) is to be understood in terms of its functions.

As for the remaining question that Green leaves us with about the difficulty in settling upon a function for characterizing all of law that isn't too myriad or too general to be jurisprudentially useful, we can start to point

[43] Thomasson, 'Public Artifacts, Intentions and Norms' 57. [44] Ibid.

to an answer by drilling down once more to the relation between token and kind, thinking about how an understanding of the nature of law as a kind points the way to a methodology for further investigation. Applying Thomasson's analysis to law suggests that in the creation of a specific law or in the making of a judicial decision there must be an intention for the law or decision to serve a more specific purpose. When it comes to legislation in a democracy with a number of voting legislators, it is likely that this intention is one that is held by legislative drafters or authors seeking to address an identifiable social problem or achieve a specific social goal.

Granted, the final form that the law takes might not be exactly as those who drafted it intended. But to the extent that those voting on it still understand their votes to be on something meant to address that social problem or pursue that social goal, they share that intention no matter what their ultimate reasons for their vote might be (e.g. the desire to stay in power). That is, we should distinguish a legislator's ultimate motivation from what she thinks she is potentially enacting with her vote. The latter is generally understood in terms of the purpose the legislation is to serve, even if that purpose is not one the legislator would personally endorse. She might vote for it to please her constituents, knowing that the vote will fail, or even that the law will fail to achieve its function once enacted.

From the theorist's perspective we can then examine the myriad purposes in those individual legal decisions and enactments in the hope of seeing some patterns or generalizations that we could use to characterize law as a whole. We already have a few candidates in guiding and coordinating behavior. Granted, these might still be too broad to be particularly valuable (although many have still made quite a bit of hay out of them), but we can imagine that further investigation will lead to more specific results.

An implication of Thomasson's analysis is that the creators of the token law need not have any of the law's general purpose in mind when drafting or deciding the token. But they do need to have some end in mind for its creation. We theorists can turn to social scientists and other legal studies researchers to begin the process of cataloging and aggregating the purposes of those tokens, which we collect and further characterize and reduce into a general theory of law.

It bears repetition that in doing so we are not necessarily in the business of looking behind the "retail" functions of these individual legal enactments and decisions to discover the invisible hand of hidden motivations, whether they be conscious or subconscious influences on individual legislators and judges (such as class biases or personal benefits that officials hope to obtain). We acknowledge the presence of these. But as general jurisprudents with hopes that our claims might have wide application, we proceed on the notion that the law need not operate according to the cynicism we so often encounter with it. We can analyze its nature by what it wears on its sleeve. This is not to proceed as if all law is perfect, but rather on the assumption that the process of creating law is perfectible at least enough such that its nature is not necessarily besmirched by the morass in which we often find it.

Thomasson's view also helps to see why artifacts are important to understand, and such an appropriate way to understand law's nature. Quoting Dipert, she notes,

> "Artifacts are the 'residue' of intentional activity." ... [W]e can broaden this to say that artifacts (at least of public, extant kinds) are the residue of human intentions and normative practices... . To see public artifacts as artifacts is to see a way of life—to take interest in public artifacts as such is to take interest in what they were made for, what norms and practices governed things like that, in the context of the broader practices and setting of a society.[45]

In other words, understanding public artifacts and what they are helps us to understand what is important in a given way of life to those who live it. Law is an outstanding example of that; by understanding it, we understand more about ourselves and what is important to us about our way of life.

C. The Jurisprudent as Modest Joiner

The word "joiner" has two definitions. One is a worker who does woodwork in a construction project, especially door and window frames as well as doors and flooring. This has the connotation of one who takes the materials with which others have worked, such as wood planks, and joins them together to fashion a new entity that is more directly useful in the building. (The other definition is one who has a penchant for joining existing groups and causes and generally has a negative connotation. This won't be the sense in which I use the term here.[46]) I am going to use the term as a kind of analogy for the theoretical method I see arising from our considerations here.

A modest joiner would be a theorist who fits together the pieces that others have tooled to make new important parts of the overall structure. The idea would be to bring together ideas from different disciplines that can shed light on the law. This person would hope to contribute to the overall

[45] Ibid 59, quoting Dipert, *Artifacts, Art Works, and Agency* 15.

[46] This other sense should, however, remain a cautionary reminder to employ wider philosophical theories and sociological research that are well conceived and hold the promise of withstanding the test of time, rather than merely twisting the latest fads to provide explanations of law. We want to be modest joiners in the carpentry sense and not in the social follower sense.

understanding of the thing being studied and, in the case of law, to the self-understanding of those who use it.

Just as joiner is perhaps a more modest position than architect, the jurisprudent is not expecting to suggest a theory that will be completely novel in every way. Yet just as door and window frames are necessary components of a building if it is not to collapse when leaving holes in the walls for windows and doors, the work of the modest joiner is important to the structure of our legal self-understanding. The creativity of the joiner is not always obvious in the structure, but may be found in novel ways in which she fits together the disparate parts tooled by others, especially when those parts come from different disciplines.[47]

What does the joiner join? Many have pointed out the inadequacies of a jurisprudence that brings to bear a variety of outdated or outmoded philosophical theories to the questions of the nature of law and the grounds of its normativity. But a modest joiner takes those bigger philosophical theories that do gain traction among the wider philosophical community and applies them to the problems of jurisprudence, adapting them to the empirical reality of legal phenomena as reported by those social scientists doing rigorous and reliable investigations. Think of the examples of ordinary language philosophy,[48] Quine's rejection of the analytic/synthetic distinction,[49] Bratman's planning theory,[50] and Searle's theory of institutional facts[51] as instances of

[47] By calling the joiner "modest" I am invoking (but not embracing) a certain side in the debate over the reach of conceptual analysis. See for example Veronica Rodriguez-Blanco, 'A Defence of Hart's Semantics as Nonambitious Conceptual Analysis' (2003) 9 *Legal Theory* 99–124; Michael Giudice, 'Conceptual Analysis and Its Critics' (2012) 6 *Problema* 3–38, 33f, rejecting the terms of the debate—with which I tend to agree. Notwithstanding this invocation, the modesty is meant here merely to suggest that the jurisprudent is not expected to provide a completely novel theory, unmoored from related philosophical and sociological work.

[48] J. L. Austin, 'A Plea for Excuses' (1956) 57 *Proceedings of the Aristotelian Society* 1–30, 7–8; Hart, *Concept of Law* 14. See also Timothy Endicott, 'Law and Language' (2002) *The Stanford Encyclopedia of Philosophy*, Edward N. Zalta (ed.) § 1 <http://plato.stanford.edu/archives/spr2014/entries/law-language>.

[49] W. V. Quine, 'Two Dogmas of Empiricism' (1951) 60 *The Philosophical Review* 20–43; Brian Leiter, 'Naturalism and Naturalized Jurisprudence' in Brian Bix (ed.), *Analyzing Law: New Essays in Legal Theory* (Oxford University Press 1998) 79–104; Brian Leiter, *Naturalizing Jurisprudence: Essays on American Legal Realism and Naturalism in Legal Philosophy* (Oxford University Press 2007). See also Dennis M. Patterson, 'Notes on the Methodology Debate in Contemporary Jurisprudence: Why Sociologists Might Be Interested' in Michael Freeman (ed.), *Law and Sociology* (Oxford University Press 2006) 254–58 at 256–58; Brian Tamanaha, 'What Is "General" Jurisprudence? A Critique of Universalistic Claims by Philosophical Concepts of Law' (2011) 2 *Transnational Legal Theory* 287–308, 301.

[50] Michael E. Bratman, *Faces of Intention: Selected Essays on Intention and Agency* (Cambridge University Press 1999); Shapiro, 'Law, Plans, and Practical Reason' (2002) 8 *Legal Theory* 387–441; Shapiro, *Legality* (Harvard University Press 2011).

[51] Searle, *Construction of Social Reality; Making the Social World*; MacCormick, 'Norms, Institutions, and Institutional Facts' (1998) 17 *Law and Philosophy* 301–45.

wider philosophical theories that have been employed to illuminate the questions of jurisprudence. These then need to be applied to instances of law as reported by social scientists, in the hope of developing a more nuanced understanding of the role of law in human society and in our (increasingly global) self-understanding.[52] Where the philosophical theory does not withstand the test of time, the jurisprudential theories that employ it are then rightfully critiqued and adapted.

In order to establish the viability of this method, we need to examine Brian Tamanaha's argument that there is an essential tension between the methodologies of those who attempt to generate a "universally applicable theory of the nature of law," like Raz and Shapiro, and those who "construct[] a theoretical framework that addresses various manifestations of law around the globe," like Tamanaha himself, William Twining, Keith Culver, and Michael Giudice.[53] The tension is that those engaged in the former kind of jurisprudential theorizing appear to argue that their theories are formed on the basis of universal necessary truths about law and hence have no room for the kinds of empirical information upon which the latter depend.[54]

Apart from some puzzling remarks by Scott Shapiro,[55] I believe that this criticism is a bit unkind to the theorists engaged in what has been called conceptual analysis, who are in search of "universal truths" about law. Giudice notes that theorists such as Raz and Jules Coleman are explicit in saying that

[52] Endorsing similar methodological ideas see William L. Twining, *General Jurisprudence: Understanding Law from a Global Perspective* (Cambridge University Press 2009) 55–56; Giudice, 'Conceptual Analysis and Its Critics' 31–32; N. Lacey, 'Analytical Jurisprudence Versus Descriptive Sociology Revisited' (2006) 84 *Texas Law Review* 944–82.

[53] Tamanaha, 'What Is "General" Jurisprudence?' 288, citing Raz, *Between Authority and Interpretation: On the Theory of Law and Practical Reason* (Oxford University Press 2009) 91–92; Shapiro, *Legality*; Brian Z. Tamanaha, *A General Jurisprudence of Law and Society* (Oxford University Press 2001); Twining, *General Jurisprudence: Understanding Law from a Global Perspective*; Keith Charles Culver and Michael Giudice, *Legality's Borders: An Essay in General Jurisprudence* (Oxford University Press 2010). See also Danny Priel, 'Jurisprudence and Necessity' (2007) 20 *Canadian Journal of Law & Jurisprudence* 173–200, 175–76. But see Giudice, 'Conceptual Analysis and Its Critics' (2012) 6 *Problema* 3–38, 15–29, seeking a combined methodology such as endorsed here and refusing to give up on conceptual analysis, citing with approval Twining, *General Jurisprudence: Understanding Law from a Global Perspective* 117; Raz, *Between Authority and Interpretation* 57–58; Coleman, 'Incorporationism, Conventionality, and the Practical Difference Thesis' (1998) 4 *Legal Theory* 381–425, 393 n. 24.

[54] Tamanaha, 'What Is "General" Jurisprudence?' 289–90.

[55] As noted by Tamanaha, ibid 290, Shapiro, *Legality* 406–07, argues that empirical social science is useless for legal philosophy because it is limited to human law and therefore would not be useful to explain the legal systems of alien civilizations, which would be necessary to include in any general or universal theory of law. Apart from Tamanaha's criticism that there is something tautological about this claim ('What Is "General" Jurisprudence?' 290 n. 16, see also 297), it seems to me that social science will simply expand to include the study of extraterrestrials so long as they possess something we can recognize as a social ordering.

while we use *our* concept of law as a starting point to investigate the nature of law wherever it is found, this does not mean that we are limited to a "rigidly parochial" concept of law. Our concept changes to become "more inclusive" as we use it in search of universal truths about law.[56] This includes the idea that our theories of law must be open to revision based on data that we get from empirical research into law as it is found around the world.

Implicit in this is the idea that our concept of law sits between our language and the social practices or other phenomena out in the world that we are trying to capture. Our concept is therefore always parochial in the sense that it is limited to the aspects of law of which we have conceived or considered.[57] But we might aspire for it to encompass as much as possible of the phenomenon as it exists (its nature).[58] Whether or not we so aspire is a contingent question based on the interests of those who use the concept and of those who study its use and the nature of the phenomenon to which it refers.[59]

When it comes to artifacts, the concepts held by those who invent a new artifact and create new tokens as they refine the design are constitutive of the nature of that kind.[60] Hence there is something to Tamanaha's idea that law is whatever a society calls "law."[61] Those who create law in each society are those that determine the nature of law within that society and the content of their parochial concept of law.

Yet we cannot be overly tempted by Tamanaha's nominalist approach, if only because we understand something more substantive with our legal concepts. As an initial matter we should distinguish here again between membership in the class of law and the notion of legal validity. While it may be true that some form of at least potential, if not actual, historical legal validity is necessary for membership in the class, we do not say that law is only what *our* society calls "law" simply because we can look at other societies

[56] Giudice, 'Conceptual Analysis and Its Critics' 21–23, quoting Raz, *Between Authority and Interpretation* 18, 33, 57–58, Coleman, 'Incorporationism, Conventionality, and the Practical Difference Thesis' 393 n. 24. See also Thomasson, 'Artifacts and Human Concepts' 62–63.

[57] Tamanaha points to this as a criticism of conceptual analysis: 'What Is "General" Jurisprudence?' 291. See also Kenneth Einar Himma, 'Do Philosophy and Sociology Mix? A Non-Essentialist Socio-Legal Positivist Analysis of the Concept of Law' (2004) 24 *Oxford Journal of Legal Studies* 717–38, 733–34, noting in a critique of Tamanaha that usage conventions for concepts can change over time.

[58] Raz, *Between Authority and Interpretation* 18–19, 31; Giudice, 'Conceptual Analysis and Its Critics' 21–22. ("The closer a concept of law comes to covering or designating successfully all instances of law, and so transcending its particular origin, the closer *explanation of that concept of law* comes to *explanation of the nature of law*": ibid 24, emphasis in original.)

[59] See Giudice, 'Conceptual Analysis and Its Critics' 1920, quoting Raz, *Between Authority and Interpretation* 57.

[60] Thomasson, 'Artifacts and Human Concepts' 64.

[61] Tamanaha, *A General Jurisprudence of Law and Society* 166.

and incorporate what they are calling law into our notion. Membership in the class of law certainly doesn't depend upon meeting *our* society's criteria of legal validity. It may depend upon meeting *some* society's criteria of legal validity at some point in time, or have some potential to do so. But that is a much more expansive set than what *we* now (or *they*) call "law." This is not to say that Tamanaha is here conflating what is locally legally valid and what a society calls "law," but rather to caution against one interpretation of his nominalist view. Also, since Tamanaha's ambitions are pluralistic, when he says that law is whatever a society calls "law," from the perspective of the theorist or social scientist, this must be understood as whatever *any* society calls law.

Let's imagine we are looking at some normative social practices of another society and that the best translation we can give to their term for those practices is our term "law." If in those normative practices we see nothing of institutionality, no codification, no officials, no notions of contextual validity, perhaps even no social pressure to conform to those norms (to the extent it is even still possible to say that they are social norms without such pressure), it seems difficult to imagine how we would even have come up with "law" as a candidate for translating their term for this practice. If we did come up with the term as a candidate for translating what they call those practices, then it would suggest that we are expanding our concept somewhat to include the differences exhibited by this other society.[62]

Tamanaha's method, when actually applied, would not be mere nominalism, since we would need to apply our parochial (yet expanding) concept of law to even see that the foreign term was translatable as "law." What Tamanaha misses is that this is not inconsistent with what many of the conceptual analysis theorists would likely endorse.

However, there is a shadow of Tamanaha's nominalism in law's institutionality. Since, as we've seen, institutions involve the conferral of statuses that are created by the institution itself, there is something to be said for the notion that law is whatever a society gives the status of law to. However, that notion of status is much more akin to legal validity. It certainly comes closer to the truth to say that anything a society considers to be legally valid (giving it the status of law by the society's own parochial lights) comes within the ambit of law. The modest joiner method would then be to harmonize philosophical theories explaining that status with data obtained from social

[62] A similar argument against Tamanha's method put in a different way is advanced by Himma, 'Do Philosophy and Sociology Mix? A Non-Essentialist Socio-Legal Positivist Analysis of the Concept of Law' 736–38, noting that the usage of concept terms is norm-governed to pick out certain features and that Tamanaha's picture is "too thin."

scientists about what practices, norms, social orderings, etc. get that status in different locations around the world (and beyond).

When I claim that law is to be understood in terms of the social functions that it performs, there is very likely some general way of characterizing those functions or aggregating them into some general notion of law's functions. Some of that data can come from the sociologists, just as the philosophers can arbitrate among them to determine which studies are focusing on the conceptually key or important aspects (from inside their parochial but expanding concept). So I am saying that we need both conceptual analysis and sociology. We need both general and specific.

To say that laws are artifacts is to say that they are best understood in terms of the functions that their creators have when they make them (and, to the extent it alters those functions, the way that they are used by people once they are implemented). We can then generalize over the functions of individual legal enactments and decisions to reach a general characterization of law's functions as a genre.

To say that it is one kind of institution is to say that law's function must be a bit more specific than merely that of conferring statuses that carry normative implications. We've seen that status conferral is more properly understood as one characteristic means by which institutions perform their functions. Institutions confer statuses that carry normative implications, and law is a specific type of institution, so it shares the status-conferral method, but the statuses must be of a specific kind or kinds. We have also seen that one characteristic of institutions is that their status conferrals carry deontic implications. This helps to explain how law creates (or at least claims to create) non-prudential reasons for action. So the status that law, as an institution, confers is a status carrying deontic powers related to the set of proper functions that law is to perform. Other institutions confer statuses conveying deontic powers that are tailored to the functions of those other institutions.[63]

I suggest beginning with the methodological working hypothesis that the concept of law is akin to a "family resemblance"[64] concept, but that we remain open to the possibility that there are functional elements that are common to all applications of the concept.[65] Any common elements will eventually get greater prominence in our explanations, which is closer to

[63] Raz discusses what distinguishes legal systems from other institutionalized normative systems in *Practical Reason and Norms* 149–54.

[64] Ludwig Wittgenstein, *Philosophical Investigations: The German Text, with a Revised English Translation* (G. E. M. Anscombe tr., 2nd (rev.) edn, Blackwell 1999 (1953)) 31–34.

[65] A similar argument is advanced by Veronica Rodriguez-Blanco, 'Is Finnis Wrong?' (2007) 13 *Legal Theory* 257–83, 278–82, calling it "core resemblance."

what Raz expects. Raz holds that there is likely a core meaning with a structured set of varied extensions.[66]

This is an important distinction for holding open the possibility that there are no essential properties to law, but yet there are some characteristics that are common to all applications. It may very well be that these core elements aren't themselves unique to law, and so the family resemblance idea will need to be retained as those elements common to all applications won't on their own serve to demarcate law from other social phenomena.

While Wittgenstein emphasized in his ideas of family resemblance that there was no one property that would be common to all instances of the concept,[67] we are only taking it as a starting possibility. We remain open to the idea that there will be some sufficiently abstract property that will be common to all instances such that we can call it provisionally necessary (but not conceptually necessary), with the understanding that more data can push us back to seeing the concept as a family resemblance.

The family resemblance idea should help to placate those like Tamanaha and Twining who insist we not neglect non-state law in developing our understanding of the practice and its implications. This is clearly important as our municipal and political legal systems developed out of systems that were more overtly religious (as there was likely originally no distinction between these two categories of legal systems).

Saying that law is akin to a family resemblance concept, however, should not mislead one into thinking that it is "essentially contested" or fundamentally interpretive (which, in Dworkin's sense, amounts to the same thing.[68]) While we might very well have some debates over certain applications of the concept, we should not be so invested in its application that we are unwilling to allow for its use in unfamiliar settings. Raz's point that the concept is "our" concept of law is important here. But once we see our role to be that of the modest joiner, we can admit that we have enough to learn from other instances that will still inform our own, keeping it open to revision.

One might raise the problem that, without a fixed notion of the concept to begin with, we will not know what to investigate in other cultures and which applications to see as legal candidates for further study. I believe this worry will be seen as misplaced once we embrace the metaphysical considerations I raise above and the resulting importance of understanding and explaining

[66] Raz, *Between Authority and Interpretation* 29.

[67] Wittgenstein, *Philosophical Investigations: The German Text, with a Revised English Translation* 32 §67.

[68] Ronald Dworkin, 'Thirty Years On (Book Review of Coleman: Practice of Principle)' (2002) 115 *Harvard Law Review* 1655–88, 1686; see also my 'Law Is Not (Best Considered) an Essentially Contested Concept' (2011) 7 *International Journal of Law in Context* 209–32, 219.

law in terms of its functions. If we take Karl Llewellyn's basic notion of the functions of law[69] as a starting point, we see that it is much more likely that the wide variation in law comes in terms of the forms it takes rather than in the general functions it performs.

This may be what gives law its family resemblance character. Starting with a relatively stable set of functions that law performs, but that do not distinguish law from other social phenomena, we can appreciate what led Green to conclude that law is more distinguished from other social phenomena by the ways in which it performs those functions (its form).[70] Yet those ways are themselves quite varied across instances and can't provide the differentiation that Green hopes for. This leads us back to seeing the functions as basic to any adequate explanation (*pace* Green), even if they are not unique to law, while still looking to sociology to provide data on the various cultural implementations and more specific functions that individual laws serve.

There will need to be a kind of reflective equilibration between the particular, empirical reports and the general, conceptual refinements. Part of the job of the legal philosopher is to arbitrate among empirical reports of particular functions that law performs to say which are important in that they further illuminate our concept or push that concept to incorporate more instances. Such determinations are to be made on the basis of what aids in our self-understanding, especially regarding what sets law apart from other institutions in the particular way that it alters norms that apply to us and for what general purposes it does so. In so doing, the legal philosopher fits these results together with the improving philosophical understandings of institutions, conventions, authority, practical normativity, etc.

Now, one might think that explanations of law in terms of its functions would perform both tasks: give us an understanding of what kind of thing it is as well as show what sets it apart from others of that kind. However, I have argued against seeing law as a functional kind, something whose function individuates it among other things. The most general functions performed by law as a kind of thing are unlikely to be terribly unique to law (although

[69] These are: settling disputes; coordinating and altering behavior; determining authority and how decisions are to be made; and implementing the institutions to perform these tasks. K. N. Llewellyn, 'The Normative, the Legal, and the Law-Jobs: The Problem of Juristic Method' (1940) 49 *The Yale Law Journal* 1355–400; see also Twining, *General Jurisprudence: Understanding Law from a Global Perspective* 105; Tamanaha, 'What Is "General" Jurisprudence?' 294. Twining avoids seeing even normativity as essential to law (although he admits its importance) as a way of keeping his theory sufficiently broad, preferring social ordering. While I have a hard time understanding how to achieve social ordering without normativity except through some form of mind-control or direct bodily manipulation, I don't think there is too much riding on this distinction for our purposes.

[70] See note 19 of this chapter.

nonetheless still key to its understanding). Hence the functions adduced for law are not going to be sufficient conditions for membership in the kind. Rather, I suggest that the functions we use to explain law are a precisification of those philosophical theories that help us to locate law as a species of institutionalized artifact, along with a generalization of the functions of specific instances of law as reported by social science. The work of the modest joiner is done in fitting these two together into a coherent whole.

7

Institutions, Artifacts, and Legal Norms*

There can be no doubt that law presents itself as a system of norms. The doubts arise when we start to ask how and to whom those norms apply, if ever. Much of the discussion in recent decades in attempts to answer those doubts has focused more on notions of validity than on the ontology of law itself. Sometimes the discussions of validity have centered on the kind of contextual, practice-centered sort of validity we know as legal validity. While some people have tried to show a direct relationship between that practice-centered validity and a wider sort of moral normativity, we've seen that the consensus (among both legal positivists and most modern natural lawyers) is that legal validity itself need not be directly dependent upon that wider validity.

Sometimes the discussions have been more directly about that wider validity: what makes it the case, if ever, that one has a good reason to obey (or at least conform one's behavior to) the law? Those discussions are not so much about the validity of law understood as it meeting a set of criteria internal to the practice, but about what might give law (at least some of) the authority it claims for itself. If that authority is legitimate, then the law's norms (where legitimate) are valid in a broader way. That is, where it is legitimate we have good reason to obey the law, where that reason applies to us as human beings or members of a given community and not merely as legal addressees.

The difficulties arise in the space between the two validities—how to get from a merely practice-dependent normativity to the wider normativity to which the law aspires. Some have tried to deflate this problem altogether, arguing it isn't really one for legal philosophers to concern themselves with, or that the way in which the law activates our wider norms is unproblematic since it cannot really create any new norms in that wider sphere.

In this chapter I want to explore the idea that it is for legal philosophers to investigate, and that there is a possibility for the law's creation of new

* An earlier and much abbreviated version of this chapter first appeared in George Pavlakos and Veronica Rodriguez-Blanco (eds), Reasons and Intentions in Law and Practical Agency (Cambridge University Press 2015).

practice-centered norms to imply the "robust" creation of new reasons applicable in the wider sphere.[1] I use the term "robust" to indicate that the reason is created anew, is applicable outside and regardless of the context of its creation, and is not an instance of merely changing a reason that already existed in another (e.g. conditional) form.[2] I contend that the possibility of the law creating new norms applicable more widely than merely within its own context is to be found not so much in an investigation of the validity conditions or the legitimization of legal authority by themselves, but in the relation between these facets and law's ontology. The fact that seeing law as an institutionalized abstract artifact helps to explain the nature and genesis of legal normativity is therefore an additional argument in favor of understanding law that way.

We have seen that to say that law is an institution is to say that it can create new desire-independent or non-prudential reasons for those subject to the institution. The focus on non-prudential reasons is justified because they are clearly more difficult to create anew and also because we are used to seeing the law create prudential reasons when it threatens us with coercion. In this latter case, "trigger" is more apt than "create" precisely because our basic prudential reasons are mostly already present.[3] It is merely by altering empirical and contingent facts that those prudential reasons are triggered. The focus on non-prudential reasons is also appropriate precisely because attempts to issue authoritative directives are attempts to create a duty,[4] and duties are a usual form that non-prudential reasons take.[5]

The question of who is subject to an institution is ultimately a question of what legitimates its authority, if it is the kind of institution we think of in

[1] That they are applicable outside the context of law does not imply that they represent some new category of reasons other than the moral and prudential ones we expect to see when not otherwise encumbered by context. I realized the need for this qualification after hearing some ideas from Fred Schauer on the subject.

[2] Be warned in what follows that Enoch will use this same term giving it the same connotation, but then will argue that robust reason-giving is still a form of changing a pre-existing reason.

[3] I say our prudential reasons are mostly present in the sense that, while happiness and well-being are the ultimate goals of prudential reasons, the paths we take to those goals can change throughout our lives, as our characters and abilities change, interests wax and wane, and new relationships are formed and lost. In distinguishing between the triggering and creation of reasons I am borrowing some ideas of David Enoch. See David Enoch, 'Authority and Reason-Giving' (2014) 89 *Philosophy and Phenomenological Research* 296–332; 'Reason-Giving and the Law' in L. Green and B. Leiter (eds), *Oxford Studies in Philosophy of Law, Volume 1* (Oxford University Press 2011) 1–38, although I don't follow his precise understanding of the nature of this distinction, as will become apparent.

[4] "[T]he distinctive feature of authorities is that the reasons they can give robustly are reasons of a special kind, *duties*." Enoch, 'Authority and Reason-Giving' 306, emphasis in original.

[5] Aesthetic reasons (insofar as they are still reasons for action as opposed to belief) are arguably another form in which we see non-prudential reasons; but they need not concern us here.

terms of authority.[6] But seeing precisely where the questions of its authority arise can allow us to understand who is appropriately subject to the institution such that its claims to impose reasons are valid more broadly.

We have seen that to say that law is an institution is to say that it is intentionally created by human beings to serve a purpose, which is to say that institutions are (generally) special kinds of artifacts,[7] albeit often abstract ones. We have also seen that artifacts themselves are special kinds of tools. Tools are objects created or adapted to perform a function. Artifacts are special in that they are created in order to be a specifically recognizable kind of tool.[8] Institutions are special in that their ability to perform their function is dependent upon some kind of collective recognition, and not merely on their structural features.[9] Hence institutions are understood in terms of their functionality, generally also involving the means of conferring a status that implies deontic powers. My contention here is that a deeper exploration of the relation of law's institutionality to its normativity will answer questions about what lends potentially wider robust validity to the norms it claims to impose, and solves problems about how to understand the law and legal systems as possibly authoritative.

A. The Challenge of Reasons and Normative Theory

When we talk about the way in which the law creates or manipulates our reasons, there are two different kinds of reasons about which we might be talking.[10] There are what are sometimes called "motivating reasons," reasons of which an agent is generally psychologically aware and which form the agent's beliefs about her justifications for her action or inaction. When an agent is weighing the pros and cons of an action and resolves the decision-making

[6] Any institution that can create non-prudential reasons for those subject to it without them giving their consent for every new such reason can be thought of as an authoritative institution.

[7] Amie L. Thomasson, 'Realism and Human Kinds' (2003) 67 *Philosophy and Phenomenological Research* 580–609, 592. See also Introduction, note 17.

[8] On the relation between tools and artifacts see Chapter 1 and Randall R. Dipert, *Artifacts, Art Works, and Agency* (Temple University Press 1993) 27–30. Amie Thomasson ultimately argues that artifacts do not have to be understood or identified in terms of their functions in order to provide for artworks, but many kinds still are best understood in terms of the functions they are to perform: Thomasson, 'Public Artifacts, Intentions and Norms' in M. Franssen, P. Kroes, T. A. C. Reydon, and P. E. Vermaas, (eds), *Artefact Kinds: Ontology and the Human-Made World* (Springer 2013) 45–62.

[9] Thomasson, 'Realism and Human Kinds' 585, citing John R. Searle, *Construction of Social Reality* (Free Press 1995) 124.

[10] My discussion here parallels that of Enoch, 'Reason-Giving and the Law' 15. See also Ulrike Heuer, 'Reasons and Actions and Desires' (2004) 121 *Philosophical Studies* 43–63, making the same distinction between "justificatory" and "explanatory" reasons.

process in favor of a specific option, the considerations weighed by the agent in favor of the option chosen and against the options rejected can be said to be the motivating reasons. There is some debate about whether an agent must ultimately have a specific reason in mind as the most important consideration prompting the action, or if the agent can act with multiple motivating reasons over-determining the action. It seems likely to me that both can happen on different occasions. But either view is acceptable for our purposes here.

Motivating reasons can also refer to each other and become nested in that a given goal of the agent might be a motivating reason behind adopting some particular course of action, which is ultimately directed at another goal. For example, one might take a vegetarian cooking class with the goal of becoming better at cooking vegetarian food, but with an ultimate goal of eating more healthy food.

The other kind of reason that we might be talking about is a normative reason, which serves as a justification for an action. Sometimes this is called an "objective reason," although that locution carries more metaphysical baggage.[11] One important facet, however, of such reasons is that the agent can have them without being aware of it. This is the kind of reason that one has to step aside when there is an anvil about to fall on one's head, even though one may be unaware of the anvil.

A more useful general example for our purposes is that one can be under an obligation without acknowledging or being aware of the obligation. If we believe in the existence of a critical morality in some form, then we are implying that the critical morality entails normative reasons. Even beyond morality, if there are goals that are valuable to all regardless of whether one has personally adopted that goal, then we would say that everyone has a normative reason to pursue that goal. An example here might be happiness, understood as the ultimate end of all prudential reasons.

A psychopath has moral reasons to be nice to people, but those moral reasons never serve as motivating reasons. The psychopath is only ever motivated by her beliefs about prudential reasons. Those are normative even if not moral. But the point here is that one's subjective beliefs about reasons are what motivates.

When we talk about the reason why someone did something we generally are talking about motivating reasons, which are psychologically present as

[11] Calling it an objective reason does not necessarily take a position in the debate between internalism and externalism about practical reasons (although I tend to favor the latter). One could believe that all of one's practical reasons are dependent upon one's "subjective motivational set" but that one could be unaware of all of the implications of the elements of that set. Bernard Williams, 'Internal and External Reasons' in T. R. Harrison (ed.), *Rational Action* (Cambridge University Press 1979) 17–28 at 18.

the balance of what the agent considered and concluded. These are generally attempts at capturing or reflecting the normative reasons.

Non-prudential reasons can be motivational and/or normative. If one's belief that one has a reason to make a sacrifice motivates one to do so, then that belief is serving as a motivating reason. Generally, however, our interest here in non-prudential reasons is in their normative flavor, since the main question is the relation between the institution of law and its putative creation of non-prudential reasons.

It might initially be supposed that there is no problem with the law creating objective normative reasons, in the sense that there is no doubt that the law exists in some form and hence there is some "reality" to the reasons it creates. If a given law is valid by the standards of validity in place for the jurisdiction in question, then it is "real" law and therefore provides a kind of objective reason, although it is then a separate question whether anyone should ever follow that law upon weighing all reasons in play. There is some merit to this way of seeing things (although it threatens to confuse legal reasons for real reasons), especially as it seems to reflect an understanding of institutional reality. But our question (put in terms of this sort of understanding) is whether and how a particular legal reason might break through to be a newly created objective normative reason for anyone to whom the law is addressed. To say that it is an objective reason for those to whom it is addressed is to imply that it has a moral character of trumping at least some other reasons held by them. That is, it may pre-empt at least some of those other reasons. This it may do by being a reason to exclude those other reasons.[12]

If the law can create or manipulate objective normative reasons at all, it must be only in virtue of its legitimate (i.e. justified) authority (and hence is limited to those cases in which it is legitimate). So it might initially appear that

[12] Here I am following Joseph Raz, *Practical Reason and Norms* (Hutchinson 1975) 39. I also follow Raz in believing that these reasons, where normative, operate to exclude counter-indicating reasons from being acted upon, rather than deliberated about: Raz, 'Authority and Justification' (1985) 14 *Philosophy and Public Affairs* 3–29, 7; *The Morality of Freedom* (Clarendon Press 1986) 39. The opposing view can be seen in Hart, *Essays on Bentham: Jurisprudence and Political Theory* (Clarendon Press 1982) 253; Scott J. Shapiro, 'Authority' in Jules L. Coleman and Scott Shapiro (eds), *The Oxford Handbook of Jurisprudence and Philosophy of Law* (Oxford University Press 2002) 382–439 at 406–07. Some are doubtful about the existence of exclusionary reasons, seeing such reasons as merely very weighty and thereby outweighing defeated reasons rather than excluding them. See, for example, D. S. Clarke, Jr., 'Exclusionary Reasons' (1977) 86 *Mind* 252–55; Chaim Gans, 'Mandatory Rules and Exclusionary Reasons' (1986) 15 *Philosophia: Philosophical Quarterly of Israel* 373–94; Michael S. Moore, 'Authority, Law, and Razian Reasons' (1989) 62 *Southern California Law Review* 827–96; Alexander, 'Law and Exclusionary Reasons' (1990) 18 *Philosophical Topics* 5–22; Philip Soper, *The Ethics of Deference: Learning from Law's Morals* (Cambridge University Press 2002) 38–48; Emran Mian, 'The Curious Case of Exclusionary Reasons' (2002) 15 *Canadian Journal of Law and Jurisprudence* 99–124, 105–08.

natural law has a point in its favor: the law is deficient if it is not legitimately manipulating objective reasons, which it can only do when it is legitimately authoritative. That requires that the legal directives be morally acceptable. Hence, the only way for the law to impose objective reasons would be if they are reflecting objective reasons we already have, since it is these pre-existing objective reasons that determine what is morally acceptable.

This is where Joseph Raz comes in to explain how the law could be manipulating objective reasons even where the law itself is only what humans have made it and subject only to the validity conditions that they make for it. On his view, law's claim to authority can only cover what is legally valid. However, what legitimates law's claim to authority is independent of that legal validity.

What generally determines whether the law's claim to authority is legitimate according to Raz is whether the law's directive helps the subject to conform better to the right balance of reasons that already apply to her than she would on her own.[13] (Hence it is piecemeal in that legal authority is only legitimate for certain laws, applied to certain people, at certain times.) So it is possible for there to be a putative legal directive that would reflect the right balance of reasons but for it not to be legally valid (e.g. a valuable piece of legislation that is unconstitutional), and of course for there to be a legally valid directive that doesn't reflect the right balance of reasons (for that person, under those circumstances). Legal validity therefore determines the practice-dependent normativity operative within the context of law. But authoritative legitimacy is the determinant for whether those contextually limited, practice-dependent norms succeed in having the wider "robust" normativity the law claims for them, and whether the law can therefore impart non-prudential reasons.[14]

Another way to approach this distinction is to consider the difference between an engaged and detached perspective from which to approach any normative system. Raz's example is of the meat-eater saying "You ought not to eat that; it has meat" to his vegetarian friend.[15] The meat-eater speaks to

[13] Raz, *The Morality of Freedom* (Clarendon Press 1986) 55–56; 'The Problem of Authority: Revisiting the Service Conception' (2006) 90 *Minnesota Law Review* 1003–1044 1018. The notion of the "right balance of reasons" reflects the idea that there is possibly a correct answer in many situations where we are weighing reasons in deciding how to act. The correct answer is what we would arrive at if we were giving all of the applicable normative reasons their appropriate weight.

[14] Most of the law's directives may take the *form* of non-prudential reasons. Nevertheless, where these are legally valid but not authoritatively legitimate, the most they actually do is trigger a prudential reason by threatening coercion for non-compliance.

[15] Raz, *Practical Reason and Norms* 175–76; see also *Authority of Law: Essays on Law and Morality* (Clarendon Press 1979) 156–57.

the friend from inside the normative system that the friend has embraced without thereby implying that he embraces it himself. From the external perspective, such as we might take as legal theorists, we can discuss the ways in which the norms operate on those for whom they are supposedly applicable without thereby implying that we endorse those norms.[16]

The problem of explaining legal normativity can therefore be understood initially to be particularly acute for someone with positivist inclinations. If, as positivists claim, law is merely a human creation, made by certain events and actions in which we engage, then it appears that whether something is a law is merely a matter of fact about a state of affairs in a given jurisdiction. More generally, statements of the form "Legally, one ought to ϕ" are merely asserting the existence of a state of affairs and not necessarily making any claims about what one ought to do, since it is always a separate question whether one should do it for that reason. To get from this fact about the law to the conclusion that "Here, one ought to ϕ," it seems like we need some argument to get us over the apparent fact/value gap, or at least a premise that we ought to act as the law requires.

David Enoch denies this is necessary or that this is a problem for positivists, claiming instead that law merely purports to activate pre-existing reasons that we already have.[17] This might often be the case, but it is hard to swallow this claim in its entirety as the law does appear to create wholly new reasons sometimes. By denying that the law creates new reasons whole-cloth (rather than merely activating pre-existing reasons), Enoch solves the problem of understanding the source of law's normativity. But his solution comes at the cost of saying that the law cannot create truly new reasons.

To say that the law cannot create new reasons goes against what seems to happen when the law sets forth how to make a valid will, or gives direction to Hart's "puzzled man,"[18] who is looking to the law for guidance. If I already have a reason to provide for my family and the law tells me that the way to do this is to make a will and that for my will to be recognized by the law it must be signed by two witnesses, I now have a reason I didn't have before to make a will and have it signed by two witnesses. If I am unsure about how to proceed on some matter and I turn to the law for guidance, when the law

[16] This is not to say that acceptance of the norms is necessary, since whether consent is necessary for legal norms to apply is a separate question for political philosophy. However, I will say that the answer to that question depends heavily on whatever legitimates authority. If authority can be legitimated without consent, and if that method of legitimization is open to the legal kind of authority, then consent will not be necessary for legal norms to be robustly applicable to those for whom it is legitimate.

[17] Enoch, 'Reason-Giving and the Law.'

[18] Hart, *Concept of Law* (Clarendon Press 1961) 40.

guides me on that matter it is giving me reasons I didn't have before. I am not saying that Enoch's triggering account cannot explain these examples as triggering. But as an initial matter, they seem more like new reasons than like instances of triggering.

If we return to the example of flag law,[19] the set of rules for how to treat the U.S. flag, which doesn't have any punishments for non-compliance, we can see that one who merely wants to be law-abiding in the United States now has a set of reasons for behaving a certain way toward the flag. Even someone who had the motivation to be respectful toward the flag may need the law to set forth some of the standards for that respectful treatment. If I were so motivated, I might be able to intuit that I should not burn the flag, or perhaps not let it touch the ground. But how am I supposed to know that "respecting the flag" includes folding it into a triangle with the stars and blue field showing, or that it should be on its right when displayed with other flags? It's not just that I had no way of knowing what "respecting the flag" required; it's that what consists in "respecting the flag" has been changed or partially created by the law. That kind of change creates new reasons rather than merely triggering pre-existing ones, since there were no reasons to associate those behaviors with "respecting the flag" before the law made that association.

While in some cases the law may merely be codifying pre-existing practices of respect, which could be discoverable by doing some kind of historical research, in other cases it may actually be creating those practices of respect by articulating them for the first time. Wherever the law is not capturing pre-existing behavioral standards but rather creating those standards, it will be creating reasons (and not merely activating reasons) for those who are motivated or have good normative reasons to comply.

After distinguishing the giving of normative (as opposed to motivating) reasons into three groups: epistemic reason-giving (reminding someone of a pre-existing reason that already applied); triggering reason-giving (activating a reason that the person already had but was not yet applicable); and "robust" reason-giving (creating a reason that didn't exist before),[20] Enoch claims that a merely legal reason is kind of like an imaginary friend, in that the most it can be on its own is a reason in the context of a practice.[21] This is akin to the idea that the rules of a game are only reasons for those already committed to playing the game. This is not particular to law, since any practice can create

[19] Flag Code, 4 United States Code §§ 1–10.

[20] Enoch, 'Reason-Giving and the Law' 4–6. As discussed shortly, he eventually claims that robust reason-giving is really just a special case of triggering reasons. David Enoch, 'Giving Practical Reasons' (2011) 11 *Philosophers' Imprint* 1–22, 9.

[21] Enoch, 'Reason-Giving and the Law' 18.

such reasons inside its own context. If we join him in seeing a clear distinction between legal reasons and real (normative) reasons, we can understand the force of Raz's point that legal reasons are claims to impose or reflect normative reasons.[22] Sometimes those claims might be true and sometimes they are false.

Law, seen this way, is a practice-context that has contextually bound reasons for people who are committed to that context in some way.[23] For those already in the game and committed to playing it, the legal rules can be real rules to the extent that the commitment is morally valid or binding. This isn't to say that once you are subject to the law in one area you are committed to playing the legal game and therefore must see those contextual reasons as real; rather, as with many other contexts, you may sometimes be bound and other times may not be bound. The rules themselves might in some cases be reasons not to participate in the context, especially if they lead one away from what one has good "real" reasons to do.

A context-dependent reason is a kind of putative reason. It becomes a real normative reason when one is in that context and (possibly) endorses or otherwise becomes committed to it. But, *pace* Enoch, contexts are not quite the same as the realm of the imagination. Some putative contextual reasons may succeed in being real reasons regardless of whether one endorses the context. We don't say moral reasons are like imaginary friends precisely because everyone has a real reason to be moral, regardless of whether they have accepted anything about the moral "context."[24] Law is somewhat weird because when seen from outside it looks more like a context such as a game, while at the same time it appears to be making the claim that it is more like morality in providing real non-prudential reasons. It is that weirdness that is and should be of interest to legal philosophers and calls for our understanding. Why should we take this general claim on the part of law seriously at all, and what about law seems to necessitate this claim?

B. Enoch's Answer

Enoch argues that robust reason-giving such as we see with law is merely a special instance of triggering reasons.[25] His argument is based on the idea that no one can give a robust reason unless the recipient already has a conditional

[22] See, for example, Raz, *Authority of Law* 30.

[23] As mentioned above, this commitment may not need to be voluntary, but it might be.

[24] The scare quotes here are merely to suggest that one is always in the moral context.

[25] For a slightly different line of attack on these ideas of Enoch, see Veronica Rodriguez-Blanco, 'Reasons in Action v Triggering-Reasons: A Reply to Enoch on Reason-Giving and Legal Normativity' (2013) 7 *Problema. Anuario de Filosofia y Teoria de Derecho* 3–25.

reason to treat the issuance as a reason.[26] If my telling you to do something can actually give you a reason to do it, this must be because you already have a reason to do that thing if and when I tell you to do it. Hence my telling you to do something merely activates the condition precedent of your pre-existing conditional reason.[27] The upshot of this is that even instances of what Enoch thinks can be considered robust reason-giving are actually still merely triggering these conditional reasons.[28]

This view strikes me as problematic in that it appears to suggest that one is born with all the reasons one will ever have in life (at least in some conditional form). There is something trivially true but also unilluminating about the claim that every reason is conditioned upon *some* conditional precedent being true. (My reason to be happy is conditioned upon my being born.) To say that all instances of robust reason-giving are merely instances of triggering because one could come up with some antecedent conditional statement that was already true is a little bit like saying that nothing completely new ever happens because we can always come up with some statement about the past that was already true and included some conditional causal antecedents about the event in question. It's not completely new because it was already the case that it would happen if the causal antecedent did.

In correspondence, Enoch has clarified that he thinks one is born with all of the "ultimate, grounding reasons" that one has in life, and that this group includes all of one's conditional reasons, with "new" reasons arriving as a result of those conditions being triggered. This has a number of implications that strike me as sufficiently strange to argue against accepting his view.

One strange implication is that the conditional reason: "I have a reason to take extra care to ensure the wellbeing of H, if I marry her" and "I have a reason to take extra care to ensure the wellbeing of H" (where H is my wife) refer to two different reasons. We will see shortly that it makes more sense to think of both of these statements as referring to the same reason.

Another strange implication is that I am born with the first (conditional) reason, although admittedly not the second. This seems to imply that I have a conditional reason to take extra care to ensure the wellbeing of everyone on the planet (or at least those I could possibly marry).[29] That is, it was true at

[26] Enoch, 'Giving Practical Reasons' (2011) 11 *Philosophers' Imprint* 1–22, 9–10.

[27] What I call "contextual reasons" could be understood as conditional reasons, but not in Enoch's sense, with which I will take issue shortly. Contextual reasons are only operative within a given context. Enoch treats conditional reasons as a separate kind of reason, one which mirrors all existing reasons and exists independently of whether the condition is satisfied.

[28] More on what distinguishes this subclass of robust reason-giving later in the chapter.

[29] I probably have a non-conditional reason to take some care to ensure the wellbeing of everyone on the planet, but only a reason to take *extra* care of a small subset of those people.

my birth that I had a reason to take extra care of H, if I marry her, but it was also true at my birth that I had a reason to take extra care of A, if I married her; B, if I married her; C, if I married her; etc. I agree that these *statements* may have been true at my birth. However, we will see that these statements weren't referring to any reasons that were valid for me at the time.

A third strange implication is that the grounds for any unconditional reason are always therefore a vast number of conditional reasons that have the unconditional reason as a consequent. When I think of the ground for a reason, I think of a more ultimate value that serves as the justification for that reason. I do not see how a tacked-on condition precedent is really a ground for that reason, even if it captures a set of empirical facts that would make the reason valid for me. We need to make a distinction here between a more general reason that serves as a ground for more particular ones, and a pre-condition that must be present for a reason to exist (or apply). It seems reasonable to suppose that I am born with a reason to take extra care to ensure the wellbeing of those with whom I form a close relationship. This is the ground for my "conditional reason" to take extra care to ensure the wellbeing of H, if I marry her. But once that condition is met, the reason is not distinct from my reason to take extra care to ensure the wellbeing of H. The statements "I have a reason to take extra care to ensure the wellbeing of H, if I marry her" and "I have a reason to take extra care to ensure the wellbeing of H" are distinct, but they refer to the same reason once the antecedent is satisfied.

The existence and applicability of the generalized grounding reason to take extra care to ensure the wellbeing of anyone with whom I form a close relationship is what makes it true at my birth that for A, B, C, if I form a close relationship with that person then I will have a reason to ensure the person's wellbeing. But those reasons never come into existence (or at least never apply to me) where those antecedents are not satisfied. They are true conditional statements about reasons that are never actualized.

I believe what is multiplying reasons for Enoch is the assumption that every logically distinct true proposition that describes a reason refers to a distinct reason. But I can describe the same reason in logically distinct ways. My reason to take extra care to ensure the wellbeing of any woman who becomes my wife and my reason to take extra care to ensure the wellbeing of the woman who does become my wife are the same reason.

Of course, there are unique things about the particular woman who became my wife that give me additional distinctive reasons that are particular to her. But on Enoch's taxonomy, I would have already had an additional conditional copy of those reasons as well before I ever met her.

Consider the following: On Enoch's view the statement "I have a reason to take extra care of H, if I marry her" was true upon my birth, although

"I have a reason to take extra care of H" was not true upon my birth. That proves to him that these are two distinct reasons, and that triggering is a form of reason creation. I claim, however, that both propositions refer to the same reason, even though one proposition was true at my birth and the other was not. The first proposition was true at my birth but the reason it described was not yet created because the things that had to happen to create the reason had not yet taken place. The proposition was true because it correctly refers to the creation conditions for that reason. My picture, in which there is only one reason, is preferable to a picture that needlessly introduces an extra category of reasons (conditional) and thereby two reasons where one would suffice.[30] This consideration should tip the scales even if the strange implications I noted above did not.

Hence a "conditional reason" with an untrue (or not yet true) condition precedent is not (yet) a reason. This shouldn't be so surprising. Assuming I can legitimately give my military subordinate a reason to clean parts of the barracks by ordering her to do so, I haven't yet changed her reasons for action by saying to her "You must clean the latrine if I order you to do so." But when I say "I order you to clean the latrine," I have given her a new reason for action, even if that is grounded on pre-existing general reasons to follow my orders regarding cleaning parts of the barracks.

While much of what I have to say about the ontology of legal norms may work even if one agrees with Enoch's picture of triggering and conditional norms (and I admit there may be other reasons to reject some of my considerations and the parsimony point that I haven't considered), I think it is important to note the reasonableness of a picture that allows for the potential for law to create norms entirely anew.

Independently of its relation to triggering reasons, Enoch gives a communicated-intention-based account of robust reason-giving.[31] This is valuable when we remember that artifacts are special in communicating the intentions of their creators and that law is a type of artifact. There are three parts to his account: I must intend to give you a reason to ϕ and communicate that intention to you; I must intend that you recognize my intention;

[30] One implication of this parsimony about reasons is that I have serious doubts about the sense of saying there is already existing a reason to (ϕ, if you ask me to ϕ), although it makes more sense to say that I could have a reason to do whatever you ask. The reason to do whatever you ask is a reason to show some kind of general deference to your wishes. That can serve as the ground to ϕ once you ask me to. But before you ask me to ϕ, I don't yet have any reason to ϕ. The reason to ϕ is a particularized one tailored to the act, your request, and the circumstances. You have to ask in order for me to have it. The reason to do whatever you ask is generalized and something I can have before you make any request of me.

[31] Enoch, 'Authority and Reason-Giving' 307–10.

and I must intend your reason to ϕ to depend on your recognition of my communicated intention to give you a reason to ϕ.

The worry then arises whether anything other than "persons or person-like organs can play the role of an authority."[32] That is, the ability to give a robust non-prudential reason such as a moral duty depends on the communication of an intention to do so, which is needed in order to distinguish the possibility of successful creation of duties from merely triggering pre-existing non-prudential reasons. However, building in this communicated-intention requirement seems to mean that only other people (or bodies) can be authorities, not the law itself.[33]

Of course, one easy solution to this problem is to say simply that the authority is vested in the law-maker, whatever person or body that might be, and that talk of the authority of law is merely metaphorical. However, this solution doesn't sit well when we think of the antiquity of some legal norms that are still apparently binding, especially when some of those legal norms are borrowed directly from jurisdictions which we would not think meet our normative requirements for political legitimacy (as is the case with the few remaining American legal norms whose legal validity is sourced in medieval British law).

This is precisely where the metaphysical questions about law become important. A better understanding of law's ontology will solve the problem of how a communicated intention can exist and possibly be robustly reason-giving when there is no identifiable human being or body we would identify as having the authority to address us directly. Creators' intentions about the content of the law and their communication to us are bound up into the law by its artifactual nature; their applicability across the ages is explained by its institutionality.

C. Authority

The answer to why we should take seriously law's claim to be more like morality in having the power to create new reasons will be found partly in understanding the metaphysics of law and partly in the nature of authority and what (if anything) legitimates law's claim to it. There is thus a two-tiered

[32] Ibid 312.

[33] To be fair, Enoch is somewhat agnostic about whether the law can communicate the necessary intentions to robustly give reasons: Enoch, 'Reason-Giving and the Law' 30, saying that if the law is capable of robustly giving reasons, it must be carrying the complex intentions of the legislature.

answer to the issue of legal normativity. The first tier is the contextual normativity of the law that arises from its institutionality, or more precisely its functionality and instrumental value. Given the particular goals a specific law is designed to achieve, those who share those goals (or have reason to) have an instrumental reason to conform with or enable it. The other tier is whether a given legal norm is legitimately normative in a wider, critical sense, which is a question that is answered by whatever legitimates authority.[34] If Raz is right then this question gets a piecemeal answer, determined by whether the legal norm gets the individual to comply better with the right balance of reasons that already apply to him (including moral reasons but also extending beyond).[35]

Both tiers incorporate issues of practical reasoning, but in different ways: the contextual norms are contingent upon the adoption of whatever ends are in question and whether those ends and the means chosen to pursue them are adopted according to institutionally cognized procedures and in accord with an important subset of other institutional norms. Their wider legitimacy depends upon whether the legal means imposed by legislation or judicial interpretation are sufficient for accomplishing those ends, as well as the ultimate value of those ends and whether they can be pursued in the manner chosen without undermining other important values. Where critical norms apply, they are necessary conclusions of practical reason.

The contextual kind of normativity is only operative on those already inside the system and to the extent that it doesn't conflict with broader reasons that might trump whatever the law is saying. That is, the instrumental value of law is only appreciable by those who have adopted whatever ends are served by law.

This is true at the level of law as a genre, such that whatever general goods law serves might not be endorsed by a given individual. Hence law's norms are not operative in their instrumental capacity on people who don't endorse and value those general goods. It is true at the level of legal systems such that certain systems might have more unique ends that they serve, which are likely to be spelled out in their constitutions or other fundamental laws. If one doesn't endorse those ends, then one will not see that particular legal system's norms as binding unless one is already endorsing the ends of law in general such that one has a reason to adopt the norms of any system not otherwise undermining the general goals or wider moral norms. It is finally even true at the level of individual legal norms in that one can feel that the

[34] As mentioned previously, this wider sense is not meant to suggest a new class of reasons besides moral and prudential reasons.

[35] Raz, *The Morality of Freedom* 74, 80.

purposes articulated for a given piece of legislation or judicial decision are not sufficiently in keeping with the communal values or goals one sees as the reason for binding oneself to the system. Alternatively, an abject failure of the legal means adopted to pursue the purposes for which they were instituted may also undermine the contextual normativity.

Hence at every level of legality, there are areas of success and failure in both ends and means that have implications for the operation of legal norms understood as merely contextual or practice-based norms. It is more than likely that endorsing the practice will encourage, if not demand, that one still abide by the legal norms with which one does not agree or which one sees as not being valuable or capable of success, just as in a game one must still abide by the decisions of the referee, even where one does not agree with those decisions.

But there are also going to be cases in which one can reject a particular contextual or practice-based legal norm while not extricating oneself from the context entirely. Cases of civil disobedience are likely examples here, as are more mundane situations such as running a red light in the middle of nowhere with no one around. One does not say in such cases that the legal norms do not apply to one's situation. Rather, one says that one remains within the system while denying the law has legitimate authority over one's actions in that situation. (Or one admits to have transgressed a legitimate norm.) At another level of generality, one can endorse the value of the legal enterprise while saying that the entire system in which one finds oneself is corrupt or otherwise not in keeping with the legal project such that none of its directives are contextually binding.

As an explanation of legal normativity once bound into the context or practice, this may work well, but the deeper problem of the fact/value gap has to do with the basis on which one ought to so bind oneself. That is, what, if any, are the independent reasons for endorsing whatever ends law serves, for entering the context and participating in the practice such that those practice-norms become applicable? After all, the law claims to bind everyone in its jurisdiction with every applicable legal norm. And it does now seem likely that this claim is false as it is made. Very few people, if any, are morally bound by every legal norm in the jurisdiction(s) in which they find themselves. There are plenty of norms that are legally valid in every jurisdiction but whose application in general or upon specific people at specific times are morally unwarranted, and hence (following Raz's view that a legal norm is a claim to be a moral norm) are not morally binding. So on what basis can we say that anyone is required to enter the legal practice-context at all?

While this question might be more aptly answered by political philosophy, one kind of answer can be seen in Raz's theory of authority. Essentially, the question is what legitimates the authority that law claims over us. If anything legitimates it, then to whatever extent that authority extends, we have a good moral reason for entering into the legal practice-context and seeing its internal norms as morally binding. That is then the way out of the problem posed by the fact/value gap. At the bottom, there isn't a dependence of a robust norm on a fact at all. Rather, we have non-context-dependent reasons for entering into the legal context and being bound by its (applicable and legitimate) norms whenever its authority is legitimate.

If someone can provide a pre-emptive or exclusionary reason, then that person is authoritative in giving that reason. Pre-emptive reasons are already present in other spheres, such as morality. The fact that stealing is morally wrong is generally a pre-emptive reason against my stealing something I want but cannot afford; it is both a reason not to steal directly and it is a reason not to act on reasons I have to steal (such as my desire notwithstanding my poverty).

Practical authorities differ in that they can create new pre-emptive reasons merely by fiat.[36] If their authority is legitimate (in that circumstance), then they are successful in creating a new pre-emptive reason. If the law was merely changing empirical circumstances so as to activate pre-existing reasons as Enoch claims, then the mere say-so of a legal official (or majority of a voting body of them) could not create new pre-emptive reasons.

To understand this we need to know a little bit about authority. Those already familiar with the literature on authority might find this introduction a bit redundant, but some might be seeing it for the first time or be in need of a brief refresher.

Authority generally comes in two flavors. One is called theoretical or epistemic authority. This is the notion of authority applied to experts in their field, but can be broadened to apply to anyone who has greater knowledge than you in a situation in which that knowledge would be useful or valuable to you. When we say that someone is an authority on a given subject, we are likely using this notion of authority. Generally speaking, such experts give you a good reason to believe what they tell you to be the case when speaking on their subject of expertise. Since their knowledge is being made accessible to you through their reports, we might say that you generally have a fairly good justification for believing what they tell you.

[36] Enoch notes that we can give each other exclusionary reasons by, for example, offering something of value on the condition that the offeree not engage in a contemplated behavior for a specific reason (like offering someone praise for giving to a charity so long as she doesn't make the gift because it will make her look good): Enoch, 'Authority and Reason-Giving' 318. But the claim to pre-empt *all* contrary reasons seems unique to cases of authority and morality. What is distinctive about practical authority is that it does so by fiat.

The other flavor of authority is what is known as practical or deontic authority. This is the authority of someone who has the right to direct your behavior.[37] We sometimes say that such a person is "in" authority rather than that they "are" an authority. Generally speaking, rights and duties are a package deal, such that someone having a right implies that someone else has a duty. We can therefore somewhat loosely say that if a practical authority has the right to direct my behavior, then I have a duty to comply with those directions.[38]

While the theoretical authority gives you good reason to believe what she says is true, the practical authority gives you good reason to act in accord with her directives. The most a theoretical authority can do to control your behavior is to offer advice based on the expertise that she has. But a (legitimate) practical authority controls your behavior by issuing directives with which you then have a duty to comply. Usually the authority of a doctor is theoretical authority, and the most the doctor can do is give advice based on your interest in staying healthy. While that advice sometimes might sound like a command, we don't say that the doctor has any right to control the behavior of other people.[39]

Some people might be in the position of being both at the same time. One's parents are almost certainly both at the same time, at least when one is relatively young. Although it is also possible that their mode of interacting with you reflects the kind of authority they are exercising. Sometimes your parents issue commands and sometimes they merely give advice.

Of the two flavors, practical authority is of more immediate interest for questions about legal normativity. When we talk about practical authority we are likely thinking about conditions that legitimate it. We sometimes do talk about de facto authorities: those who have power over us (in the non-normative sense of being able to compel us), how they came to have the power to enforce their will upon others or came to be treated as having the right to direct the behavior of others. However, the difference between

[37] On the Hohfeldian analysis, this is best understood as a power since "right" is ambiguous: Wesley Newcomb Hohfeld, *Fundamental Legal Conceptions as Applied in Judicial Reasoning and Other Legal Essays* (Yale University Press 1919) 50–60.

[38] Technically, the content of the right and duty would have to be the same. Hence it would be more correct to say that I have a duty to comply with the authority's directives where the authority has a right to have me comply with her directives. But the idea of the authority having a right to direct the behavior of subjects is common in the literature, so we will stick with that formulation here.

[39] One counterexample might be in cases of mental incapacitation, where a diagnosing doctor might have the right to direct the behavior of the patient and others who are in a position to restrain the patient against his will. However, even this is probably better understood as a delegated legal authority, a power given to doctors by law.

someone who may be in authority and someone who is *merely* exercising (non-normative) power is the claim of right. The robber in the street does not claim to have a right to take your money, just the power to force you to comply by threat of harm. The tax official, however, claims a right to take your money independently of the threats she may use to enforce compliance. Where the claim is false, the person is just exercising power.

If what distinguishes practical authority from mere power is the fact that the former involves a right to exercise that power, a right to direct the behavior of others that is coupled with a duty on their part to comply, then the very conditions that bestow practical authority on those who have it are the conditions that would legitimate any claim to it. Hence the real issue for any theory of practical authority is to determine what its legitimacy conditions are.

This is where the disagreements tend to start. Some deny the possibility of anything legitimating practical authority at all,[40] arguing that individuals can never (justifiably) give up their autonomy or that all supposed instances of practical authority are just veiled threats and advice about how to avoid more unpleasant consequences. But others find that there is a case to be made for sometimes saying that others have the right to direct one's behavior.

Take the example of one's parents. It is certainly plausible to say that, even as adults, we have some duty to comply with the reasonable directives of our parents (even if that duty is easily outweighed). Perhaps that duty is based on the fact that we owe our existences and lives to them; perhaps it is based on requirements to honor them such as those spelled out in the Ten Commandments or the Laws of Manu. This is not to say that there is nothing they can do to lose that right. And it is not to say that the right applies to whatever they might tell you to do. But neither of these qualifications should be surprising, as one's background rights and moral duties can come in to trump impositions on them even where those impositions are sometimes otherwise justified.

So if a robust possibility of legitimate practical authority remains open, the big question is what legitimates it. Some political and moral theorists hold that there are ways in which we might voluntarily submit to the will of another and, once having done so, we are then duty-bound to conform to his directives. But this voluntary option doesn't apply to all instances of authority that seem potentially legitimate (think of the example of one's parents again), nor does it reflect what actually appears to happen in many political contexts.

[40] Robert Paul Wolff, *In Defense of Anarchism* (University of California Press 1998 (1970)); Heidi M. Hurd, 'Challenging Authority' (1991) 100 *The Yale Law Journal* 1611–77.

Raz's insight is that there is a way to base practical authority on a wider view of theoretical authority without reducing the former to the latter, as done by those who deny the possibility of legitimate practical authority. The idea is that practical authority is generally legitimate where the authority is basing its directives on reasons that already apply to you and when following that directive would get you to comply with the correct balance of those reasons better than you would do if left to your own devices.[41]

While there is copious literature on practical authority attempting to spell out its legitimating conditions, I cite Raz's theory as a convenient and, to my mind, fairly sound view on the matter. It is also one that gives legitimating conditions for practical authority more generally, which are then applied to law. Therefore, it doesn't presuppose a specific political or substantive moral viewpoint on which to rest the legitimization of legal authority.[42]

What is distinctive about legal authority as one form of practical authority is that it claims unlimited authority over anyone and anything within the jurisdiction to which the legal system applies.[43] Other forms of practical authority, even one's parents', tend to be much more circumscribed in their claims and may not make claims of authority at all, even when they would be legitimate.

That claim to unlimited authority is almost never true in Raz's theory since the legitimization of any authoritative directive must be done on a piecemeal, case-by-case basis. Even if Raz's isn't one's favorite theory, or one believes that a specific political belief or organization is necessary to legitimate legal authority, the point here is that the way to say which legal directives are robustly normative in a morally binding sense is to have an answer that stems from whatever it is that legitimates the authority of those directives.

This isn't a solution to the is/ought problem because it calls for a moral theory to legitimate those directives, a theory that would have a normative claim about where and when authoritative directives are legitimately binding. Hence we would certainly have a normative premise in an argument about what one ought to do. But it is a solution for the legal positivist trying to explain how a merely fact-based legal system could still have the potential for legitimately morally robust demands that it places upon its subjects.

[41] Raz, *The Morality of Freedom* 47, 53.

[42] Raz distinguishes legal authority from political authority, saying the former is both narrower and broader than the latter: Raz, *Between Authority and Interpretation: On the Theory of Law and Practical Reason* (Oxford University Press 2009) 127 (noting that legal obligations sometimes have nothing to do with the political aspect of the community and that political obligations may require more than the law actually requires such as a duty to support the government). But in most of the literature the two are generally treated interchangeably.

[43] Joseph Raz, *Practical Reason and Norms* (Oxford University Press 1999 (1975)) 150–53.

D. Obedience and Compliance

To obey a directive is to conform one's behavior to the directive with the directive itself as the primary motivating reason. To (merely) comply is to conform one's behavior to the directive with other reasons (or none) as the primary motivators. Raz's theory does not require one to obey a legitimate directive; one need only comply with it.[44] This is seen in the fact that a legitimate directive does not exclude the reasons one may already have to act in conformity with the directive.[45] That is, Raz's theory is that where authoritative directives are morally legitimate, they pre-empt or exclude the subjects' existing *contrary* reasons: reasons she may have to act contrary to the directive. Since they only exclude contrary reasons, if the subject had other reasons to act in conformity with the law, then those reasons are still permitted to be acted upon. But where the subject does not have any of those independent reasons to act in conformity with the law, it would appear that the only remaining reason that is possible for acting in accord with the law is the directive itself and the fact of its moral legitimacy.

To be clear: this is very likely to be an exceedingly rare set of circumstances. In general, since for a directive to be authoritative it must be based upon or reflect dependent reasons that the subject already has, it is very likely that there will be plenty of pre-legal reasons to act in the way that the law directs. (They are "pre-legal" in the sense that they existed before that particular directive was issued, but they may still be other kinds of legal reasons that are serving as dependent reasons.) Hence, in most cases, the most the law does is trigger or activate pre-existing reasons when it issues directives.

Take a common example of a coordination problem that the law helps to solve, such as which side of the street to drive on. By picking a side, the law makes one solution to the coordination problem salient, thereby activating, triggering, or precisifying the pre-existing reason to drive on the side that everyone else is driving on. (The law is not here performing what Enoch would call epistemic reason-giving since, at least if we imagine a new law where it is not yet a common practice to drive on one side or the other, it is making it the case that a given side is the correct side by fiat.) So, in most cases, the law's apparent claim that one should follow it merely because it is the law falls on partially deaf ears. We follow it for our own reasons, although

[44] Joseph Raz, *The Authority of Law: Essays on Law and Morality* (2nd edn, Oxford University Press 2009 (1979)) 144–45.

[45] Joseph Raz, 'Postema on Law's Autonomy and Public Practical Reasons: A Critical Comment' (1998) 4 *Legal Theory* 1, 17 n. 39; *Authority of Law* 144.

perhaps it is because those reasons are telling us to conform to the law's directive on that issue.

Yet, there are possible rare cases in which, by excluding all contrary reasons, the law has left us with only one possible reason in favor of compliance, and that is the legal directive itself. This would be a case in which it is truly possible to obey the law merely because it is the law, since there would be no other reason for compliance. These are rare precisely because we have to assume that contrary dependent reasons which are being reflected by the directive (which *ex hypothesi* is legitimate) are being excluded by them at the same time. This would happen whenever the dependent reasons would militate in favor of a given course of behavior, but merely by stepping in the law gives a legitimate pre-emptive reason against that course of behavior.

An analogy along Enoch's lines of thought might help here. Enoch's example of robust reason-giving is that of a request.[46] The request provides a reason beyond any antecedent or ancillary reason to act so as to please the requester for instrumental reasons such as career enhancement.

The problem with this particular example is that it doesn't bear any direct relation to a case of authority, so we need to see an example that displays issues of authority at the same time as being a case of robust reason-giving. Imagine that one does have a moral duty to respect one's parent and that this moral duty has not been defeated or out-weighed more generally by prior misbehavior of the parent. It is certainly reasonable, as many cultures maintain, to imagine that even adults maintain this duty of respect for one's parent.

Now imagine the parent makes a demand for you to perform a behavior that doesn't involve the violation of a moral duty but does involve acting against all one's prudential reasons in a minor way. We have to imagine that the prudential reasons are rather minor lest the parent's demand itself lose its legitimacy. Perhaps the parent has just perfected the art of cigar-rolling and instructs you to try one,[47] although you are not a smoker. Imagining there are no issues with workplace drug-testing or health insurance agreements that would be violated, the only major reason not to comply is that the cigar poses a danger to your health. But this one instance would be relatively minor considering that you are not a regular smoker. The idea is that the only reason you have for trying the cigar is the demand of your parent. If the duty to respect your parents would extend to this example, then it would seem that the demand has robustly given you a reason to smoke the cigar.

[46] Enoch, 'Authority and Reason-Giving' 299.

[47] While this is more likely to come in the form of a request, we need to raise the request to the level of a demand in order for it to be a clear case of the exercise of authority. I'm sure many readers

If we can imagine the demand as an instance of a legitimately authoritative directive on Raz's model, it is because we have dependent reasons that include honoring our parents' wishes that are reflected here and we are assuming that the correct balance of reasons requires that you smoke the cigar. Yet before the demand was made, there was no reason to smoke the cigar, and the demand hasn't merely altered some empirical fact that triggered a pre-existing reason. The duty to respect one's parents was already present.[48] If authority can be brought into Enoch's picture of robust reason-giving then it appears possible for the law to display instances of it as well.

While this may be a rare occurrence, glimpses can be seen whenever someone obeys the law merely because it is the law and holds it to be legitimate, even when their other reasons militate against what the law is telling them to do. One example of this might be stopping at a red light in an area one knows is deserted (imagine it has been evacuated). Where all chances of accident or detection have been removed, many will simply run the light. But some will still stop and they are likely so acting because it is the law that is giving them a reason to stop.

Under Raz's theory, what makes this possible is the fact that when it is successfully getting a subject to comply with the correct balance of reasons better than she would do if left to her own devices, the subject thereby gets a moral reason to obey the law. It must be a moral reason for it to be an instance of robust non-prudential reason-giving when it is not merely triggering a pre-existing moral or prudential reason.

E. The Authority of Institutions

We now have more information in order to answer questions about why legal normativity is an important issue for legal philosophers, and also more of a window into how it is legitimated. If we start with an account of law's institutionality, we have an explanation of how it comes to assert the ability to impose non-prudential reasons on those subject to it. That is an aspect of institutions more generally.

can easily imagine a parent issuing what is actually a demand in a form that sounds superficially like a mere request.

[48] There is a problem with this analysis in that it is possible to understand that the demand triggers or precisifies the duty to respect one's parents. But on Enoch's analysis this would still be an instance of robust reason-giving in his terminology and we will stick to his picture in order to see how the law could display a robust instance of reason-giving.

As mentioned earlier, institutions can be understood as a subclass of artifacts, although institutions may be abstract in that they might not be identical to whatever concrete entities they may be associated with. Institutions like universities are not identical to any set of physical entities such as their students, faculty, administrators, buildings, or land. Laws and legal systems are certainly abstract institutions in that they are not identical with the people constituting the legal officials, the words written in books or scrolls of law, or the geographic area of their jurisdiction.[49]

Even if abstract institutions frequently confer status on physical objects, the object should not be confused for the institution that conferred the status. Money is an institution; a piece of currency is not, although we can say whether a given piece of paper is money is an institutional fact about the paper. This is why John Searle speaks of institutional facts more than institutions themselves.

As we have already seen, under Searle's theory an institutional fact is created by the collectively intended application of a status function by using a constitutive rule.[50] That status function conveys deontic powers, which is to say that the bearer of the status can "provide desire-independent reasons for action,"[51] including non-prudential reasons. The key is the collective acceptance of some set of conditions, which, if fulfilled, brings the institution into existence. The immediate questions for us here are what are the normative grounds for that collective acceptance, that is, what is a good reason to accept those conditions; how wide must that collective acceptance be; and how does the status function convey deontic powers.

The status function generally carries deontic powers that apply to anyone within the ambit of the institution. The constitutive rules themselves set the conditions for membership and hence applicability of the institution's norms. Some institutions are relatively static and do not require much alteration after their creation. In these, there may not be much room for roles or offices. But in other, more dynamic institutions, there will generally be roles or offices, themselves creations of the institution and which carry deontic powers to alter the (institutionally context-bound) normative space of those subject to the institution.

[49] See Thomasson, 'Realism and Human Kinds' 587.

[50] Searle, *Construction of Social Reality* 23–28. Remember that status functions are akin to the mathematical use of the term "function" and not to the explanatory sense on which we are focusing in general. Also the constitutive rules creating institutional facts for Searle tend to take the form "X counts as Y in context C." Thomasson broadens this to account for abstract institutional entities, which are not applied to pre-existing objects: Thomasson, 'Realism and Human Kinds' 587–88. Searle has also noted the need not to be bound by this particular form, in part for the same reasons: Searle, *Making the Social World: The Structure of Human Civilization* (Oxford University Press 2010) 19–20.

[51] Searle, *Making the Social World* 23.

In a legal institution, those deontic powers are themselves legal creations and are to be characterized as such. (As noted above, the law itself is a kind— or "genre"—of institution, but also special in that one of its key functions is the creation of other institutions; legal systems are therefore institution-generating institutions.) The deontic powers are held by officials, or possibly by individual laws and regulations themselves if they can operate without official intervention.[52] They have a system or practice-based normativity applicable to anyone subject to that system.

As detailed above, we can analyze that normativity in two ways. The first way is merely in terms of the system itself as a practice and seeing the normativity it imposes through the creation of its institutional deontic powers. In this way we can analyze legal normativity in an external but engaged fashion, speaking about legal reasons as applying to whomever the system claims it applies, treating those legal subjects as practice participants. In doing so we are thinking of legal normativity as akin to the rules of a game or another social practice in which one may or may not participate. (It is far from unusual for other social institutions and practices to make normative claims upon more people than those who belong to it or acknowledge the authority of the institution to do so. Organized religions are certainly one example.)

The other way to analyze that normativity is to ask what might give someone a robust reason for being bound by those system norms. This is to inquire into the conditions for legitimating the claims that the law makes that all its directives are morally binding on those to whom they are directed. If they are truly morally binding, then those who are subject to them have a good reason to see themselves as bound, whether or not they acknowledge that reason.

Whether the norms are viewed contextually or robustly, however, what is important here is that it is possible for institutions to be created anew, usually by a kind of declaration that is collectively accepted.[53] The new status that is created consists partially in the deontic powers that are conferred by the acceptance of the constitutive rule that creates that new status. This self-referentiality is an important feature of how collective acceptance confers status and creates norms. For something to have the properties of a given institutional kind, it must be believed to be of that kind; the belief that it is of that kind makes it so.[54] Hence, part of what it is to have an

[52] I am here imagining some kind of system that automatically generates and sends a violation notice to motorists who trip a camera when running a red light, where the notice is issued without human intervention.

[53] Thomasson, 'Realism and Human Kinds' 589; Searle, *Making the Social World* 85–86.

[54] Thomasson, 'Realism and Human Kinds' 585, citing Searle, *Construction of Social Reality* 32. See also Thomasson, 'Artifacts and Human Concepts' 58, noting that any member of an essentially artifactual kind must be the result of an intention to create that sort of artifact and therefore exhibits the same kind of self-referentiality Searle mentions.

institutional status is the ability to create new reasons for those subject to the institution.

If the institution persists, then the new reasons it creates for those subject to it may also persist. Since the status and the new reasons created by the deontic powers are so closely linked, we can say that part of what it is for the institution to persist is for the reasons it creates to continue to apply. Conversely, by the time none of its created reasons any longer apply to anyone, the institution has ceased to exist (although other associated artifacts might continue to exist).

With these considerations we have the beginnings of an answer to the question of why reasons created by people long dead and not authoritative (over us) in the properties they had when alive can continue to be applicable to us today. Those reasons retain their context-dependent normativity just in case their institutionality is still retained; they retain any robust normativity to the extent they are (now) legitimately authoritative to their addressees. They can continue to address people long into the future so long as the institution itself persists (or is somehow incorporated into or validated by another institution) and that persistence depends on continued collective acceptance. The procedures that created certain legal norms in medieval England would not suffice for legal validity in modern U.S. law, but some of those legal norms have been institutionally incorporated into modern U.S. law by the relevant U.S. officials continuing to see them as legally valid.

As for the questions of how the institution generates norms and who is in the ambit of collective acceptance, Amie Thomasson has a compelling argument that because an institution is a self-conscious creation, the group who collectively accepts the institutional status cannot be ignorant of or in serious error as to its nature or contents.[55] The collective acceptance of the relevant set of conditions that are declared sufficient for the creation of the institution make it the case that those conditions are sufficient to create the institution.[56] And we cannot be massively wrong about the instantiation of those conditions since it is generally just our perception of those conditions that we declare to be sufficient for creation of the institution.[57] Since the content of the institutional status is (partially) the desire-independent reasons it purports to create, those parts of the collective acceptance of the institution cannot be massively wrong about the creation of its norms.

[55] Thomasson, 'Realism and Human Kinds' 588–90.

[56] We can be wrong about necessary conditions and other conditions that are not criterial of the institution: ibid 590.

[57] The dispute between inclusive and exclusive legal positivists can be understood to be over whether the conditions sufficient for the creation of a legal institutional entity must be perceptions (or beliefs). Both would agree that we cannot be wrong about the conditions sufficient for the

This does not tell us anything about the scope or nature of that collective acceptance which creates the institution.[58] It simply states that, where there is an institution, there is some group whose collective acceptance confers that institutional status, thereby implying the power to give reasons and alter the normative space for those subject to it. But it does have the implication that the protection from possible error does not extend to individuals or to groups outside the collective whose acceptance creates and sustains the institution.[59]

This opens up the possibility for empirical research or discovery and highlights the importance of social scientific investigation into the conditions creating the institutions in which we and others believe. A social scientist engaged in research will generally need to take an external viewpoint on the topic of that research (at least provisionally). The investigation must take place without assuming the correctness of or buying into the collective acceptance of the institutional norms. Hence the investigator's perspective is not protected from errors about the nature of those norms.

We also have an answer for Enoch, which says that he got the picture partially right but was wrong in not allowing that questions of what makes legal normativity morally legitimate may still be an apt subject for legal philosophers. The reason why it is an apt subject is precisely that the law is claiming moral legitimacy. Hence, it is certainly within our dossier to comment upon that claim and to investigate the circumstances in which it may be accurate.

In doing so, we may be admitting that the law is usually merely activating reasons that already apply, even when it does have moral legitimacy. But by acknowledging its institutional nature, we are open to the possibility that it creates new norms that weren't originally present and merely activated by the law. They may be akin to pretend norms, as Enoch claims would be the

creation of a legal institution (i.e., that the legal validity conditions are as the community determines them to be); they disagree about whether we can be wrong about whether those conditions are instantiated (i.e., whether there can be an element of those validity conditions the instantiation of which is beyond our epistemic access). This view of institutions suggests (but is not dispositive) that exclusive positivism is the correct picture. The more serious or massive the error that inclusive positivism allows, the less likely it is consistent with this understanding of the metaphysics of institutions.

58 Thomasson says her theory of artifacts doesn't depend on collective intentionality, although it appears that her theory of institutions as a subset does: Thomasson, 'Artifacts and Human Concepts' 52; 'Public Artifacts, Intentions and Norms' 54. Nevertheless, this understanding of institutions also appears compatible with a range of different theories of collective intentionality. See ibid 55 n. 10, citing Searle, *Construction of Social Reality*; Bratman, *Faces of Intention: Selected Essays on Intention and Agency*; Margaret Gilbert, *Living Together: Rationality, Sociality, and Obligation* (Rowman & Littlefield Publishers 1996).

59 Thomasson, 'Realism and Human Kinds' 591.

case with any merely practice-based norms. But where the law's claim to moral legitimacy is accurate (if ever) and where that accuracy coincides with the creation of a new norm that didn't already apply to the subject, there is a space for law to make a real normative difference that Enoch doesn't acknowledge.

One might object here that, insofar as we are seeing legitimacy along Razian lines, in order for just about any legal directive to be legitimately authoritative, it must be based upon pre-existing, "dependent" reasons. These are reasons that already apply to the person who is subject to the directive.[60] If that is the case, the objection might go, then Enoch may still be right, since the law is merely activating these pre-existing dependent reasons.

The key here is that, for a directive to be legitimately authoritative under Raz, it need not be based directly on these dependent reasons; it need only *reflect* those reasons.[61] While there must ultimately be underlying dependent reasons that apply to the subject, it is not the case that the law's directive must be directly based on those underlying reasons in order to be legitimate. If it is not based on those underlying reasons but merely reflecting them, then it opens up a space to say that the law is doing more than simply activating existing reasons.

The best way to see this is to remind ourselves of the complexity of reasons and how they are created. In order to be legitimately authoritative, the law's directives must generally at least reflect those underlying dependent reasons (at least according to Raz). This means that legal directives must ultimately aid the subject to comply with the correct balance of those reasons that already apply to her. The reasons that already apply to her are the dependent reasons.

Hence, on this model, it is easy to see a view like Enoch's get off the ground: if the law is merely reflecting pre-existing reasons when legitimate, then the most it can do is either to remind us of the applicability of that pre-existing reason (an "epistemic" form of reason-giving in his taxonomy) or to activate those pre-existing reasons, perhaps marshalling them to coordinate behavior or otherwise provide the kind of guidance we need in order

[60] Raz, *The Morality of Freedom* 41.

[61] The dependence thesis does not exclude the authority from acting for other reasons which apply to it alone, and not to its subjects. All it requires is that its instructions will reflect the reasons which apply to its subjects, that is that they should require action which is justifiable by the reasons which apply to the subjects. Sometimes the best way to reach decisions which reflect the reasons which apply to the subjects is to adopt an indirect strategy and follow rules and considerations which do not themselves apply to the authority's subjects. Sometimes, in other words, one has to act for non-dependent reasons in order to maximize conformity to dependent reasons: ibid 51.

to comply with the best balance of all those reasons (a "triggering" form of reason-giving in his taxonomy). Since the law is merely changing social facts, the most it can do is trigger a pre-existing normative reason that one already had but which was not yet applicable.[62]

For Enoch, to trigger a reason, a fact need only be "normatively significant."[63] But to provide a robust reason is for the communication itself to make the normative difference. That is, a robust instance of reason-giving requires, on Enoch's view, the creation of the reason merely from facts about the communication, such as the intention to create such a reason in the listener, and that the communication itself serve as the listener's reason.[64] The idea is to capture the distinction between seeing a request as a reason to comply and seeing making the requester happy as an instrumental reason given further goals or values of the listener.

Most of the time when we accede to the law's demands of us, we are very likely seeing any reason-giving on the part of the law as triggering in Enoch's sense. But the law does purport to give us reasons merely because it is the law and not by triggering reasons that we already have. Is there a way to say that when it commands compliance merely because it is the law it is robustly reason-giving, even if that command is only legitimate where it reflects pre-existing reasons we already have? This depends again on whether one is sufficiently internal to the practice to see the law's reason-giving as robust, which itself depends on whether the directive is legitimate.

F. The Communication of Intention in Institutionalized Artifacts

Here is where it becomes important to see law as a genre of artifacts. Laws are artifacts in that they are specialized creations of human intentionality that serve specific purposes and are designed in order to be recognized as such. Laws are fashioned and implemented in such a way as to be recognized and used precisely as laws by following the procedures for such recognition and use set by the system that validates them. Following the pattern or mold set by the particular legal system allows the officials tasked with such recognition to recognize and incorporate the newly designed law or newly created legal norm, seeing it as a fully operable member of the class of valid law within that system. The recognition of the wider society

[62] Enoch, 'Reason-Giving and the Law' 26. [63] Ibid 27.
[64] Ibid 12–13.

is then parasitic upon the officials with the institutionally specified task of that recognition.[65]

As we've seen, artifacts themselves are a special case of tools, which would be anything adapted for a human purpose. Artifacts are distinct in that they are designed to be recognizable as the specific kind of tool that they are. That means at the very least that the creator of the artifact has in mind that others will see the artifact for the kind of thing it is supposed to do (where, as with law, we are dealing with public artifacts that are understood in terms of the function they are to perform). This is a kind of communication between creator and those who will in the future come into contact with the artifact.

Hence if Enoch is right that communicated requests can be sufficient for robust reason-giving, then it seems likely that artifact creators can perform a similar kind of communication merely through the creation of objects that are intended to be seen by others in a certain way. This doesn't mean that they are creating a reason to treat the object in a very precise way such that we are normatively bound not to repurpose those objects. But it does seem likely, as Amie Thomasson notes, that the identity of an artifact as a certain kind of thing does sometimes provide some robust norms of treatment.[66]

Imagine I create a token flag of the sovereign country in which we happen to be located (assume for the sake of simplicity that the country has no laws about how to treat its flag). There are likely all sorts of (non-legal) norms that are thereby created with regard to this object I've made. And they may not be precisely the norms I intended to create. For example, I might hate the government of that country and have created the flag with the intention that you burn it. Nonetheless, I still intend that the object be recognized as the country's flag and not, for example, as a dinner napkin. That creates a reason for you to treat it as a flag, even if one intended treatment in this case is to burn it.

Now, in making the flag-token I am also calling up its institutional status. Not only is it an artifact with a clearly recognizable identity, but also its association with that nation and its institutions cannot be missed. Hence, even if I wish you to burn the flag I created, if the norms of those institutions are

[65] Writing of norms of "recognition" with regard to artifacts should not be misinterpreted to mean these are merely epistemic norms. These are always to be understood as (practical) norms of treating the artifact in a certain way. I thank Cindy Phillips for pointing out the need for this clarification.

[66] Thomasson, 'Public Artifacts, Intentions and Norms' 51. As we've already seen, Thomasson's aim in this article is to show that artifacts need not have intended functions so that she can generalize her theory of the metaphysics of artifacts to include works of art. She acknowledges, however, that some kinds of artifacts do have intended functions and are to be understood in terms of those functions: see ibid 48. Given that analysis, it seems likely that individual laws have intended functions on her analysis and that law, as a genre of artifact, is therefore to be understood in terms of those functions. In conversation, she confirmed the likelihood of this being a correct application of her theory to law.

legitimate, that could undermine the reason-giving efficacy of my specific intention for you to burn it. Notwithstanding my hatred of the country, it might actually be a very just place that provides for its inhabitants well, helping them to flourish without unjustly imposing upon others around the world. Then even if there are no laws against flag-burning, saying the norms of the institution are generally legitimate is to say that it is providing a valuable service in the creation of those norms. As a result there are likely moral reasons not to burn its flag even if there are no legal reasons not to do so. Hence when I create the flag-token, some of my communicated intentions may be successfully norm-creating (e.g. see this as the country's flag and not a dinner napkin) and others (e.g. burn it) may not be.

Recall that on Thomasson's analysis, something is an exemplar of an ("essentially")[67] artifactual kind

> only if it is the product of a largely successfully executed intention to make [an exemplar of that kind,] where the maker must have a substantive concept of the nature of [those artifacts] that largely matches that of some prior [] makers (if any) and intend to realize that concept by making an object with [] relevant features [of the kind].[68]

We can broaden this to include institutional entities that are the result of collective creation and recognition. The key for our purposes (and hers) is to recognize that some of those relevant features are "receptive." That is, they are "intended ways in which the object is to be regarded, used, or treated."[69]

This is not to say that the creator of the artifact must create it with the intention that it actually be recognized as a member of that kind. Rather (for public artifacts, which are our primary focus, as previously mentioned), it is only necessary that the creator intended it to be "recognizable" at least to an intended audience.[70]

For many genres of public artifacts, the main (sometimes the only) thing that distinguishes them is the norms of treatment they receive, and hence the

[67] "[A]n essentially artifactual kind is a kind that necessarily has in its extension all and only artifacts – considered as intended products of human action": ibid 49 n. 5. See also Thomasson, 'Artifacts and Human Concepts' in E. Margolis, and S. Laurence (eds), *Creations of the Mind: Theories of Artifacts and their Representation* (Oxford University Press 2007) 52–73, 58, giving gold spheres as an example of a non-essentially artifactual kind since it is only a contingent fact that all gold spheres (we know of) are artifacts.

[68] Thomasson, 'Public Artifacts, Intentions and Norms' 49, citing 'Realism and Human Kinds' 599–600.

[69] Thomasson, 'Public Artifacts, Intentions and Norms' 49.

[70] Ibid 50. As we've already seen, the limitation to "public artifacts" excludes artifacts that are designed not to be recognizable to anyone, or only to the creator. Certainly institutions, requiring collective acceptance as they do and as a special subset of artifacts, come within the class of public artifacts.

recognizability of the artifact carries with it those norms of treatment.[71] That is, for many such artifacts, what it is to be that artifact is to bear those norms of treatment and it is the intention of its creator that it carry those norms, which are thereby at least partially constitutive of its identity.[72]

Now we are closer to seeing how it must be possible to create completely new reasons for action upon creating artifacts and hence to do so through laws as a species of artifact. Since it is possible to create new artifact types,[73] as well as to create new exemplars of existing artifact types that still differ from their predecessors in some of their structural or receptive features,[74] it must be possible to create new norms of treatment that are constitutive of these new entities. To the extent that the artifact is a public kind, then those norms are addressed to the community that comprises the potential users of the artifact.

This is not to say that the creator of a wholly new artifact type is necessarily successful in the particular norms of treatment that she might intend for her artifact, just as I was not successful in my intentions by creating the flag of a just society for you to burn. But for her creation to be successful at all, it generally will have to be recognizable as a member of a more general kind that comes with some norms already in place. When people recognize its value as a distinct type they will then start to generate additional norms of treatment that may or may not be in line with her intentions.

The key for us to take away from this discussion of artifacts is the possibility of new norms, not from where they come or to whom they might apply. But when we think of institutions as a sub-class of these public artifacts then we start to see a clearer picture of how people in certain roles might have privileged places from which to ensure those new norms are what they

[71] Ibid 51, citing Roman Ingarden, *Ontology of the Work of Art: The Musical Work, the Picture, the Architectural Work, the Film* (Raymond Meyer tr., Ohio University Press 1989 (1962)) 260–61. Thomasson notes that these are genuine norms and not regularities of behavior, as "misuse" of the artifact or "improper" behavior with regard to it are subject to "correction or rebuke": Thomasson, 'Public Artifacts, Intentions and Norms' 53.

[72] Thomasson, 'Public Artifacts, Intentions and Norms' 56. The relevance of the intention of creators to the identity of artifacts is not to be seen as implying any specific interpretive theory or strategy in the legal context. This is a method for explaining the nature of law and not an argument about how it is to be applied.

[73] Ibid.

[74] Beth Preston calls this phenomenon of artifacts "reproduction with variation" and we've discussed it as one of several phenomena characteristic of artifact functions that must be accommodated by any complete theory of artifacts. Preston, 'Philosophical Theories of Artifact Function' in *A Philosophy of Material Culture: Action, Function, and Mind* (Routledge 2013) 216–17 and previously in Chapter 6. As she and Thomasson both note, even new artifact types tend to be improvements upon existing broader artifact types in some way: Thomasson, 'Public Artifacts, Intentions and Norms' 56, noting the Wright brothers' flyer was intended to be a transportation device and not an object of religious worship.

intend them to be and how to apply them to that group within the institution's ambit. We also see how the law, as an artifact, can be a medium for the communication of intentions that can create new reasons for addressees of the law.

Law as a genre is a type of institutionalized abstract artifact. That it is a type of artifact means that it has some receptive features, some of which are norms of treatment that its tokens tend to share. The creators of those tokens (legislation, judicial decisions, administrative rules, etc.) intend for what they create to be publicly recognizable as law and generally to share in those norms of treatment. Since part of what it is to be an exemplar of that type of artifact is that it bears some of those norms, to the extent that the creation is successful (determined in law by the criteria of legal validity), the token carries some of those general norms of treatment as well as possibly creating new ones in terms of what is distinctive about that exemplar.

That it is a type of institution means that it confers a special status on some members or other elements within its ambit. That special status tends to include deontic powers to give non-prudential reasons by the institution's own lights. Where those reasons are legitimately authoritative, the institution has successfully created the non-prudential reasons as it claims to have done. Where they are not legitimately authoritative, they merely alter empirical facts about how members of the institution are likely to treat actions in compliance and non-compliance with those contextual norms (implying a possible triggering of prudential reasons to comply). This picture therefore holds out the possibility of the law creating entirely new reasons for action, even acknowledging a positivist picture of law as entirely a product of human creation, and explains the contours of that normativity.

8
The Functions Themselves

Up until this point, this book has been primarily about why and how functions are so central to understanding the nature and normativity of law, not so much about what those functions actually might be. Nevertheless, the careful reader will have seen several descriptions of what other theorists have considered the primary explanatory functions of law along the way.

We have discussed Dworkin's view that the function of law is to justify the state's use or withholding of force and seen problems with using that kind of function to explain law.[1] Since for Dworkin law is an interpretive activity, anything that is not performing its justificatory function cannot count as law. Dworkin's understanding of this function therefore runs afoul of the idea that for any function to be a candidate for a satisfactory explanation, it must accommodate the possibility of malfunction.

If we were to jettison the notion of law as an interpretive activity in Dworkin's sense and revert to a positivist notion of law, it would be difficult to see how the justification of force could then still be the function of law. If law were whatever society posits, then it could not justify the state's use or withholding of force in relation to wider principles. Fiat in itself cannot provide a justification for a moral decision about how to use force (at least not since Socrates trounced Thrasymachus in Plato's *Republic*). While one might be tempted to think of this as a kind of phantom function, like that of the perpetual motion machine—always doomed to failure—we have also seen that law is not the kind of artifact about which we could be so radically wrong about its chances for success in the function that explains it.[2]

One might imagine a kind of detached "Dworkinesque" approach, in which the function of a legal system is to implement or impose the moral and political principles that a community holds dear.[3] This is Dworkinesque in that it is a function organized around the community's moral and political

[1] See Chapter 3 and Ronald Dworkin, *Law's Empire* (Belknap Press 1986) 93.

[2] See Chapter 7 section E text accompanying note 58.

[3] I am indebted to Norvin Richards for this suggestion.

values, but is inconsistent with his theory in that it makes no wider claim that the law is interpretive or that we must see those values and the law's operation in the best light.

This could be understood to be a claim about particular legal systems, in which case there would be nothing inconsistent in it with our larger considerations about law as a genre. If certain jurisdictions organize their legal systems around implementing their chosen values, that would be consistent with the law itself having different wider functions that are true of it everywhere.

It could also be understood to be a claim about law in general: that legal systems everywhere share the function of implementing the community's values. That is most certainly the case as well, as long as we realize that we are not necessarily talking about all of the community's values. The question is whether this is jurisprudentially useful or explanatory. As we've seen, there is a strong and important relationship between any public artifact and the goals its designers see it accomplishing. If we are talking about an artifact that is fashioned over time by many hands, each of whom has the good of some subset of the community in mind (even if that subset is only himself), then we can group those goods together and say that they are at least a subset of the community's values. Hence there is something trivially true (and therefore not so explanatorily useful) in saying that law is a genre of public artifact with the function of implementing the community's values. Anything best understood in terms of its functions will thereby be best understood in terms of its instrumental utility in actualizing some perceived value. So if we are talking only of some subset of the community's values, we would already be saying it has this function just by saying that law is a public artifact, and we wouldn't be learning very much more about it.

On the other hand, if we are talking about a *specific* subset of the community's values, as suggested by saying it is their moral and political commitments, then we are in either of two situations. One option is that we are closer to a natural law point of view. Even if the theorist is not himself required to endorse any particular community's moral and political values in making this explanation, this kind of explanation would include an endorsement of having law as a political structure that is responsive to the community's moral and political values for democratic reasons. The other option is not to endorse having such a political structure at all, recognizing that this function can be fulfilled by a legal system even if that particular community has truly reprehensible moral and political values. But once we say that the moral and political values could be reprehensible, we are back to a fully legal positivist picture, and this articulation of law's function threatens to become trivial again. If the moral and political values can be reprehensible, then there is no obvious reason to separate the moral and political values from any other subset of the community's values and we are saying again merely that the function of law is to implement some subset of value, which is true of everything that is explained functionally.

Other views of law's function are not quite so problematic. Where problems have arisen, it has generally been not so much with the function articulated to explain law, but rather with the particular way in which that explanation is fleshed out or the way the theorist understands the relation of law to its function. Sometimes those problems arise because of the theorist's understanding of what a function is. Other times the problems arise because of the theorist's understanding of the explanatory power the function was to have in the explanation.

When it comes to the actual functions articulated by theorists, the ideas of legal positivists and of natural lawyers are not necessarily so far apart. Most focus in some way on coordination and dispute settlement. Some positivists, however, may formulate these functions in ways that avoid or deemphasize the value or values inherent in the goals attached to the functions.

The natural lawyer John Finnis adopts the common view that the function of law is to organize behavior so that society members can solve coordination problems and cooperate in pursuit of their common good.[4] As with those of many other natural lawyers, the function Finnis articulates is one whose value is hard to deny. Hence, while it might be possible to retain some neutrality about whether positive law is the best means available for achieving this function, it is not generally open to doubt whether the function itself is valuable. As such, a certain kind of theoretical neutrality is closed off and the theorist is engaged in both an explanatory and a normative enterprise. Since the law is supposed to be doing good, the theorist needs to explore what aspects of law best enable it to succeed.

Lon Fuller (a natural lawyer of a different stripe) holds that the function is to "achiev[e] a certain kind of order … through subjecting people's conduct to the guidance of general rules by which they make themselves orient their behavior."[5] While his theory then focuses on the internal or contextual values that law must meet in order to be fit for purpose (rather than measuring its operation directly according to some fleshed-out notion of the common good), his particular way of doing so tends to hold that success in the

[4] John Finnis, *Natural Law and Natural Rights* (Clarendon Press 1980) 153–54, 276, 334–36. See also Veronica Rodriguez-Blanco, 'Is Finnis Wrong?' (2007) 13 *Legal Theory* 257–83, 265–66; John Gardner, 'Law's Aims in *Law's Empire*' in Hershovitz, S. (ed.), *Exploring Law's Empire* (Oxford University Press 2006) 207–24, 209–10.

[5] Lon L. Fuller, 'A Reply to Professors Cohen and Dworkin' (1965) 10 *Villanova Law Review* 655–66, 657.

performance of this function is a membership condition in the class of law. It is similarly clear that the theorist is not expected to remain neutral about the value of that "certain kind of order" for society.

Fuller also embraced the coordinative function for law.[6] It may be that the coordinative function is a better explanation of Fuller's understanding of a function to explain law in our sense, given Green's complaint that subjecting behavior to the governance of rules sounds more like a statement of means than ends.[7]

On the other hand, Chaim Gans argues that even coordination is an instrumental function, done for the sake of some external "cooperative purpose."[8] Gerald Postema makes the same point: "Coordination is intelligible just when it can be seen in service of other intelligible ends, aims, values, or principles."[9] It does seem clear that coordination for its own sake cannot be what is meant by explaining law's function in this way. Rather, the focus must be upon coordination *problems*: situations where significant values or ends are at stake that individual (and group) actions must be coordinated to achieve.[10] It may be that law is singularly placed to achieve (or at least pursue) some specific subset of those values that would be difficult or impossible to achieve without it performing its coordinative function.

This talk of values should not be misinterpreted to imply that they are necessarily natural or moral values. The ends to be pursued might only be valuable to a subset of the population. Nevertheless, it is also likely that some morally valuable ends do require something like law's coordination ability in order to pursue. This is something that many legal positivists certainly agree with.[11]

H. L. A. Hart thought that law's function was to "provid[e] guides to human conduct and standards of criticism of such conduct"[12] (deemphasizing the explanatory role this function was to serve in his theory, but without realizing that it still perhaps held a more prominent place within his theory than he gave it credit for). Scott Shapiro focuses a bit more on coordination

[6] Lon L. Fuller, 'Human Interaction and the Law' (1969) 14 *American Journal of Jurisprudence* 1–36, 23.

[7] Leslie Green, 'Law as a Means' in P. Cane (ed.), *The Hart-Fuller Debate in the Twenty-First Century* (Hart Publishing 2010) 169–88, 173, and Chapter 6 section A.

[8] Gans, 'The Normativity of Law and Its Co-Ordinative Function' (1981) 16 Israel Law Review 333–49, 342–43.

[9] Gerald J. Postema, *Legal Philosophy in the Twentieth Century: The Common Law World*, vol. 11 (Enrico Pattaro ed., Springer 2011) 531.

[10] See for example Postema, 'Coordination and Convention at the Foundations of Law' (1982) 11 *Journal of Legal Studies* 165–203, 173–74 for more detail.

[11] See for example Shapiro, *Legality* (Harvard University Press 2011) 36; Gardner, 'Nearly Natural Law' (2007) 52 *American Journal of Jurisprudence* 1–23.

[12] Hart, *The Concept of Law* (Clarendon Press 1961) 249.

when he claims that the function is to correct the moral problems associated with a system of public planning.[13] This "moral aim" of law is part of what sets it apart from other planning systems. It also helps to show how close modern natural law and legal positivism have become, notwithstanding problems with the presumption of rationality described in the chapter on natural law. This somewhat whittles away the theorist's neutrality, leaving it intact primarily when considering whether the law is the best means for accomplishing these undeniably valuable goals.[14] However, the positivist can still maintain a neutral position about whether law is the best or even an adequate means for achieving its valuable purpose, while the natural lawyer's presumptions of the rational purpose to law require her to believe in the possibility of success.

We can understand the social guiding or ordering and coordination functions together, since it is precisely the kinds of difficulties that become coordination problems that are usually understood to require guiding or social ordering. This is a very common view of the overall function of law in the wider historical and sociological literature. For example, in an address by Edward Jenks to the Sociological Society in 1923, he claimed that "law is, historically, and still, in the main, actually, an attempt to prevent the individual encroaching on the interests of his fellows, or, to put it in another way, its object is the regulation of social conduct."[15]

The influential German sociologist Niklas Luhmann held a similar view that one goal of law was to enable individuals to recognize the interests of others.[16] In this view, the social problems that law is primarily supposed to solve are those created by individuals interfering with others as they try to pursue their own personal plans. All larger coordination problems could be characterized this way.

The legal scholar, theorist, and historian Anton-Hermann Chroust—perhaps presaging one key point I make in this book, as well as Shapiro's theory, by sixty years—understood law to be "an instrument for ordering

[13] Shapiro, *Legality* 213–14.

[14] See also Gardner, *Law as a Leap of Faith: Essays on Law in General* (Oxford University Press 2012) 169–72.

[15] Edward Jenks, 'The Function of Law in Society' (1923) 5 *Journal of Comparative Legislation and International Law 3d Ser* 169–77, 171 (commas as in original). See also Philip Allott, 'The True Function of Law in the International Community' (1998) 5 *Indiana Journal of Global Legal Studies* 391–414, 399, arguing that law is to show how private choices can still be to the public benefit: "Private wellbeing and public wellbeing are reconciled through law." But see ibid at 396, arguing that there are myriad incompatible functions adduced for law.

[16] Niklas Luhmann, *The Differentiation of Society* (Columbia University Press 1982) 94; see also John W. Murphy, 'Niklas Luhmann and His View of the Social Function of Law' (1984) 7 *Human Studies* 23–38, 33.

certain aspects of human conduct through social planning and social engineering."[17] This might seem to leave open which aspects of human conduct need ordering, but it is precisely the ones that need to be coordinated that are most ripe for planning and social engineering. Harry Jones echoed this idea that the law is a tool for social ordering in response to certain problems that arise as a result of social change; hence the law needed to be responsive to social change.[18]

Another view that can be harmonized with the coordination function is the need for subjects to be able to predict how the organs of government will react to their actions and choices. This view should not be confused for a reductivist account holding that law is merely a prediction of what courts or other legal officials will do. Rather, the utility of law is understood in terms of its predictive value even as it is still understood to be an institution of rules and norms. This is the view that Dworkin uses in his caricature of legal positivism as conventionalism,[19] and can also be seen in Luhmann's claim that the function of law in "traditional societies" was "to provide for coherence of [the political system's] decisions over time."[20] As the comparative legal scholar Richard Kay claims, "The promotion of [a] regime of certainty and predictability [about the circumstances of the intrusion of the collectivity into the lives of individuals] is the singular peculiar value of the institution of law."[21]

While I am not sure that it is "singular" or "peculiar," it is clear that the predictive function is another aspect of the coordination function, even if it appears to be the converse of the function that Jenks articulates above. The need for the individual to coordinate her choices in light of what others are likely to do is as pressing as the need for the community to solve for the imposition of individual choices upon everyone else. Both are forms of coordination.

One therefore need not be overly worried that the philosophers and the sociologists would have radically different things to say about law's functions. Jose Bengzon canvassed the sociological theories of his day, leading him to

[17] Anton-Hermann Chroust, 'The Managerial Function of Law' (1954) 34 *Boston University Law Review* 261–90, 261. See also Allott, 'The True Function of Law in the International Community' 399, stating that law enables a society to choose its future.

[18] Harry W. Jones, 'The Creative Power and Function of Law in Historical Perspective' (1963) 17 *Vanderbilt Law Review* 135–46, 139.

[19] Dworkin, *Law's Empire* 117.

[20] Niklas Luhmann, 'Differentiation of Society' (1977) 2 *Canadian Journal of Sociology* 29–53, 38.

[21] Richard S. Kay, 'Judicial Policy Making and the Peculiar Function of Law' (2008) 40 *Connecticut Law Review* 1261–86, 1281–82.

say that sociology was backing up a functional ascription much the same as that made by H. L. A. Hart in his discussion of the minimum content of natural law.[22] This is the idea that since people have relatively fragile bodies, are about equal in strength, are not completely altruistic, have to share resources, and have limitations in their understanding and convictions, all legal systems must at least have rules to prevent these features from undermining the social order.[23]

Some sociologists of law do prefer to maintain a greater generality in their characterization of the function of law along these lines. For example, Ann and Robert Seidman and their co-author Michael McCord hold that "All law aims at solving social problems that consist of repetitive patterns of social behaviours characterized by law-makers as undesirable. Law constitutes government's principal tool for channeling behaviours in desired ways."[24]

Some aspect of these considerations might therefore be a slight addition to the coordination and ordering functions; perhaps a further specification of the situations in which coordination problems are of the type that law is best qualified to solve. While it is possible that the need for a corrective on these features of social life is itself a kind of coordination problem in some circumstances, it might be more correct to say that this corrective is simply a more basic need and add it to the coordination idea as an additional basic proper function. After all, the need for basic rules against the free use of violence is not best described as a coordination solution, as the actions those rules seek to prevent are not generally themselves best understood as coordination problems.

Once again, however, there is no reason to say that we must reduce the law's functions to a unitary overarching descriptor. We can be happy with a listing of general descriptions of functions laws tend to perform wherever they are found.

While coordination is certainly one key function that law performs, it may come across on its own as more of a modal characteristic than a functional one. Green points out that most coordination problems are solved without law and that there are many other kinds of social means of solving them.[25]

[22] Jose P. Bengzon, 'Law as a Function of the Social Order' (1968) 43 *Philippine Law Journal* 699–737, 703–06.

[23] Hart, *Concept of Law* 193–200. See also Michael Giudice, *Understanding the Nature of Law* (Edward Elgar Pub Ltd 2015) 73.

[24] Ann Seidman, Robert B. Seidman, and Michael McCord, 'Theory and Methodology for Investigating the Function of Law in Relation to Governmental Institutions: The Case of the Development Bank of Southern Africa' (1993) 1993 *Acta Juridica* 263–78, 264.

[25] Leslie Green, 'Law Co-Ordination and the Common Good' (1983) 3 *Oxford Journal of Legal Studies* 299, 312.

He also notes that some laws may work to maintain coordination problems rather than solve them.[26] We've seen that the first point is only a problem if we think of law as a functional kind, a notion that should be rejected.[27] The second point is not really a problem in itself either, as it is entirely possible that the maintenance of certain coordination problems actually prevents or solves certain higher order (or simply distinct) coordination problems that are deemed more pressing.

Postema notes further that law itself may create just as many, or more, coordination problems as it solves.[28] But this is also not a reason in itself for doubting the explanatory value of saying that law has a coordination function. Many tools and artifacts create other instances of the problems they are designed to solve. They are only useful if they are successful at accomplishing their purposes without creating more serious problems of another kind. So those who see a value in law can say something similar about it: the coordination problems that law seeks to solve[29] are serious enough to risk the multiplication of coordination problems that are a result of law.[30]

The possibility of generalizing from more specific functions to some description that starts to capture a large set of those specifics is exemplified by some work by Joseph Raz. In an earlier paper,[31] Raz set out a classification scheme for law's social functions. The law's "direct functions" are those that it fulfills via obedience to or application of the law. The law's "indirect functions" are those that it fulfills via "attitudes, feelings, opinions, and modes of behaviour which are not obedience to laws or the application of laws, but which result from the knowledge of the existence of the laws ore from compliance with and application of the laws."[32] The direct functions are further divided into law's primary functions of "Preventing Undesirable Behaviour and Securing Desirable Behaviour," "Providing Facilities for Private Arrangements between Individuals," "The Provision of Services and the Redistribution of Goods," and "Settling Unregulated Disputes."[33] These are all the functions that form the primary justification for the existence of

[26] Ibid 301. [27] See Chapter 2, section E.

[28] Postema, 'Coordination and Convention at the Foundations of Law' 187f.

[29] "First-level" coordination problems in Postema's taxonomy: ibid 182–6.

[30] "Second- and third-level" coordination problems in Postema's taxonomy (second-level coordination problems are those between legal officials and citizens; third-level coordination problems are among legal officials): ibid 182, 186–94. The point I make here is not meant to imply that Postema would deny it. As he notes, the law generally works to solve these higher-level coordination problems as they are created.

[31] Joseph Raz, 'On the Functions of Law' in A.W.B. Simpson (ed.), *Oxford Essays in Jurisprudence (Second Series)* (Clarendon Press, Oxford 1973) 278–304, reprinted in *The Authority of Law: Essays on Law and Morality* (Clarendon Press 1979).

[32] Raz, *Authority of Law* 167–68. [33] Ibid 169–72.

the law and deal directly with the general population. There are two secondary functions (which are still direct): specifying procedures for making changes to the law and regulating bodies that apply the law.[34] The indirect functions are ones that might generally be seen as attitudinal byproducts of the direct ones, such as inculcating beliefs in certain values or enhancing respect for authority.[35]

One thing that is clear in some of the functions given by Raz is that they are themselves instrumental goals serving whatever wider end may be in view of those creating and implementing the law. Functions such as providing services or redistributing goods might be cited by Leslie Green as the kind of "functions" that point to law's modality being more central to its understanding than the ends it serves.[36] That is, the obvious next questions would be which services, and redistributing goods from whom to whom. Hence those functions look again more like means than ends. But as we have seen, some focus on instrumental goals that serve a wider end does not itself undermine the centrality of function in the explanation. Driving nails is never the ultimate end of whatever wider activity or project in which the hammer-user is engaged. Yet this fact does not undermine the centrality of driving nails to the explanation of hammers. So too with law: that some of its central functions can only be understood within the context of a wider social project does not undermine the explanatory importance of those functions.

That Raz himself realizes the possibility of generalizing from the more specific functions law serves to a more general categorization can be seen from the fact that he also articulates wider ends that law serves in addition to the more specific functions mentioned above. One example is that it shares in the function of authority more generally: to mediate between people and the reasons that apply to them.[37] This shows that Raz agrees with the idea that law's functions can be systematized and generalized from more particular functions that some laws may serve but not others, to broader characterizations of law's functions that apply to every instance. Some laws redistribute goods while others are not written with that in mind. Others focus on settling private unregulated disputes by providing for a public and official procedure to settle them. While this might make the law in general look more like a Swiss Army knife, Raz shows that there can still be a general way of characterizing the myriad functions it serves.

I agree that most of the functions that have been listed here are good ways to start examining the law's functions. I also think that the various

[34] Ibid 175. [35] Ibid 176–77. [36] Green, 'Law as a Means' 183.

[37] Raz, 'The Problem of Authority: Revisiting the Service Conception' (2006) 90 *Minnesota Law Review* 1003–44, 1018.

generalizations of those functions into characterizations like "solving coordination problems" and "helping people better conform to the reasons that already apply to them" are also all on the right track. However, my argument that we see the law as an institutionalized abstract artifact is also meant to add something to the most general list of law's functions.

To generalize from law's nature as an artifact, we have seen that one general function is to create new reasons for those subject to the law through serving as the medium for the communication of an intention to do so by those who author, implement, endorse, or ratify the law. Of course, this may not always be successful, in that some of the reasons such officials are attempting to create may not be legitimate. But by thinking of it as a kind of artifact, we are seeing it as such a medium for communicating intentions to create reasons with regard to behaviors under it in much the same way that a physical artifact communicates intentions to create reasons for behaviors regarding that artifact.

Seeing law as a medium for communicating intentions to create reasons in this way should be distinguished from another common view of law having a communicative function, although I don't mean to suggest that I reject that other function out of hand. This is the view perhaps made most famous by Lawrence Lessig and Cass Sunstein,[38] that law is a tool for expressing the society's attitudes and values. If anything, this way of understanding the expressive function of law would be a more specific instance of the communicated intentions view I hold for artifacts. Furthermore, Richard McAdams has harmonized the expressive function with the coordination function, subordinating the former to the latter.[39] If that is correct, then it would just be seen as another method within the coordination function.

[38] Lawrence Lessig, 'The Regulation of Social Meaning' (1995) 62 *University of Chicago Law Review* 943–1046; Cass R. Sunstein, 'On the Expressive Function of Law' (1996) 144 *University of Pennsylvania Law Review* 2021–54. See also, for example, Dan M. Kahan, 'What Do Alternative Sanctions Mean?' (1996) 63 *University of Chicago Law Review* 591–654; Dan M. Kahan, 'Social Influence, Social Meaning, and Deterrence' (1997) 83 *Virginia Law Review* 349–96, 363; Mark Tushnet and Larry Yackle, 'Symbolic Statutes and Real Laws: The Pathologies of the Antiterrorism and Effective Death Penalty Act and the Prison Litigation Reform Act' (1997) 47 *Duke Law Journal* 1–86, 75–76; Elizabeth S. Anderson and Richard H. Pildes, 'Expressive Theories of Law: A General Restatement' (2000) 148 *University of Pennsylvania Law Review* 1503–76; Richard H. McAdams, 'An Attitudinal Theory of Expressive Law' (2000) 79 *Oregon Law Review* 339–90; Oona A. Hathaway, 'Do Human Rights Treaties Make a Difference?' (2002) 111 *Yale Law Journal* 1935–2042, 2004f. For criticism see generally Matthew D. Adler, 'Expressive Theories of Law: A Skeptical Overview' (2000) 148 *University of Pennsylvania Law Review* 1363–502. Lon Fuller may have presaged this view slightly in noting the expressive function of rituals in customary law, which is carried over into developed legal systems: Fuller, 'Human Interaction and the Law' 6.

[39] Richard H. McAdams, 'A Focal Point Theory of Expressive Law' (2000) 86 *Virginia Law Review* 1649–1730.

Also, the law and economics literature has generalized the expressive function to any effect by law upon behavior beyond deterrence.[40] That would threaten to remove the functionally explanatory component of the expressive view, since it would avoid any notion of ends that the law is serving. If it is any non-deterrence impact upon behavior whatsoever, then it does not carry any notion of what ends those impacts are supposed to have. However, since this is in the context of the law and economics view, there is a solution in the wider theory of law and economics itself: that law is to incentivize behavior to maximize economic efficiency. Whether that operates as a natural effect of law on the problem of social costs, as a corrective to market failures, or as a prescriptive theory of how to mitigate both legal and market failures,[41] I leave aside as beyond the scope of this work.

By seeing law as an institution, we can be a bit more precise about the reasons being communicated and how they are created and addressed. Specifically, it creates reasons—rights and duties—by creating and altering statuses. It is the quintessential institution for creating other institutions and hence for specifying which other institutions (and the statuses they create and convey) will be afforded the social recognition within its ambit. Generally (but not always), this is the widest possible social institutional recognition within a given society. Furthermore, it suggests that the statuses and their attendant rights and duties ("deontic powers") created or altered according to its specifications are the ones that the apparatus of the state (or other systemic body) is prepared to respect and guarantee in some way.

To understand this, consider again the role codification plays within Searle's theory of institutions.[42] An institution that can codify the conditions for membership becomes a formal institution in that it thereby specifies its members by type.[43] It sets constitutive rules for what will count as having the

[40] Dhammika Dharmapala and Richard H. McAdams, 'The Condorcet Jury Theorem and the Expressive Function of Law: A Theory of Informative Law' (2003) 5 *American Law and Economics Review* 1–31. See also Patricia Funk, 'Is There an Expressive Function of Law? An Empirical Analysis of Voting Laws with Symbolic Fines' (2007) 9 *American Law and Economics Review* 135–59, 136.

[41] See generally Francesco Parisi, 'Positive, Normative and Functional Schools in Law and Economics' (2004) 18 *European Journal of Law and Economics* 259–72.

[42] We discussed this in more detail in Chapters 2 and 6. See also John R. Searle, *Construction of Social Reality* (Free Press 1995) 53, 87–88; *Making the Social World: The Structure of Human Civilization* (Oxford University Press 2010), 91.

[43] By "members" I mean people filling offices or roles as well as objects, activities, practices, statuses, and relations. Anything about which we can formulate a proposition that is a candidate for an institutional fact whose truth is set by the codified rules of the institution is a member of that (formal) institution. We have also called these "instances" (although I prefer the term "member" when including people). See Chapter 2, section D; N. MacCormick and O. Weinberger, *An Institutional Theory of Law: New Approaches to Legal Positivism* (D. Reidel Pub. Co. 1986) 54; Dick W. P. Ruiter, 'Structuring Legal Institutions' (1998) 17 *Law and Philosophy* 215–32, 215–16.

institutionally defined status by specifying generally what features a member must have. The ability to specify those properties generally allows membership to be fixed by type rather than by token. Hence the institution need not endow the statuses upon its members one by one (although it may still do so for some statuses).

Codification therefore sets the parameters of institutional validity—what will count as a valid member of the institution, getting the status specified by the institution, and having those rights and responsibilities recognized and guaranteed by the systemic body. For formal institutions, codification is the wider institutional equivalent of legal validity. Just as codification sets the truth conditions for institutional facts of formal institutions, legal validity determines the truth conditions for legal propositions such as "Legally, one may not park one's car here."

The function of law that I am here proposing to add to our starting list is therefore that of providing for such an institutional framework for the specification, recognition, and protection of contextual rights and duties (deontic powers) by institutions generally within the widest possible social setting (and thereby setting them apart for a specific kind of emphasis). It is the broadest institution whose function it is to generate and/or validate institutions. Since the general function of institutions is to allow people to effect their wills, pursue their plans, and solve other social problems or challenges they may encounter by creating or altering artificial statuses conveying contextual deontic powers, one key function of law is to coordinate and enable that institutional function as widely as possible.

9

Conclusion

This book has been an attempt to answer certain difficulties in understanding what law is and how it creates reasons for those who are subject to it. I have put forward the case that the law is a genre of institutionalized abstract artifact with the implication that the best way to investigate and understand the law is by examining the functions it serves in society.

I began by differentiating law into different levels of generality: individual legal enactments; legal systems; and law as a genre of human endeavor. Individual enactments are institutionalized abstract artifacts. Legal systems are systematized collections of these artifacts, although they can also be understood as artifacts in themselves in that they are generally express creations of founders or collections of lawmakers mindful of the interplay of individual laws within the system. Legal systems can be analogized to an operating system designed to be an environment for creating more software. The individual pieces of software must be fashioned according to the rules of the operating system and for use in that environment, but the operating system is still also an artifact itself. Law in general is then understood to be a type of institutionalized artifact.

We then moved on to a discussion of functions, noting that the explanatorily useful notion to be used for law would be the design or proper function: the characteristic ends that it is supposed to yield that explain its presence, development, or selection. We distinguished this from (and rejected) Cummins functions, which are the benefits a trait contributes to a wider system. Related to this rejection, I argued for keeping the explanatory focus on artifact functions rather than biological functions in that the former are less problematic than the latter. We also saw the very important point that for something to be ripe for functional explanation, it must be capable of failure in the performance of that function.

Artifacts were differentiated from instruments (anything used for a purpose) and tools more generally (anything adapted for a purpose) as tools that are designed to signal their identity in some way (when limiting our focus on artifacts to public artifacts). That identity is usually conceived of as arising out of the artifact's function. Those whose identities are not understood as relating to their functions are generally works of art. We also saw that membership in a given class of artifacts does not require that a token artifact is intended to be used as are other members of the class, nor that it be successful.

We then saw that institutions are special kinds of artifacts, involving the creation and assignment of roles or statuses which carry rights and responsibilities ("deontic powers"). I focused primarily on the theory of John Searle, in which a "status function" (here akin to the mathematical use of "function") is assigned to something via a constitutive rule (thereby possibly creating that thing) and collectively accepted as such. The status functions convey deontic powers to alter desire-independent reasons for action, perhaps creating a new kind of activity. These statuses are generally the means by which the institution performs its function. As with other artifacts, the institution itself is then understood in terms of that function. Formal institutions convey their statuses by type rather than token, by codifying their status functions. This creates the possibility of validity rules and counterfeit instances of the institution where those validity rules are not met. The notion of official codification allows us to understand law as a special institution-type for generating other institutions.

We have also seen that the explanatory role that functions play is not necessarily to distinguish law from all other human endeavors. Hence it should not be expected that performance of, or aiming at, a particular function is sufficient for membership in the class of law. (Law is not a functional kind.) Law's functions are still only one part of an overall explanation of law and need not set law apart from other human endeavors all on their own. Nor is the performance or pursuit of these functions necessary for membership in the class of law. As we learned with artifacts more widely, failure must be a possibility and some tokens may not even be intended to pursue the function that identifies the class. Rather, my point is that its functions are *explanatorily* essential for understanding law without distinguishing it on their own or being necessary for membership in the class.

Then we began our tour of the role of functions in contemporary philosophy of law with the ideas of Ronald Dworkin. We saw that Dworkin's understanding of law's function was to justify the state's use or withholding of force. This ties it to the moral and political commitments of the community, but also introduces the notion that there must be a right answer to any legal interpretation, representing the best justification of the relevant situations in which the state will use force or refrain from doing so. This leads him to deny that there are any gaps in the law, since there is always a correct interpretation "out there" and that would lend a truth value to any legal proposition.

The problem with Dworkin's view is that his articulation of the justification function for law, along with the right-answer thesis, entail that true law can never fail to perform its function. Since interpretations that do not successfully justify the state's use or withholding of force are not valid legal interpretations or applications, the law can never fail. There are four possible solutions to this problem: that legal validity and non-defectiveness are distinct; that legal validity and membership in the class of law are distinct; that law is not to be understood by its function; or that the law has gaps. However, none of these solutions are open to Dworkin.

We then turned to natural law, another theory that puts its picture of law's function at center stage. The idea is that the function of law is to reproduce and precisify the requirements of reason or morality in the pursuit of the common good. We saw that some natural lawyers explicitly took the Aristotlean tack of requiring successful performance of this function for something to be a member of the class of law. This position likely runs afoul of the requirement that something to be explained by its function be capable of failure.

We focused instead on the "weak natural law thesis" of John Finnis and Mark Murphy, according to which laws that fail to perform their function are understood to be merely defective members of the class, rather than excluded from it. One problem is that Murphy considers law to be a functional kind and so incorporates the notion of characteristic activities into his notion of function in order to differentiate law from other areas of human activity. Yet it is clear that many other institutions and human practices perform similar functions and employ similar means of doing so. Hence, even with this addition, it is difficult to see law as a functional kind. Additionally, the inclusion of characteristic activities threatens again to exclude non-standard instances from the class of law.

We saw that the weak natural law thesis leads many to wonder what is left to separate natural law and legal positivism, given that some legal positivists say they can embrace the weak natural law thesis. Positivists would certainly agree that irrational or immoral laws are defective. One possible distinction is whether the deficiencies are characteristically *legal* ones. Putting rationality at the center of law's functionality makes irrational laws legally deficient, while one who does not link law's function with rationality so closely would say that it is a moral or rational deficiency without being a legal one.

Some positivists, like John Gardner (following a reasonable interpretation of Joseph Raz), admit that immoral laws are legally deficient, thereby decreasing the space between natural law and legal positivism even further. The remaining distinction between the two theories is whether to say that law is "defeasibly morally binding" (a positivist position) and whether to say that it is "presumptively morally binding" (as Finnis does). The former does not carry any assumption that a given legal enactment is binding. To presume that law is morally binding is to see a close connection between the non-defectiveness condition and the criteria for membership in the class of law. To infer from the fact that law has a moral aim the conclusion that it is presumptively morally obligatory implies that law is well suited to accomplish its function. If there were other (accessible) means of accomplishing that moral goal that were more likely to succeed, there would be no reason to presume law was morally obligatory. So the weak natural law position still requires an assumption that the law is the best means available for accomplishing its function, an assumption that legal positivists avoid.

In looking at legal positivism, we saw that it was best able to embrace the idea that law is a kind of artifact and hence should be comfortable with the notion that it is best understood in terms of its functions. Yet H. L. A. Hart underemphasized the role of functions in his own theory. Perhaps this was because of how he saw it (mis-)used by Lon Fuller and Dworkin. Nevertheless, Hart appealed to law's functions at several key points in his own theory, especially in articulating its behavior guidance function, in explaining the role of primary and secondary rules, and in his discussion of the minimum content of natural law. This shows both that the behavior guidance function is not so broad as to be jurisprudentially useless, and as forming the basis for the practical difference thesis that legal norms be capable of governing conduct without reference to the underlying norms that may legitimate them.

We then saw that the debate between inclusive legal positivists (who hold that moral criteria *may* be included among the conditions for legal validity in a given system) and exclusive legal positivists (who hold they may not) can be understood as a debate over what the law must be in order to accomplish its functions. Exclusive positivists appeal to the behavior guidance function of law to say that allowing moral criteria into the conditions for legal validity makes it impossible for law to perform that function, since agents must then look directly to morality for guidance, bypassing the law. One solution offered by Jules Coleman is to distinguish between the criteria of identification and the criteria of validity, linking law's function with its identification and not its validity. But these may not come apart in the right way. Another solution, offered by Wil Waluchow, is to say that any sacrifice to the practical difference law makes (and hence to the guidance function) made by including robust moral requirements in the legal validity conditions is also made by seeing that moral term as merely increasing officials' discretion. Both theories therefore make identical sacrifices of law's ability to provide guidance. However, this argument works by seeing that moral requirement as one of moral acceptability rather than seeing it as imposing an objective standard.

So an exclusivist rejoinder might be that limiting the focus to acceptability means that the validity of law only depends upon the acceptance of officials anyway. Also, there is not much practical difference between the two camps, except perhaps in the implications for some rhetorical positions about legal validity.

We then turned to an examination of Scott Shapiro's social planning theory of law and saw that it was broadly compatible with the view I endorse here. However, there were two problems with the theory that help to show it is preferable to see law as a type of institutionalized abstract artifact, rather than the more limited understanding of it as a social plan. The first problem was the fact that the normativity of the law extends beyond the authority that creates it. Shapiro's planning theory makes the law out to be more ephemeral than it is, while understanding the law's institutionality along Searlean lines does a better job of capturing its persistence. The second problem stems from Shapiro's claim that legal systems get a presumption of validity from superior jurisdictions. This was seen as ad hoc and open to too many counterexamples.

Next I laid out an argument that we must first settle certain metaphysical questions about law's nature before determining the best methodology for investigating it in greater detail. A clearer picture of its ontology will also help differentiate it from other areas of human life. So we explored in more detail the reasons for seeing that law is a kind of institutionalized artifact, and then followed this with an argument against the instrumentalist view that law is better understood in terms of how it does what it does, rather than what it is supposed to accomplish. We then went into greater detail about law's signaling function, employing some of Amie Thomasson's ideas about artifacts. This signaling function is further marshalled against the instrumentalist view, showing that some of what it holds to be law's means can still be understood as ends.

Having settled some of those metaphysical issues, we then examined my idea of the "modest joiner" methodology in which the jurisprudent takes successful philosophical theories from the wider literature and applies them to law, using empirical information to hone them. To do this, we needed to smooth out apparent tensions between a method employing conceptual analysis and one that is open to empirical data from sociology and anthropology. We followed Michael Giudice in saying that there is no real inconsistency between the two methods, arguing against Brian Tamanaha on this point while endorsing his methodology with some important caveats.

We then explored the implications of this understanding of law for the problem of explaining legal normativity, especially in a legal positivist context within which law is grounded in social fact and addressing David Enoch's challenge that doing so is not the job of the legal philosopher. We saw that there is a two-tiered form of normativity in law: its institutional nature explaining a contextually bound tier and its artifactual nature explaining a more basic form of reason-giving that is not contextually bound. Whatever legitimizes its authority still governs whether we should ultimately adopt the contextually bound normativity and see ourselves within law's ambit. But the communicated intentions represented by an artifact's signaling function show it is not a category mistake to say that legal norms can be grounded in social facts. Those social facts are bundled with the artifactual norm (communicated by its creators) to treat laws as exemplars of the kind of thing they are: a norm that may be weak and easily defeated, but a norm nonetheless.

Finally, we examined several different statements of law's function(s) and what their strengths and weaknesses might be, as well as how they might fit within the picture I have painted here. We saw that behavior guidance, social ordering, predicting the state's response to personal choices, communicating the society's values, mitigating the demands of the individual upon others, and mitigating the demands of others upon the individual can all be harmonized within the idea that one primary function of law is to solve coordination problems. Some aspects might fall outside that conception, but there is no reason to think that we must reduce the law's function to a singular articulation. Our canvass also showed that the ideas of legal philosophers and those of legal historians and sociologists are not necessarily so far apart. Joseph Raz's catalog of law's functions also highlighted the possibility of harmonizing some more particular functions within a wider description without losing the value of articulating those more particular functions. The contribution of seeing law as a kind of institutionalized abstract artifact adds to the list the function of setting a framework for the specification, recognition, and protection of contextually bound rights and duties within the widest possible social setting (setting them apart for a particular kind of emphasis), that is, the generation and validation of other institutions. This is also an aspect of its wider coordination function.

Is this too general to be jurisprudentially or explanatorily useful? I don't think so. It certainly can be used to suggest avenues for empirical sociological research about the practices and limits of legal validity (which institutions are thereby validated) and the reasons for those limits. I have also suggested ways in which this understanding can be used to explain more clearly the generation of legal norms, their nature and applicability. It can be used to guide further theoretical and practical explorations into how our understandings of law change with new socio-political developments around the world (and possibly beyond, *pace* Shapiro.[1])

[1] See Chapter 6, section C, note 55.

So much is done with law precisely because so much *can* be done with law. It can serve so many of our myriad purposes, plans, and goals. But this doesn't mean that we cannot gain some fresh insights into what those purposes, plans, and goals are and how we use law to pursue them. In doing so we are seeking to better understand those purposes, plans, and goals, and, ultimately, ourselves.

References

Flag Code, 4 United States Code §§ 1-10

Bond v. U.S. 572 U.S. ___ (2014) (Docket No. 09-1227)

In re Erickson 815 F.2d 1090 (7th Cir.,1987)

Texas v. Johnson 491 U.S. 397, 109 S.Ct. 2533 (1989)

Trop v. Dulles 356 U.S. 86 (1958)

U.S. v. Eichman 496 U.S. 310 (1990)

Achinstein, P., 'Function Statements' (1977) 44 *Philosophy of Science* 341–67

Achinstein, P., *The Nature of Explanation* (Oxford University Press 1983)

Adler, M. D., 'Expressive Theories of Law: A Skeptical Overview' (2000) 148 *University of Pennsylvania Law Review* 1363–502

Alexander, L., 'Law and Exclusionary Reasons' (1990) 18 *Philosophical Topics* 5–22

Allott, P., 'The True Function of Law in the International Community' (1998) 5 *Indiana Journal of Global Legal Studies* 391–414

Anderson, E. S. and Pildes, R. H., 'Expressive Theories of Law: A General Restatement' (2000) 148 *University of Pennsylvania Law Review* 1503–1576

Anscombe, G. E. M., 'On Brute Facts' (1958) 18 *Analysis* 69–72

Austin, J. L., 'A Plea for Excuses' (1956) 57 *Proceedings of the Aristotelian Society* 1–30

Baker, L. R., 'The Metaphysics of Malfunction' (2009) 13 *Techne* 82–92

Beever, A., 'The Law's Function and the Judicial Function' (2003) 20 *New Zealand Universities Law Review* 299–319

Bengzon, J. P., 'Law as a Function of the Social Order' (1968) 43 *Philippine Law Journal* 699–737

Bigelow, J. and Pargetter, R., 'Functions' (1987) 84 *Journal of Philosophy* 181–96

Bloom, P., 'Intention, History, and Artifact Concepts' (1996) 60 *Cognition* 1–29

Bloomfield, P., 'Archimedeanianism and Why Metaethics Matters' in Shafer-Landau, R. (ed.), *Oxford Studies in Metaethics Vol. 4* (Oxford University Press 2009) 253–302

Boorse, C., 'A Rebuttal on Functions' in Ariew, A., Cummins, R., and Perlman, M. (eds), *Functions: New Essays in the Philosophy of Psychology and Biology* (Oxford University Press 2002) 63–112

Bratman, M. E., *Faces of Intention: Selected Essays on Intention and Agency* (Cambridge University Press 1999)

Burazin, L., 'Can There Be an Artifact Theory of Law?' (forthcoming 2016) *Ratio Juris*

Chroust, A.-H., 'The Managerial Function of Law' (1954) 34 *Boston University Law Review* 261–90

Clarke, D. S. Jr. 'Exclusionary Reasons' (1977) 86 *Mind* 252–55

Cohen, F. S., *Ethical Systems and Legal Ideals: An Essay on the Foundations of Legal Criticism* (Falcon Press 1933)

Cohen, F. S., 'The Problems of a Functional Jurisprudence' (1937) 1 *Modern Law Review* 5–26

Cohen, F. S., *The Legal Conscience: Selected Papers* (Yale University Press 1960)

Cohen, G. A., 'Functional Explanation, Consequence Explanation, and Marxism' (1982) 25 *Inquiry: An Interdisciplinary Journal of Philosophy* 27–56

Coleman, J. L., 'Negative and Positive Positivism' (1982) 11 *Journal of Legal Studies* 139–64

Coleman, J. L., 'Incorporationism, Conventionality, and the Practical Difference Thesis' (1998) 4 *Legal Theory* 381–425

Coleman, J. L., 'Constraints on the Criteria of Legality' (2000) 6 *Legal Theory* 171–83

Coleman, J. L., *The Practice of Principle: In Defence of a Pragmatist Approach to Legal Theory* (Oxford University Press 2001)

Coleman, J. L., 'Methodology' in Coleman, J. and Shapiro, S. (eds), *The Oxford Handbook of Jurisprudence and Philosophy of Law* (Oxford University Press 2002) 311–51

Culver, K. C. and Giudice, M., *Legality's Borders: an Essay in General Jurisprudence* (Oxford University Press 2010)

Cummins, R., 'Functional Analysis' (1975) 72 *The Journal of Philosophy* 741–65

Dasgupta, S., 'On the Plurality of Grounds' (2014) 14 *Philosophers' Imprint* 1–28

Delacroix, S., 'Six Paths to Vertigo-Free Legal Theory' in Freeman, M. and Harrison, R. (eds), *Law and Philosophy*, vol. 10 (Current Legal Issues series, Oxford University Press 2007) 36–48

Dharmapala, D. and McAdams, R. H., 'The Condorcet Jury Theorem and the Expressive Function of Law: A Theory of Informative Law' (2003) 5 *American Law and Economics Review* 1–31

Dickson, J., *Evaluation and Legal Theory* (Hart 2001)

Dipert, R. R., *Artifacts, Art Works, and Agency* (Temple University Press 1993)

Dipert, R. R., 'Some Issues in the Theory of Artifacts: Defining "Artifact" and Related Notions' (1995) 78 *Monist* 119–35

Dworkin, R., 'Judicial Discretion' (1963) 60 *The Journal of Philosophy* 624–38

Dworkin, R., 'Hard Cases' (1975) 88 *Harvard Law Review* 1057–109

Dworkin, R., 'No Right Answer?' (1978) 53 *New York University Law Review* 1–32

Dworkin, R., *Taking Rights Seriously* (Harvard University Press 1978)

Dworkin, R., *Law's Empire* (Belknap Press 1986)

Dworkin, R., 'On Gaps in the Law' in Amselek, P. and MacCormick, N. (eds), *Controversies about Law's Ontology* (Edinburgh University Press 1991) 84–90

Dworkin, R., 'Indeterminacy and Law' in Guest, S. (ed.), *Positivism Today* (Dartmouth 1996) 1–9

Dworkin, R., 'Objectivity and Truth: You'd Better Believe It' (1996) 25 *Philosophy and Public Affairs* 87–139

Dworkin, R., *Law's Empire* (Hart 1998)

Dworkin, R., 'Thirty Years On (Book Review of Coleman: Practice of Principle)' (2002) 115 *Harvard Law Review* 1655–1688

Dworkin, R., 'Hart's Postscript and the Character of Political Philosophy' (2004) 24 *Oxford Journal of Legal Studies* 1–37
Ehrenberg, K. M., 'Archimedian Metaethics Defended' (2008) 39 *Metaphilosophy* 508–29
Ehrenberg, K. M., 'Defending the Possibility of a Neutral Functional Theory of Law' (2009) 29 *Oxford Journal of Legal Studies* 91–113
Ehrenberg, K. M., 'The Anarchist Official: A Problem for Legal Positivism' (2011) 36 *Australian Journal of Legal Philosophy* 89–113
Ehrenberg, K. M., 'Law is Not (Best Considered) an Essentially Contested Concept' (2011) 7 *International Journal of Law in Context* 209–32
Elster, J., *Ulysses and the Sirens: Studies in Rationality and Irrationality* (Cambridge University Press 1979)
Endicott, T., 'Law and Language' (2002) *The Stanford Encyclopedia of Philosophy*, Edward N. Zalta (ed.) available at <http://plato.stanford.edu/archives/spr2014/entries/law-language>
Enoch, D., 'Giving Practical Reasons' (2011) 11 *Philosophers' Imprint* 1–22
Enoch, D., 'Reason-Giving and the Law' in Green, L. and Leiter, B. (eds), *Oxford Studies in Philosophy of Law, Volume 1* (Oxford University Press 2011) 1–38
Enoch, D., 'Authority and Reason-Giving' (2014) 89 *Philosophy and Phenomenological Research* 296–332
Essert, C., 'Legal Obligation and Reasons' (2013) 19 *Legal Theory* 63–88
Finnis, J., *Natural Law and Natural Rights* (Clarendon Press 1980)
Finnis, J., 'The Authority of Law in the Predicament of Contemporary Social Theory' (1984) 1 *Notre Dame Journal of Ethics and Public Policy* 115–37
Finnis, J., 'Law and What I Truly Should Decide' (2003) 48 *American Journal of Jurisprudence* 107–30
Fuller, L. L., 'Positivism and Fidelity to Law – A Reply to Professor Hart' (1958) 71 *Harvard Law Review* 630–72
Fuller, L. L., 'A Reply to Professors Cohen and Dworkin' (1965) 10 *Villanova Law Review* 655–66
Fuller, L. L., 'Human Interaction and the Law' (1969) 14 *American Journal of Jurisprudence* 1–36
Fuller, L. L., *The Morality of Law* (revised edn, Yale University Press 1969 (1964))
Funk, P., 'Is There An Expressive Function of Law? An Empirical Analysis of Voting Laws with Symbolic Fines' (2007) 9 *American Law and Economics Review* 135–59
Gans, C., 'The Normativity of Law and Its Co-Ordinative Function' (1981) 16 *Israel Law Review* 333–49
Gans, C., 'Mandatory Rules and Exclusionary Reasons' (1986) 15 *Philosophia: Philosophical Quarterly of Israel* 373–94
Gardner, J., 'The Legality of Law' (2004) 17 *Ratio Juris* 168–81
Gardner, J., 'Law's Aims in *Law's Empire*' in Hershovitz, S. (ed.), *Exploring Law's Empire* (Oxford University Press 2006) 207–24
Gardner, J., 'Nearly Natural Law' (2007) 52 *American Journal of Jurisprudence* 1–23

Gardner, J., *Law as a Leap of Faith: Essays on Law in General* (Oxford University Press 2012)
Geach, P., 'Teleological Explanation' in Körner, S. (ed.), *Explanation* (Basil Blackwell 1975) 76–95
Gilbert, M., *Living Together: Rationality, Sociality, and Obligation* (Rowman & Littlefield Publishers 1996)
Giudice, M., 'Conceptual Analysis and Its Critics' (2012) 6 *Problema* 3–38
Giudice, M., *Understanding the Nature of Law* (Edward Elgar Pub Ltd 2015)
Gizbert-Studnicki, T., 'The Social Sources Thesis and Metaphilosophy' in Gizbert-Studnicki, T., Dyrda, A., and Banas, P. (eds), *Metaphilosophy of Law* (Hart forthcoming 2016)
Golding, M. P., 'Realism and Functionalism in the Legal Thought of Felix S. Cohen' (1981) 66 *Cornell Law Review* 1032–1057
Green, L., 'Law Co-ordination and the Common Good' (1983) 3 *Oxford Journal of Legal Studies* 299–324
Green, L., *The Authority of the State* (Clarendon Press 1988)
Green, L., 'The Functions of Law' (1998) 12 *Cogito* 117–24
Green, L., 'Law as a Means' in Cane, P. (ed.), *The Hart-Fuller Debate in the Twenty-First Century* (Hart Publishing 2010) 169–88
Greenberg, M., 'How Facts Make Law' in Hershovitz, S. (ed.), *Exploring Law's Empire* (Oxford University Press 2008) 225–64
Griffiths, P. E., 'Functional Analysis and Proper Functions' (1993) 44 *The British Journal for the Philosophy of Science* 409–22
Hallpike, C. R., *The Principles of Social Evolution* (Clarendon Press 1986)
Hart, H. L. A., 'Positivism and the Separation of Law and Morals' (1958) 71 *Harvard Law Review* 593–629
Hart, H. L. A., *The Concept of Law* (Clarendon Press 1961)
Hart, H. L. A., 'Legal and Moral Obligation' in Flathman, R. E. (ed.), *Concepts in Social and Political Philosophy* (Macmillan 1973) 187–200
Hart, H. L. A., *Essays on Bentham: Jurisprudence and Political Theory* (Clarendon Press 1982)
Hart, H. L. A., *Essays in Jurisprudence and Philosophy* (Clarendon Press 1983)
Hart, H. L. A., 'Comment: Legal Theory and the Problem of Sense' in Gavison, R. (ed.), *Issues in Contemporary Legal Philosophy* (Clarendon 1987) 35–42
Hart, H. L. A., *The Concept of Law* (Bulloch, P. A. and Raz, J. (eds), 2nd edn, Clarendon Press 1994 (1961))
Hathaway, O. A., 'Do Human Rights Treaties Make a Difference?' (2002) 111 *Yale Law Journal* 1935–2042
Hempel, C. G., 'The Logic of Functional Analysis' in Martin, M. and McIntyre, L. C. (eds), *Readings in the Philosophy of Social Science* (MIT Press 1994) 349–75
Heuer, U., 'Reasons and Actions and Desires' (2004) 121 *Philosophical Studies* 43–63
Hilpinen, R., 'Artifact' (2011) *The Stanford Encyclopedia of Philosophy*, Edward N. Zalta (ed.) available at <http://plato.stanford.edu/archives/win2011/entries/artifact/>

Himma, K. E., 'Do Philosophy and Sociology Mix? A Non-Essentialist Socio-Legal Positivist Analysis of the Concept of Law' (2004) 24 *Oxford Journal of Legal Studies* 717–38

Himma, K. E., 'The Ties That Bind: An Analysis of the Concept of Obligation' (2013) 26 *Ratio Juris* 16–46

Hindriks, F. A., 'The New Role of the Constitutive Rule' (2003) 62 *American Journal of Economics & Sociology* 185–208

Hohfeld, W. N., *Fundamental Legal Conceptions as Applied in Judicial Reasoning and Other Legal Essays* (Yale University Press 1919)

Holmes, O. W., 'The Path of the Law' (1897) 10 *Harvard Law Review* 457–78

Hume, D., *A Treatise of Human Nature* (London: printed for John Noon 1739)

Hurd, H. M., 'Challenging Authority' (1991) 100 *The Yale Law Journal* 1611–1677

Husserl, E., *Studies in the Phenomenology of Constitution* (Rojcewicz, R. and Schuwer, A. trs, Kluwer Academic 1989)

Ingarden, R., *Ontology of the Work of Art: The Musical Work, the Picture, the Architectural Work, the Film* (Meyer, R. tr, Ohio University Press 1989)

Jenks, E., 'The Function of Law in Society' (1923) 5 *Journal of Comparative Legislation and International Law* 3d Ser 169–77

Jones, H. W., 'The Creative Power and Function of Law in Historical Perspective' (1963) 17 *Vanderbilt Law Review* 135–46

Kahan, D. M., 'What Do Alternative Sanctions Mean?' (1996) 63 *University of Chicago Law Review* 591–654

Kahan, D. M., 'Social Influence, Social Meaning, and Deterrence' (1997) 83 *Virginia Law Review* 349–96

Kay, R. S., 'Judicial Policy Making and the Peculiar Function of Law' (2008) 40 *Connecticut Law Review* 1261–1286

Khalidi, M. A., 'Three Kinds of Social Kinds' (2015) 90 *Philosophy and Phenomenological Research* 96–112

Kincaid, H., 'Assessing Functional Explanation in the Social Sciences' in Martin, M. and McIntyre, L. C. (eds), *Readings in the Philosophy of Social Science* (MIT Press 1994) 415–28

Kitcher, P., 'Function and Design' (1993) 18 *Midwest Studies in Philosophy* 379–97

Kramer, M., 'How Moral Principles Can Enter into the Law' (2000) 6 *Legal Theory* 83–108

Kramer, M. H., 'Legal and Moral Obligation' in Golding, M. P. and Edmundson, W. A. (eds), *The Blackwell Guide to the Philosophy of Law and Legal Theory* (Blackwell Publishing 2005) 179–90

Kretzmann, N., 'Lex Iniusta Non est Lex – Laws on Trial in Aquinas' Court of Conscience' (1988) 33 *American Journal of Jurisprudence* 99–122

Lacey, N., 'Analytical Jurisprudence versus Descriptive Sociology Revisited' (2006) 84 *Texas Law Review* 944–82

Leiter, B., 'Naturalism and Naturalized Jurisprudence' in Bix, B. (ed.), *Analyzing Law: New Essays in Legal Theory* (Oxford University Press 1998) 79–104

Leiter, B., *Naturalizing Jurisprudence: Essays on American Legal Realism and Naturalism in Legal Philosophy* (Oxford University Press 2007)

Leiter, B., 'The Demarcation Problem in Jurisprudence: A New Case for Scepticism' (2011) 31 *Oxford Journal of Legal Studies* 663–77

Lessig, L., 'The Regulation of Social Meaning' (1995) 62 *University of Chicago Law Review* 943–1046

Letsas, G., 'Monism, Interpretivism, and Law's Aim' in Freeman, M. and Harrison, R. (eds), *Law and Philosophy*, vol. 10 (Current Legal Issues series, Oxford University Press 2007) 49–59

Llewellyn, K. N., 'The Normative, the Legal, and the Law-Jobs: The Problem of Juristic Method' (1940) 49 *The Yale Law Journal* 1355–1400

Luhmann, N., 'Differentiation of Society' (1977) 2 *Canadian Journal of Sociology* 29–53

Luhmann, N., *The Differentiation of Society* (Columbia University Press 1982)

Lyons, D., *Ethics and the Rule of Law* (Cambridge University Press 1984)

McAdams, R. H., 'An Attitudinal Theory of Expressive Law' (2000) 79 *Oregon Law Review* 339–90

McAdams, R. H., 'A Focal Point Theory of Expressive Law' (2000) 86 *Virginia Law Review* 1649–1730

MacCormick, N., 'Law as Institutional Fact' (1974) 90 *Law Quarterly Review* 102–29

MacCormick, N., 'Norms, Institutions, and Institutional Facts' (1998) 17 *Law and Philosophy* 301–45

MacCormick, N., *Institutions of Law: An Essay in Legal Theory* (Oxford University Press 2007)

MacCormick, N. and Weinberger, O., *An Institutional Theory of Law: New Approaches to Legal Positivism* (D. Reidel Pub. Co. 1986)

McLaughlin, P., *What Functions Explain: Functional Explanation and Self-Reproducing Systems* (Cambridge University Press 2001)

Malinowski, B., *Magic, Science and Religion, and Other Essays* (Doubleday 1954)

Marmor, A., 'The Nature of Law' (2001) *The Stanford Encyclopedia of Philosophy*, Edward N. Zalta (ed.) available at <http://plato.stanford.edu/archives/win2011/entries/lawphil-nature/>

Marmor, A., 'Farewell to Conceptual Analysis (in Jurisprudence)' in Waluchow, W. J. and Sciaraffa, S. (eds), *Philosophical Foundations of the Nature of Law* (Oxford University Press 2013) 209–29

Merton, R. K., *Social Theory and Social Structure* (1968 enl. edn, Free Press 1968)

Mian, E., 'The Curious Case of Exclusionary Reasons' (2002) 15 *Canadian Journal of Law and Jurisprudence* 99–124

Miller, S., 'Institutions, Collective Goods and Moral Rights' (2003) 18–19 *ProtoSociology* 184–207

Miller, S., 'Social Institutions' (2007) *The Stanford Encyclopedia of Philosophy*, Edward N. Zalta (ed.) available at <http://plato.stanford.edu/archives/fall2012/entries/social-institutions/>

Millikan, R. G., *Language, Thought, and Other Biological Categories: New Foundations for Realism* (MIT Press 1984)

Millikan, R. G., 'An Ambiguity in the Notion 'Function'' (1989) 4 *Biology and Philosophy* 172–76

Millikan, R. G., 'In Defense of Proper Functions' (1989) 56 *Philosophy of Science* 288–302
Millikan, R. G., *White Queen Psychology and Other Essays for Alice* (MIT Press 1993)
Millikan, R. G., 'Wings, Spoons, Pills and Quills: A Pluralist Theory of Function' (1999) 96 *Journal of Philosophy* 191–206
Millikan, R. G., 'Biofunctions: Two Paradigms' in Ariew, A., Cummins, R., and Perlman, M. (eds), *Functions: New Essays in the Philosophy of Psychology and Biology* (Oxford University Press 2002) 113–43
Moore, M. S., 'Authority, Law, and Razian Reasons' (1989) 62 *Southern California Law Review* 827–96
Moore, M. S., 'Law as a Functional Kind' in George, R. P. (ed.), *Natural Law Theory: Contemporary Essays* (Clarendon Press 1992) 188–242
Murphy, J. W., 'Niklas Luhmann and His View of the Social Function of Law' (1984) 7 *Human Studies* 23–38
Murphy, M. C., 'Natural Law Jurisprudence' (2003) 9 *Legal Theory* 241–67
Murphy, M. C., 'Natural Law Theory' in Golding, M. P. and Edmundson, W. A. (eds), *The Blackwell Guide to the Philosophy of Law and Legal Theory* (Blackwell Publishing 2005) 15–28
Murphy, M. C., *Natural Law in Jurisprudence and Politics* (Cambridge University Press 2006)
Murphy, M. C., 'The Explanatory Role of the Weak Natural Law Thesis' in Waluchow, W. J. and Sciaraffa, S. (eds), *Philosophical Foundations of the Nature of Law* (Oxford University Press 2013) 3–21
Neander, K., 'Functions as Selected Effects: the Conceptual Analyst's Defence' (1991) 58 *Philosophy of Science* 168–84
Neander, K., 'The Teleological Notion of "Function"' (1991) 69 *Australasian Journal of Philosophy* 454–68
Parisi, F., 'Positive, Normative and Functional Schools in Law and Economics' (2004) 18 *European Journal of Law and Economics* 259–72
Patterson, D. M., 'Notes on the Methodology Debate in Contemporary Jurisprudence: Why Sociologists Might Be Interested' in Freeman, M. (ed.), *Law and Sociology* (Oxford University Press 2006) 254–58
Pavlakos, G., 'The Metaphysics of Law: From Supervenience to Rational Justification' in Brozek, B., Rotolo, A., and Stelmach, J. (eds), *Supervenience and Normativity* (Springer forthcoming 2016)
Pavlakos, G. and Rodriguez-Blanco, V. (eds), *Reasons and Intentions in Law and Practical Agency* (Cambridge University Press 2015)
Perlman, M., 'The Modern Philosophical Resurrection of Teleology' (2004) 87 *Monist* 3–51
Perry, S., 'Hart on Social Rules and the Foundations of Law: Liberating the Internal Point of View' (2006) 75 *Fordham Law Review* 1171–1210
Perry, S. R., 'Hart's Methodological Positivism' (1998) 4 *Legal Theory* 427–67
Plunkett, D., 'A Positivist Route for Explaining how Facts Make Law' (2012) 18 *Legal Theory* 139–207

Postema, G. J., 'Coordination and Convention at the Foundations of Law' (1982) 11 *Journal of Legal Studies* 165–203

Postema, G. J., *Legal Philosophy in the Twentieth Century: The Common Law World*, vol. 11 (Pattaro, E. ed, Springer 2011)

Preston, B., 'Why is a Wing Like a Spoon? A Pluralist Theory of Function' (1998) 95 *The Journal of Philosophy* 215–54

Preston, B., 'Philosophical Theories of Artifact Function' *A Philosophy of Material Culture* 213–34

Preston, B., *A Philosophy of Material Culture: Action, Function, and Mind* (Routledge 2013)

Priel, D., 'Jurisprudence and Necessity' (2007) 20 *Canadian Journal of Law & Jurisprudence* 173–200

Quine, W. V., 'Two Dogmas of Empiricism' (1951) 60 *The Philosophical Review* 20–43

Radcliffe-Brown, A. R., *Structure and Function in Primitive Society* (Cohen & West 1952)

Rawls, J., 'Two Concepts of Rules' (1955) 64 *Philosophical Review* 3–32

Raz, J., 'On the Functions of Law' in Simpson, A. W. B. (ed.), *Oxford Essays in Jurisprudence (Second Series)* (Clarendon Press 1973) 278–304

Raz, J., *Practical Reason and Norms* (Hutchinson 1975)

Raz, J., 'Legal Validity' (1977) 63 *Archiv für Rechts und Sozialphilosophie* 339–53

Raz, J., *The Authority of Law: Essays on Law and Morality* (Clarendon Press 1979)

Raz, J., 'Hart on Moral Rights and Legal Duties' (1984) 4 *Oxford Journal of Legal Studies* 123–31

Raz, J., 'The Obligation to Obey: Revision and Tradition' (1984) 1 *Notre Dame Journal of Ethics and Public Policy* 139–55

Raz, J., 'Authority and Justification' (1985) 14 *Philosophy and Public Affairs* 3–29

Raz, J., 'Authority, Law and Morality' (1985) 68 *Monist* 295–323

Raz, J., *The Morality of Freedom* (Clarendon Press 1986)

Raz, J., *Practical Reason and Norms* (2nd edn, Princeton University Press 1990 (1975))

Raz, J., *Ethics in the Public Domain: Essays in the Morality of Law and Politics* (Clarendon Press 1994)

Raz, J., 'Postema on Law's Autonomy and Public Practical Reasons: A Critical Comment' (1998) 4 *Legal Theory* 1–20

Raz, J., *Practical Reason and Norms* (Oxford University Press 1999 (1975))

Raz, J., 'The Problem of Authority: Revisiting the Service Conception' (2006) 90 *Minnesota Law Review* 1003–44

Raz, J., *The Authority of Law: Essays on Law and Morality* (2nd edn, Oxford University Press 2009 (1979))

Raz, J., *Between Authority and Interpretation: On the Theory of Law and Practical Reason* (Oxford University Press 2009)

Rodriguez-Blanco, V., 'A Defence of Hart's Semantics as Nonambitious Conceptual Analysis' (2003) 9 *Legal Theory* 99–124

Rodriguez-Blanco, V., 'Is Finnis Wrong?' (2007) 13 *Legal Theory* 257–83
Rodriguez-Blanco, V., 'Reasons in Action v Triggering-Reasons: A Reply to Enoch on Reason-Giving and Legal Normativity' (2013) 7 *Problema. Anuario de Filosofia y Teoria de Derecho* 3–25
Rosen, G., 'Abstract Objects' (2012) *The Stanford Encyclopedia of Philosophy*, Edward N. Zalta (ed.) available at <http://plato.stanford.edu/archives/spr2012/entries/abstract-objects/>
Roversi, C., 'Acceptance is Not Enough, but Texts Alone Achieve Nothing' (2012) 43 *Rechtstheorie* 1–30
Roversi, C., 'Legal Metaphoric Artifacts' in Brozek, B. and Stelmach, J. (eds), *The Emergence of Normative Orders* (Copernicus Center Press 2015) 215–80
Roversi, C., Borghi, A. M., and Tummolini, L., 'A Marriage is an Artefact and Not a Walk that we Take Together: An Experimental Study on the Categorization of Artefacts' (2013) 4 *Review of Philosophy and Psychology* 527–42
Ruiter, D. W. P., 'Structuring Legal Institutions' (1998) 17 *Law and Philosophy* 215–32
Schauer, F., 'A Critical Guide to Vehicles in the Park' (2008) 83 *New York University Law Review* 1109–1134
Schick, K. D. and Toth, N. P., *Making Silent Stones Speak: Human Evolution and the Dawn of Technology* (Simon & Schuster 1993)
Searle, J. R., 'Collective Intentions and Actions' in Cohen, P. R., Morgan, J. L., and Pollack, M. E. (eds), *Intentions in Communication* (MIT Press 1990) 401–16
Searle, J. R., *The Construction of Social Reality* (Free Press 1995)
Searle, J. R., 'Social Ontology and the Philosophy of Society' in Margolis, E. and Laurence, S. (eds), *Creations of the Mind: Theories of Artifacts and their Representation* (Oxford University Press 2007) 3–17
Searle, J. R., 'Language and Social Ontology' (2008) 37 *Theory and Society* 443–59
Searle, J. R., *Making the Social World: The Structure of Human Civilization* (Oxford University Press 2010)
Sebok, A. J., 'Comment on "Law as Means"' in Cane, P. (ed.), *The Hart-Fuller Debate in the Twenty-First Century* (Hart 2010) 189–98
Seidman, A., Seidman, R. B., and McCord, M., 'Theory and Methodology for Investigating the Function of Law in Relation to Governmental Institutions: The Case of the Development Bank of Southern Africa' (1993) 1993 *Acta Juridica* 263–78
Shapiro, S. J., 'On Hart's Way Out' (1998) 4 *Legal Theory* 469–507
Shapiro, S. J., 'Law, Morality, and the Guidance of Conduct' (2000) 6 *Legal Theory* 127–170
Shapiro, S. J., 'Authority' in Coleman, J. L. and Shapiro, S. (eds), *The Oxford Handbook of Jurisprudence and Philosophy of Law* (Oxford Universty Press 2002) 382–439
Shapiro, S. J., 'Law, Plans, and Practical Reason' (2002) 8 *Legal Theory* 387–441
Shapiro, S. J., 'Was Inclusive Legal Positivism Founded on a Mistake?' (2009) 22 *Ratio Juris* 326–38

Shapiro, S. J., *Legality* (Harvard University Press 2011)
Shapiro, S. J., 'Massively Shared Agency' in Varga, M. and Yaffe, G. (eds), *Rational and Social Agency* (Oxford University Press 2014) 257–93
Simon, H. A., *The Sciences of the Artificial* (3rd edn, MIT Press 1996)
Smith, B., 'John Searle: From Speech Acts to Social Reality' in Smith, B. (ed.), *John Searle* (Cambridge University Press 2003) 1–33
Smith, B. and Searle, J., 'The Construction of Social Reality: An Exchange' (2003) 62 *American Journal of Economics & Sociology* 283–309
Soper, P., *The Ethics of Deference: Learning from Law's Morals* (Cambridge University Press 2002)
Sorabji, R., 'Function' (1964) 14 *Philosophical Quarterly* 289–302
Sperber, D., 'Seedless Grapes: Nature and Culture' in Margolis, E. and Laurence, S. (eds), *Creations of the Mind* (Oxford University Press 2007) 124–37
Sunstein, C. R., 'On the Expressive Function of Law' (1996) 144 *University of Pennsylvania Law Review* 2021–2054
Tamanaha, B., 'What is "General" Jurisprudence? A Critique of Universalistic Claims by Philosophical Concepts of Law' (2011) 2 *Transnational Legal Theory* 287–308
Tamanaha, B. Z., *A General Jurisprudence of Law and Society* (Oxford University Press 2001)
Thomasson, A. L., *Fiction and Metaphysics* (Cambridge University Press 1999)
Thomasson, A. L., 'Realism and Human Kinds' (2003) 67 *Philosophy and Phenomenological Research* 580–609
Thomasson, A. L., 'Artifacts and Human Concepts' in Margolis, E. and Laurence, S. (eds), *Creations of the Mind: Theories of Artifacts and their Representation* (Oxford University Press 2007) 52–73
Thomasson, A. L., 'Artifacts in Metaphysics' in Meijers, A. (ed.), *Philosophy of Technology and Engineering Sciences* (Elsevier 2009) 191–212
Thomasson, A. L., 'Public Artifacts, Intentions and Norms' in Franssen, M., Kroes, P., Reydon, T. A. C., and Vermaas, P. E. (eds), *Artefact Kinds: Ontology and the Human-Made World* (Springer 2013) 45–62
Tushnet, M. and Yackle, L., 'Symbolic Statutes and Real Laws: The Pathologies of the Antiterrorism and Effective Death Penalty Act and the Prison Litigation Reform Act' (1997) 47 *Duke Law Journal* 1–86
Twining, W., 'A Post-Westphalian Conception of Law' (2003) 37 *Law & Society Review* 199–258
Twining, W. L., *General Jurisprudence: Understanding Law from a Global Perspective* (Cambridge University Press 2009)
Waldron, J., 'All We Like Sheep' (1999) 12 *Canadian Journal of Law and Jurisprudence* 169–86
Waldron, J., 'Does Law Promise Justice?' (2001) 17 *Georgia State University Law Review* 759–88
Waldron, J., 'Is The Rule of Law an Essentially Contested Concept (in Florida)?' (2002) 21 *Law and Philosophy* 137–64
Waluchow, W. J., *Inclusive Legal Positivism* (Clarendon Press 1994)

Waluchow, W. J., 'Legality, Morality, and the Guiding Function of Law' in Grant, C., Colburn, B., Hatzistavrou, A., and Kramer, M. (eds), *The Legacy of H. L. A. Hart, Legal, Political, and Moral Philosophy* (Oxford University Press 2008) 85–98

Wetzel, L., 'Types and Tokens' (2014) *The Stanford Encyclopedia of Philosophy*, Edward N. Zalta (ed.) available at <http://plato.stanford.edu/archives/spr2014/entries/types-tokens/>

Williams, B., 'Internal and External Reasons' in Harrison, T. R. (ed.), *Rational Action* (Cambridge University Press 1979) 17–28

Wittgenstein, L., *Philosophical Investigations: The German Text, with a Revised English Translation* (Anscombe, G. E. M. tr, 2nd (rev.) edn, Blackwell 1999)

Wolff, R. P., *In Defense of Anarchism* (University of California Press 1998)

Woodfield, A., *Teleology* (Cambridge University Press 1976)

Wright, L., 'Functions' (1973) 82 *The Philosophical Review* 139–68

Zvolenszky, Z., 'Abstract Artifact Theory about Fictional Characters Defended' (2013) 5 *Proceedings of the European Society for Aesthetics* 597–612

Index